CELESTIAL EMPIRE

CELESTIAL EMPIRE

The Emergence of Chinese Science Fiction

NATHANIEL ISAACSON

WESLEYAN UNIVERSITY PRESS

Middletown, Connecticut

Wesleyan University Press
Middletown CT 06459
www.wesleyan.edu/wespress
© 2017 Nathaniel Isaacson
Manufactured in the United States of America
Designed by Richard Hendel
Typeset in Miller and Gill types by
Tseng Information Systems, Inc.

Library of Congress Cataloging-in-Publication
Names: Isaacson, Nathaniel, author.
Title: Celestial empire: the emergence of Chinese science fiction /
Nathaniel Isaacson.
Description: Middletown, Connecticut: Wesleyan University Press, 2017. |
Includes bibliographical references and index.
Identifiers: LCCN 2016028269 (print) | LCCN 2016046258 (ebook) |
ISBN 9780819576675 (cloth: alk. paper) | ISBN 9780819576682
(pbk.: alk. paper) | ISBN 9780819576699 (ebook)
Subjects: LCSH: Science fiction, Chinese—History and criticism.
Classification: LCC PL2275.S34 I83 2017 (print) | LCC PL2275.S34 (ebook) |
DDC 895.13/0876209—dc23
LC record available at https://lccn.loc.gov/2016028269

5 4 3 2 1

CONTENTS

ACKNOWLEDGMENTS

When I first began research for this project as a PhD student at UCLA, I was under the impression that I would be able to cover the entire twentieth century and that the paucity of available materials would mean that the decisions about what to include and what to exclude had already been made for me. As I neared completion of the dissertation, my adviser confessed to me that when I had originally proposed the project, he had thought it was not feasible at all. I am eternally grateful to him for having the patience and wisdom to let me find out the answer to this question on my own. In the intervening years, I think that it is safe to say that both of us have been proven wrong. Chinese science fiction has emerged as a field in its own right, with scholars producing research and translation at a breakneck pace. This research continues to expand the field of Chinese science fiction, examining its relationship to China's own literary canon and to science fiction as a global phenomenon.

I would like to thank North Carolina State University and UCLA for supporting this research from its earliest stages up through publication. Travel and research funding from North Carolina State University, which allowed me to conduct research at libraries in Beijing and Shanghai, and a dissertation-year fellowship from UCLA and a Distinguished Teaching Assistant fellowship were especially helpful. I owe special debts to Theodore Huters, David Schaberg, Jack Chen, Shu-mei Shih, Andrea Goldman, and Robert Chi for their mentorship during my PhD studies. I also owe a great debt to Paola Iovene for her careful review of my dissertation, which played a significant role in the revisions that went into this manuscript. I am grateful to Carlos Rojas, Andrea Bachner, Chris Hamm, and Eileen Chow for their mentorship and support, especially in presenting and revising various versions of chapter 5 at Duke University for the *Oxford Handbook of Modern Chinese Literature* and for the Triangle East Asia Colloquium. Song Ming-wei and Wu Yan have also been particularly crucial mentors in guiding me through the field of Chinese science fiction. Jennifer Feeley, Sarah Wells, and all the panelists at the 2011 "Visions of the Future: Global Science Fiction Cinema" conference in Iowa City, Iowa, were instrumental in convincing me that truly interdisciplinary work was worth the toil. I am also grateful for the support and encouragement of my graduate cohort at UCLA: David Hull, Maura Dykstra, CedarBough T. Saeji, Brian Bernards, Jennifer T. Johnson, Matthew Cochran, Aynne Kokas, Winnie Chang, Hanmo Chang, Ma Lujing, and Makiko Mori. In China, I would also like thank Li Guangyi, Ren Dongmei, and Jia Liyuan for their guidance and support.

I would also like to express my sincerest appreciation to the reviewers of my articles and book manuscript. Thanks are also due to Arthur Evans, Parker Smathers, and the rest of the staff at Wesleyan University Press for their guidance, expertise, and support through the process of writing and revision.

Finally, I would like to express my gratitude to my wonderful and supportive wife, Kaori Isaacson, and our two children, Kenzo and Karina, for their patience during the past years. My father and mother, Ken and Martha Isaacson, my brother and sister, Tyler and Natasha, continue to be an inspiration as well. This book is dedicated to them.

CELESTIAL EMPIRE

INTRODUCTION
COLONIAL MODERNITY
AND CHINESE SCIENCE
FICTION

 This interdisciplinary cultural study of early twentieth-century Chinese popular science writing and science fiction (hereafter SF)[1] and its relationship to the colonial project and industrial modernity traces the development of the genre in China from its early history in the late Qing dynasty through the decade after the New Culture Movement (roughly 1904–1934). The emergence of Chinese SF was a product of the transnational traffic of ideas, cultural trends, and material culture that was engendered by the presence of colonial powers in China's economic and political centers. In particular, I argue that the relationship between SF and Orientalist discourse is a defining feature of the genre in early twentieth-century China. Through readings of historical accounts of the introduction and institutionalization of science in China, pictorial representations of real and imagined scientific and technological innovations, writing on the role of science in the quest for national renewal, and a number of original works of Chinese SF, I demonstrate that late Qing and Republican period intellectuals through the 1930s were preoccupied with the question of the relationship between science, fiction, and empire. In the context of the colonial threat, a profound pessimism emerged about China's fate as a nation, and this pessimism permeates discourses on science and works of SF from this period.

I engage with a number of fields, principally modern Chinese literary studies, modern Chinese intellectual history, postcolonial studies, SF studies, and utopian studies. For China scholars, especially cultural and intellectual historians and literary scholars, I provide a survey of the relationship between the emergence of Chinese-language SF and the emergence of modern Chinese literature. For scholars of SF studies, I demonstrate how a previously neglected subset of the SF tradition has been influenced by the legacy of empire and expand the geographic scope of global SF studies. In order to make this work more accessible to those unfamiliar with early twentieth-century China's intellectual history and its more long-standing historical resonances, I provide biographical notes and citations of accessible English-language studies whenever possible.

This study parallels other emerging work examining the role of genre fiction in the history of modern Chinese literature and its relationship to an ongoing project of moral and political education through fiction. SF has occupied and continues to hold a unique position in China's literary scene, as a tool of popularization of scientific knowledge, a vehicle for expressing anxieties and hopes for modernization and globalization, and a medium of social and historical critique. Related to the problems and questions that arise in attempting to define SF as a genre is the question the genealogy of SF in China: while some scholars see prototypical examples of SF in premodern Chinese genres such as fantasy and "stories of the strange" (*zhiguai*), others have argued variously that SF did not appear in China until the 1930s, 1950s, and even the post-Mao period. I demonstrate that SF emerged as the product of two converging factors during the late Qing: first, the crisis of epistemological consciousness brought about by China's semicolonial subjugation to European powers, and second, the imperialist imagination of global exchanges and conquest that led to the emergence of the genre in the West and its translation into Chinese via Japan. Writers and readers of SF drew upon China's tradition of fantastic writing in terms of thematic content and in borrowing many of the formal features of premodern fiction genres. In many cases, late Qing SF also borrowed from the classical tradition in the search for interpretive and epistemological frameworks for European science.

In my reading of early Chinese SF, I identify a deep-seated anxiety about the emancipatory potential of a genre closely associated with the colonial effort. Late Qing and early Republican Chinese authors were ambivalent about the question of whether the discursive knives of genres associated with empire could be successfully turned against their wielders, and if so, what the implications of adopting such discourse were. One might anticipate Occidentalism[2] — a dialectical inversion of Orientalism—as a likely response to such bodies of discourse, and this study explores the extent to which this was the case, finding that the response to Orientalism visible in reportage, political discourse, fiction, and visual culture associated with science was far more complex. Orientalism was (and is) a self-generating process, creating and created by the geopolitical realities of the modern world. As Edward Said observed, Orientalism produced knowledge about the East and the West, but this was often simultaneous with or even subsequent to the existence of the political and economic imbalances inherent in the colonial project—Orientalism did not merely represent reality but was in many ways constitutive of it (Said 1979, 13). This impact was so far-reaching and profound that while counter-discourses and acts of subversion were a possibility, fictional discourses of Eastern superiority could not overcome their contextual reality.

The political reality of Orientalism visibly contradicted what few Occidentalist fictions there were. Efforts to come to grips with Orientalism and the often vain attempts to create counter-discourses and imagine alternate historical trajectories for Chinese and Asian history are at the center of visual and print representations of science emerging in China during this period, but rarely, even in fiction, were they able to overcome the realities of an expanding military and economic European empire. In the context of expanding European and Japanese empire, the perturbing nature of essentialized discourses between East and West proved difficult to counter or surmount, and the prospect of national extinction seemed a palpable threat for many Chinese writers. In the search for lasting solutions, a vexing and perennial issue was what the relationship between Chinese and Western epistemologies would be.

In broad strokes, the findings and implications of this study are principally concerned with the ways in which Orientalist discourse and the specter of social Darwinism played a critical role in intellectual and popular discourses on modernization and national metamorphosis of the early twentieth century. Some authors tried to carve out spaces in which both would stand on equal footing, while others argued for the superiority of native systems of knowledge. Still others attempted to postulate the terms by which an instrumentalist approach to the material world could work in symmetry with Chinese metaphysical and moral philosophy. In many cases, the perceived binaries between modernity and tradition, East and West, civilization and barbarity, erupted into a kaleidoscopic fractal where long-term solutions were difficult to perceive.

Many of the metaphors, motifs, and linguistic concerns of the works of SF that I examine are familiar figures in the history of modern Chinese literature at large. One of the most salient images in modern Chinese literature is the iron house (*tie wuzi*) metaphor of Lu Xun (1881–1936) in his introduction to *A Call to Arms* (*Nahan*, 1923), where he describes Chinese society as "an iron house: without windows or doors, utterly indestructible, and full of sound sleepers—all about to suffocate to death. Let them die in their sleep, and they will feel nothing. Is it right to cry out, to rouse the light sleepers among them, causing them inconsolable agony before they die?" (*Lu Xun quanji* [hereafter *LXQJ*], 1:437).[3]

The figure of the intellectual who is cognizant of the crisis at hand but finds himself unable to intervene appears again in "New Year's Sacrifice" ("Zhu fu," 1924) when the I-narrator is unable to offer any solace to the beleaguered widow Xianglin Sao,[4] also appears throughout the work of Lu Xun. Prior to Lu Xun's adoption of this narrative persona, this character was also a common protagonist of early Chinese SF, where he most often takes on the role of a traveler, viewing allegorical representations of China through the eyes of an outsider. Emerging in these narratives is a pseudo-ethnographic mapping of the collision of internal and external pressures that faced Chinese society in the early decades of the twentieth century. The similarity of the ethnographic discovery of a benighted populace unaware of their impending doom, for whom salvation appears unlikely, often extends to the image of suffocation itself. Beset by such a sense of crisis, Utopia/Eutopia, I argue, was an unlikely spatio-temporal mode of representation: transcending the iron house as a mode of fantastic writing did not emerge as a characteristic of early Chinese sf. Which is to say, where both Fredric Jameson and Darko Suvin have attempted to elucidate the isomorphisms between sf and utopian narrative, I argue that the genres rarely overlapped in the late Qing.[5] Furthermore, this same sense of crisis and unavailing struggle is often figured in terms of bodily metaphors of illness and medicinal cures—again, seminal metaphors associated with Lu Xun that would go on to become some of the most salient imagery of modern Chinese literature.[6] A parallel concern is the relationship between past and present, or tradition and modernity, through which similar crises of figuration emerge.

In early Chinese sf, I identify prototypical versions of a number of metaphors that would go on to become central to the May Fourth reassessment of China's cultural heritage, and traditionally associated with Lu Xun, that later were ensconced as central themes in modern Chinese literature in general. These metaphorical figurations already featured prominently in the work of late Qing authors and are visible in the very first works of Chinese-language sf. This observation is not intended to diminish the status of Lu Xun or to remove him from his canonical status as the father of modern Chinese literature. Rather, I intend to bring nuance to the understanding of Lu Xun's work by demonstrating the ways in which it crystallized a set of already existing tropes rather than inventing them outright. These tropes included metaphors of illness and mental health as allegories of national strength; the imagery of cannibalism as the sign of a society in decline; metaphors of cultural suffocation and the iron house in the literary figuration of the prospects for national salvation; and extensive ruminations regarding the fraught relationship between the intelligentsia and the common man. In late Qing sf, many of the most salient metaphors of the May Fourth period, and of modern Chinese literature at large, were already prevalent.

While this crisis manifests itself metaphorically in Chinese sf through confrontations between the beasts of mythical tradition and modern machineries of warfare, it also manifests textually in the mode of representation chosen by authors. A wide range of stylistic and lexicographic modes is visible in the primary texts analyzed in this study. I argue that through rereading of Lu Xun's early works and in our reading of early Chinese SF, and through a deepened understanding of how the most salient metaphors of May Fourth authors were already prevalent in late Qing fiction, we broaden our horizons on the transition from literary to vernacular writing. Thus, I hope not only to contribute to the understanding of the relationship between science and empire in the world of early twentieth-century Chinese letters, but also to contribute to an evolving view of the ways in which China's New Culture Movement should be understood as part of an ongoing debate over the centrality of vernacular writing. Contemporaneous to this debate, early Chinese SF also offers a window on the labor pains of this mode of writing, as authors educated in the examination system struggled to articulate themselves in a new and evolving literary mode. Finally, this study contributes to the understanding of SF as a global media phenomenon.

I do not frame the emerging discourses through which Chinese intellectuals and eventually the reading public apprehended science and technology in the oversimplified terms of stimulus and response. An important aspect of the condition of colonial modernity is the extent to which these relationships constituted a feedback loop of mutually reinforcing conditions. Europe's colonial efforts were made possible by a limited set of scientific and technological advantages, and these advantages became more significant as a result of the material and intellectual gains that colonial possessions enabled. Territorially and financially, possession and occupation of new land, labor, and capital holdings allowed for continued colonial expansion. Intellectually, this simultaneously necessitated and facilitated the creation of new networks and contexts of scientific discovery. In the realm of letters, the imagination of such territorial holdings and networks of scientific discovery led to the emergence of new genres like SF and the adventure novel, through which the desire for such expansion was expressed and engendered in the metropolitan population back home. In China, the crisis of consciousness was compounded by a pervasive understanding that internal cultural failings were as much to blame for the inability to resist semicolonial subjugation as foreign aggression was. This overdetermined sense of national peril was catalyzed by the impression that the only way to overcome foreign incursion was to take up the discursive and material arms of the enemy and the knowledge that doing so would be a signal of complicity with the imperial project. In other words, a central concern for this study and for the writers of early Chinese SF was whether Western science and SF could be co-opted to turn the knives of empire upon their wielders, and in so doing what issues inevitably arose.

Kexue Xiaoshuo

An anomaly of the emergence of science fiction in China is that while the genre itself saw its beginnings as a Western import through translation,[7] the term "science fiction" (*kexue xiaoshuo*) began to appear regularly as a literary genre category associated with specific stories in publication in China (c. 1904) *before it did in the English-language press*.[8] In China, the term *kexue xiaoshuo* was first used to describe a work of fiction in the table of contents of Liang Qichao's[9] magazine *Xin xiaoshuo* (New fiction), which began publication in Japan in November 1902. Like most genre labels, the term was not so much a taxonomically derived category as it was a label of marketing convenience for the budding urban publishing industry, and there was considerable overlap between this and other genres, especially fantasies, travel narratives, and futuristic utopias. Barring a few caveats, "science fiction" was arguably a concrete publishing category in China before it was in the West, even as it predominately featured translations of Western works.[10] The term itself is a portmanteau of two neologisms imported via Japan. *Kexue* (Jp. *kagaku*) gradually supplanted *gezhi*, the "investigation of things and extension of knowledge," as the Chinese equivalent of science, paralleling an intellectual shift from neo-Confucian positivism to categorical and experimentally verifiable data as the foundations of knowledge of the material world. At the same time, the prose category *xiaoshuo* (fiction) had begun to supersede poetry as the primary written mode of social and political critique. Thus, the Chinese translation of "science fiction," *kexue xiaoshuo*, recapitulates two of the major intellectual developments of twentieth-century Chinese intellectual history—the introduction of Western science and the growing importance of the novel.

Other magazines soon followed suit in their use of *kexue xiaoshuo* as a genre designation, appearing next to the stories' title in the contents and on the first pages of stories in popular serial fiction magazines. Works labeled *kexue xiaoshuo* initially included translations and creative adaptations of English works, often based on Japanese translations of original texts like Jules Verne's adventure stories or Camille Flammarion's *La fin du monde* (1893; translated as *Shijie mori ji*, 1903). Within the broader prose category of *xiaoshuo*, a veritable explosion of genre designations emerged during the late Qing, all of them bearing clear allegiance to the cause of popular education and national renewal. In an article published in *Xinmin congbao* (New citizen), Liang listed ten genres of fiction: historical (*lishi xiaoshuo*); governmental (*zhengzhi xiaoshuo*); philosophic-scientific (*zheli kexue xiaoshuo*); military (*junshi xiaoshuo*); adventure (*maoyan xiaoshuo*); mystery (*tanzhen xiaoshuo*); romance (*xieqing xiaoshuo*); stories of the strange (*yuguai xiaoshuo*); diaries (*zhajiti xiaoshuo*); and tales of the marvelous (*chuanqiti xiaoshuo*) (Wu Xianya, 43). Liang was particularly inspired by the political novel, which he argued was a driving force in the modernization and political fortitude of countries like the United States, Great Britain, Germany, France, Austria, Italy, and Japan, elsewhere arguing that literature had the power to elevate the reader to the level of the fictional heroes he read about (Lee, 146–147). In publication, a number of other genre labels were attached to titles in the contents of serial fiction like *Yueyue xiaoshuo* (The all story monthly), including nihilist (*xuwu xiaoshuo*), utopian (*lixiang xiaoshuo*), philosophical (*zheli xiaoshuo*), social (*shehui xiaoshuo*), national (*guomin xiaoshuo*), comical (*huaji xiaoshuo*), and short stories (*duanpian xiaoshuo*).[11] As specific as these distinctions may appear, the narrative and formal barriers between these categories were much less clear in the tumultuous intellectual terrain of China at the twilight of the Qing dynasty.

The Political Crisis of the Late Qing

By the early twentieth century, the Opium Wars and the first Sino-Japanese War had brought an end to the long-held local perception of China as the "Middle Kingdom," presiding over a Pax Sinica,[12] and left the most economically, socially, and politically important regions of China subject to de facto foreign rule. A continuing crisis of political and epistemological consciousness saw the last remnants of political legitimacy slipping from the hands of the fiscally and militarily benighted Qing government. China was unable to repel foreign incursion; Confucianism, the examination system, traditional Chinese theories of political and social organization, and the very understanding of the world order and China's position in it were shaken to the core. The long-term repercussions of the Taiping Rebellion (1850–1864) were compounded by political strife following the Japanese victory in the first Sino-Japanese War (1894–1895). The failure of the Hundred Days' Reform (1898), which was soon followed by the Boxer Rebellion (1899–1901) and the ensuing indemnity China was forced to accede to as punishment, confirmed the overdetermined combination of political insolvency in the face of foreign incursion. In the wake of this series of foreign and domestic political failures, the Chinese intellectual framework seemed suddenly inadequate and incompatible with modern global politics. Weakened confidence in traditional philosophy indicated a necessity to grasp both the practice and spirit of science, which had enabled Western advances (Kwok, 6). So intense was the sense of peril that the governor of Hunan declared: "Our country can no longer survive in the world" (quoted in Murthy, 56). A succession of crises led to the conclusion that devotion to the study of Western science would be a critical element of China's fate as a country (Reardon-Anderson, 9). The establishment of the republic in 1911 (which was soon followed by Yuan Shikai's attempt to reestablish a monarchy) and the presentation of Japan's Twenty-One Demands in 1915 illustrated once again that beyond political and material reform, Chinese society itself was in need of fundamental reorganization (Kwok, 8).

The need for social and political reorganization was part of a decades-long struggle with the paradox of reform: many perceived it to be the case that in order to stave off extirpation, China would have to transform itself in a manner so profound and radical that it would hardly resemble the object that intellectuals had set out to preserve in the first place. The disruption of the tribute system signaled China's loss of status as the center of the Asian world and represented the emergence of a new world order. The Middle Kingdom had suddenly been shifted to the periphery as new networks of industrial production in Europe combined with related networks of economic and military power, engendering an entirely new set of institutional formations and relationships in a radically altered global environment. The late Qing crisis of reform brought about a radical shift to long-standing approaches to science and literature.

Two critical issues separate the engagement with European sciences at the end of the nineteenth and early twentieth centuries from the Ming and the rest of the late Qing: First, until the Qing defeat in the Opium Wars and the first Sino-Japanese War, *Yangwu* arguments justifying the importation of Western ideas and technology on the grounds that they were ultimately of Chinese origin were more or less sustainable, and Western science was not taken seriously until the last decade of the nineteenth century (Wright 1996, 2). The material advantages that are often mistaken for European superiority in the realm of scientific inquiry did not emerge until the industrial revolution. Chinese civilization, over the course of nearly half a millennia, had undergone a period of incorporation of foreign epistemology and a simultaneous reassessment of native tradition. After the first Sino-Japanese War, it became increasingly clear that regardless of the intellectual gymnastics it took to get there, the adoption of European science and technology, especially in the field of military armaments, was absolutely necessary. This change in perspective was precipitated by a sense that the nation was faced with a hitherto unseen moment of crisis, and that regardless of misgivings about science and technology, their adoption was a matter of life or death.

Second, prior to the end of the nineteenth century, the imperial throne closely guarded any new knowledge introduced by European missionaries, seeing to it that this information remained a part of the theater of imperial power, used in the ritual demonstration of the relationship between the throne and heaven; this knowledge was not popularized, and there was little imperative to do so. In Europe, popularization of technical knowledge in the European industrial revolution occurred as a result of the material need for greater expertise in the processes of mass production—scientific education was not made accessible for its own sake, but for the sake of the vested interests of industrial capital. Moreover, in China, scientific knowledge was not popularized until it was apparent that local national/imperial interests could not be sustained without such an effort.

Science and Empire

For centuries Western science had found its way into China, often at the hands of Jesuit missionaries, destined to become a closely held instrument of political influence for the imperial throne. From the late Ming on, Jesuit mathematicians played an important role in helping to assist court mathematicians in correcting problems with mensuration and cartography. Ming and Qing rulers were quick to discern the scientific from the religious, and were adept at turning what was meant to be a symbol of papal and (Christian) divine power into symbols of Chinese (imperial) divine power. Jesuits introducing Gregorian calendrical reforms to China in the early seventeenth century offered a powerful predictive model of the universe, one that played a vital role in the maintenance of imperial power. Their teachings on the predictive power of mathematics, the sciences, and experimentally verifiable evidence were presented alongside the doctrine that the universe was the product of a divine creator and that only Christianity could render an understanding of the relationship between humankind and this creator. Jesuits who first came to China in the early seventeenth century found that their acceptance at the Ming and Qing courts was dependent largely upon their knowledge of astronomy and cartography and their calendrical acumen. The rise and fall of Jesuit influence was closely tied to the fate of the Qing dynasty. Favor bestowed upon the Jesuits by the Qing court resulted in their resentment by non-Manchu literati (Elman 2006, 63–149).[13] These factors limited the scope of Jesuit influence, effectively curtailing the popularization of scientific knowledge.

For both the Ming and Qing courts, interest in knowledge of astronomy, cartography, and mensuration was a matter of their potential use as instruments of empire, particularly in terms of agricultural rituals defining the sovereign's connection between heaven and man, and cartographic work defining geographic territory. The ability to predict cyclical occurrences related to agricultural production and less regular astronomical events was closely guarded by the imperial court and used as evidence that imperial rulers had the Mandate of Heaven (Elman 2006, 15–35). Missionaries like Matteo Ricci believed that the introduction of such principles as Euclidean mathematics "would prepare the Chinese for the higher truths of Christianity," but Qing intellectuals were adept at separating the Christian and scientific content of the mathematical, astronomical, and cartographical skills that Jesuit priests had to offer (Elman 2006, 26, 107). Ricci's clocks, maps, and globes aided him in securing permission to open a mission west of Canton, in his attempts to gradually move north to Beijing, and these clocks quickly supplanted indigenous Chinese timekeeping devices. These demonstrations of technological superiority were meant to be seen by imperial courts as a demonstration of the superiority of European technological and spiritual civilization (Landes, 40–45).[14] Thus, science and technology were introduced to China with the specific objective of gaining a new flock of Christian believers and expanding the influence of the church. Science, as much as religion or the sword, was a tool of imperial expansion. Clockwork gears were part of Matteo Ricci's arsenal of soft power.

Nevertheless, clocks came to embody an affront to China's sense of self-regard, and timekeeping was one field among many where Chinese intellectuals began to argue for a Chinese origin to what had by then become a clearly superior European technology. Chinese scholars began to argue that Western clocks were derived from the Chinese clepsydra, and that such methods had since been lost to Chinese craftsmen. Others argued that clocks were merely playthings, and of no real intellectual or practical use. Despite such self-serving rhetoric, "timepieces were among the few Western artifacts the Chinese were ready to pay for" in the early nineteenth century, and such objects were one of the few goods that Chinese merchants were interested in trading for highly valued tea, porcelain, and other goods that brought the British Empire such extreme trade deficits in the run-up to the Opium Wars (Landes, 46–50). The introduction of timepieces, astronomical methodologies, and techniques of mensuration were understood by both sides of the exchange as tools of empire. Chinese rulers' interest in science was aimed at using its predictive power to reaffirm the legitimacy of their own dominion by arguing that it was expressed in the natural world.

The shift that distinguished the nineteenth century from previous eras was the sense that Western science and technology were indeed superior and that an adequate response demanded their popularization. The increasingly undeniable superiority of Western science at the close of the nineteenth century[15] and the social implications of Darwinian theories of evolution brought challenges not only to Chinese conceptions of time and their place in world, but also to the Chinese framework of cosmology and nature.[16] A combination of factors contributed to an increasingly widening scientific and technological gap between Britain and France on the one hand and China on the other that emerged during the eighteenth century. This included Jesuit resistance to adopt Newtonian calculus into their mathematical repertoire, an information gap between Jesuits in China and their European counterparts, the diminished status of the Jesuit order in the eyes of the papacy, and an inward turn beginning during the Kangxi reign (Elman 2006, 169, 183–189). "The Newtonian revolution in physics and engineering in Britain and France was not transmitted to China until the Taiping Rebellion (1850–1864) via French engineers at the Fuzhou Shipyard and British machine workers at the Jiangnan Arsenal" (244).[17] A simultaneous Jesuit "muddling" of Newtonian physics and a Qing turn inward prevented China from adapting the engineering and technological expertise that sparked off the industrial revolution in Europe.

At the same time, the eighteenth century saw a restoration of Chinese mathematical and medical classics and a diminished interest in foreign bodies of knowledge. In a familiar process of empire building, Qing rulers oversaw efforts to gather and assimilate the historical, literary, and scientific achievements of previous dynasties. For the Qing, this effort often entailed a process of reconstruction and extraction that attempted to discern Han and pre-Han texts from their Song dynasty neo-Confucian scholarly traditions (Elman 2006, 225–280). These restorative efforts eventually led to the *Yangwu*, or Foreign Affairs Movement, the argument that European technologies and scientific methods were derived from Chinese origins, a pervasive intellectual trend that saw its strongest expression in the years between 1860 and 1895.[18] This argument played an important role both as a balm for China's defeat at the hands of European powers and, as some have argued, as an explanation for why it was acceptable to adopt so-called foreign concepts. This term was at the center of an intellectual and political paradox—in order to survive as a nation, China would have to give up the epistemological system that defined it; or, in other words, in order to repel their Western aggressors, China would have to adopt a substantial portion of the Western worldview. Arguments in favor of the importation of Western technologies often had recourse to this notion, though it is unclear whether this was out of real conviction or political expediency. This idea arose as a response to a series of agonizing defeats at the hands of European colonial aggression, and in the words of Theodore Huters, "the relationship between domestic and foreign learning has been one of the most enduring issues in determining the intellectual direction of modern China" (Huters 2005, 23).

In "The Fate of 'Mr. Science' in China" (1995), Wang Hui argues that an instrumentalist orientation, focused on function and progress, with little interest in the idealist pursuit of knowledge for its own sake, defined late imperial Chinese approaches to science. For a period of centuries Chinese scientists, especially mathematicians and astronomers, were engaged in a process of engaging with Western science, technology, and theology. At the same time, they were engaged in a constant reassessment of their own traditions, among other things attempting to uncover the "true essence" of Han dynasty learning before it passed through the hands of Song scholars. The early to high Qing saw a renewed interest in Chinese mathematics and a reexamination of the universal principles of Zhu Xi's neo-Confucian *lixue* ("teaching of the principle"). During the late nineteenth century, "science" in the Chinese context began a transition of both terminology and ideology. Originally, the term "science" was translated and understood using the vocabulary and philosophical orientation of the neo-Confucian interpretation of the "Greater Learning" (*Daxue*).[19] "Investigation-extension" (*gezhi*), "investigation of things," "the study of probing thoroughly the principle" (*qiongli zhi xue*), and "to investigate things so as to extend knowledge" (*gewu zhizhi*) all emphasize the importance of personal experience and cognition. *Gezhi* is an internal process of individual cultivation and cognition that leads to the subjective apprehension of knowledge and results in the capacity to bring universal order (Wang Hui, 2–14; Qiu Ruohong, 63–67; Yue, 13–17). Initially, the Chinese understanding of European sciences was characterized by an attempt to frame Western sciences in neo-Confucian terms. A parallel trend was the philological shift that saw a reassessment of Song textual studies and attempts to recover early Chinese textual traditions from exegetical traditions that emerged during and after the Song dynasty (Elman 1984). Vestiges of this mode of translation remain to this day: the Chinese term for physics, *wuli*, is an abbreviation of the term *gewu qiongli*, investigation of things and fathoming of principles, from the same section of the *Greater Learning* (Kioka and Suzuki, 35–51).

Nineteenth-century Atlantic trade networks were not as significant in terms of financial and capital accumulation as they were for their role in expanding Europe's limited supply of land and energy. Europe of the seventeenth to the nineteenth century was indeed Europe, the Americas, and colonial Africa (Pomeranz, 23–24, 264–297). The development of European science and technology was inextricably intertwined with the expansion of European empire. Fa-ti Fan refers to the negotiations between various interest groups, aesthetic principles, horticultural practices, natural history, folk knowledge, and Sinology that occurred in colonial contact zones in coastal China and helped drive the development of British natural history from the second half of the nineteenth century onward as "scientific imperialism," noting the "symbiotic, even integral relationship between scientific and imperialist enterprises" (Fan, 4; see also Secord, 37). From the sixteenth century on, European exploration and the expansion of scientific knowledge were often dependent on one another. Scientific institutions played a major role in the dissemination of "energy, manpower and capital on a worldwide basis and an unprecedented scale" (Brockway, 6). Botanical knowledge of economically valuable plants helped aid the expansion of empire by assisting colonial entrepreneurs in the establishment of new plantations with raw materials and knowledge necessary for those plantations to succeed. Rubber and cinchona (used to make quinine) were two key products, transplanted from one colonial holding to another, which played a key role in European penetration into South and Southeast Asia, the Middle East, and Africa. Both of these products were necessary war matériel in such military efforts.[20] In tropical colonial holdings, the material and knowledge-oriented capital met with relatively abundant labor, in various forms of servitude and at low cost to entrepreneurs.

Global commercial networks made use of diffuse access to local knowledge to make local observations in building universal understandings of fields as diverse as astronomy and gravitation, in efforts to catalog the natural world, and in the formation of Darwin's theories of evolution. Darwin's work on natural selection was enabled by a global network of collaborators, connected first through the postal system, steamships, and print culture and later through the telegraph (Secord, 32–37). Merchant ships did not only carry goods; they also carried people devoted to the production of knowledge, and in many cases the merchants aboard these ships were themselves involved in the production and dissemination of knowledge (Delbourgo and Dew, 7). In other words, the expansion of our scientific understanding of the world, the expansion of Atlantic and Asian trade networks, and the expansion of empire were simultaneous and mutually reinforcing processes, often occurring aboard the same oceangoing vessels and at the same colonial outposts. These developments resulted from cooperative efforts of colonial administrators and local collaborators. Recognition of the reciprocal nature of these intellectual and material exchanges offers the opportunity to move beyond both the impact-response and China-centered approaches to China's intellectual history, understanding history in terms of global relationships (Fa-ti Fan, 5).

Colonial Modernity

Chinese SF is arguably best geographically and culturally contextualized in terms of Tani Barlow's "colonial modernity." This critical framework approaches the changes of the early twentieth century in terms of the transnational traffic of ideas, cultural trends, and material culture engendered by the expansion of European colonialism. This heuristic perspective elucidates the relationship between local developments and global exchanges, acknowledging the pervasive influence of colonialism upon these exchanges. In Barlow's words,

> "Colonial modernity" can be grasped as a speculative frame for investigating the infinitely pervasive discursive powers that increasingly connect at key points to the globalizing impulses of capitalism. Because it is a way of posing a historical question about how our mutual present came to take its apparent shape, colonial modernity can also suggest that historical context is not a matter of positively defined, elemental, or discrete units—nation states, stages of development, or civilizations, for instance—but rather a complex field of relationships or threads of material that connect multiply in space-time and can be surveyed from specific sites. (Barlow, 6)

Critiques of colonial modernity bring to light the uneven terrain in which the economic and intellectual relationships that emerged in the colonial context were established, and the cultural hybridity that these exchanges engendered.

Labeling China's position in the global political sphere, especially in a way that recognizes the cultural uniqueness of port cities like Shanghai that found themselves at the vanguard of colonial modernity, is no easy task. While coastal cities relevant to global trade were incorporated into the European colonial project, much of the Chinese interior remained under Chinese rule. Meng Yue notes that one might identify Shanghai as a peripheral city in Wallerstein's "world systems" (1989), feeding the European core with labor and resources. Yue imagines Hardt and Negri (2000) labeling Shanghai as a "node" in the global "empire of capital." As a counterpoint, Yue suggests that Andre Gunder Frank (1998), Hamashita Takeshi and Kawakatsu Heita (1991), or Peter Perdue (2005), with their competing visions of an Asian-oriented world economy, might have emphasized the degree to which Shanghai was in many ways a global core city, especially in terms of late imperial China's relationship to central and Southeast Asia prior to the rise of European and Japanese colonial empires, ultimately concluding that "Shanghai is found somewhere between semi-colonialism and cosmopolitanism" (Yue, viii–xi).

A complex web of relationships among China, Japan, Europe, and the United States, colonial modernity resulted in an eclectic and often contradictory array of responses to the transnational traffic of ideas, cultural trends, and material culture that characterized coastal Chinese cities in the late Qing. Both Lydia Liu and Wang Hui have devoted critical attention to the question of how this unevenness played out in the translation of notions of individualism, science, literature, and modernity into the Chinese lexicon, often via the distorting lens of Meiji Japan.[21] Colonial modernity was a global phenomenon characterized by transnational exchanges in the context of imperial expansion, the colonial presence, and its accompanying economic and sociological discourses, which resulted in widely variegated local responses that often shared similar core features.[22] These responses were in turn conditioned by changing historical and social conditions, by varying levels of wealth and education, by conflicting and occasionally opposing ideological and philosophical approaches, and in many cases by creative misunderstandings, misreading, and artistic license.

Empire, science, and the fictional imagination that propelled imperial expansion were inextricably intertwined. Asia and the Americas provided both material resources and networks for scientific research that played a vital role in the creation of modern Europe.[23] The Western world was "only able to create the great transformation of the nineteenth century in a context also shaped by Europe's privileged access to overseas resources" (Pomeranz, 4). Europe was not the "unshaped shaper of everything else" (Pomeranz, 10); the geopolitical shifts of early modernity through the twentieth century, though unequal, were nevertheless mutual.

The ways in which Western science and technology were appropriated and acculturated are as multifaceted as the ways in which indigenous Chinese culture and intellectual life were modified, reimagined, and often reinvented. Charlotte Furth also adds that the transformations engendered by this encounter were far from unilateral: "One danger of the concept [of a Chinese 'response to the West'], however, is its tendency to suggest that the process was one of linear substitution of 'Western' ideas for native ones; and that Chinese played an intellectually passive role" (Furth 2002, 15).

The challenges of European military hegemony most certainly provided a stimulus to the intellectual field of late nineteenth- and early twentieth-century China, but the response was far more complex than a matter of dialectical antithesis. In other words, colonial modernity enabled a repertoire of linguistic, symbolic, and cultural practices that may be deployed in formulating perspectives on one's self and society. These often included the internalization or repetition of Orientalist discourse, but also encompassed strategies of appropriation, resistance, subversion, and filtration that were both consciously and unconsciously deployed, to varying degrees of success. Likewise, the resulting short- and long-term outcomes have proven to be much more complex than simple replacement or synthesis. Thus, there are conceivably as many iterations of modernity as there are individuals, or perhaps more. As a socially contingent phenomenon, local iterations of colonial modernity are often constructed around shared experiences or understandings; however, they are neither essentialized nor universal. The parallels and intersections visible in the experiences of modernization, urbanization, and the response to Westernization common to China, Korea, Japan, and Vietnam should by no means mask the vast historical and individual differences in these countries' encounters with these forces.

Colonial modernity is the hybrid offspring of the encounter between margin and periphery in the context of imperial expansion. Hardt and Negri define empire as the exercise of virtual forces of control at the margins, intervening in "breakdowns in the system" (38–39). I contend that it is at these marginal locations where the influence of empire is experienced most immediately, in the form of the constant presence of the colonial order. For China, the imperial form also had already taken on the diffuse character that Hardt and Negri argue contemporary techno-scientific empire is destined for, as power executed through international treaties. The military defeats of the Opium Wars and the first Sino-Japanese War were, historically speaking, relatively short-lived, but their ongoing consequences—the "lease" of Hong Kong and other treaty ports, and the annexation of Taiwan—were felt as ongoing effects of the war, and produced hybridizing exchanges of knowledge and technology, especially in turn-of-the-twentieth-century Shanghai. Meng Yue argues that Shanghai was a space between both "overlapping territories" and "overlapping temporalities" whose rise was in many ways facilitated by the domestic and international failures of the Qing Empire (Yue, vii–xxix).

The introduction of Western science to China was inextricably intertwined with the rising tide of European and Japanese empire. In exchanges between Jesuits and the Ming and Qing courts prior to the Sino-Japanese War, the first forays into popular scientific publication, the production and distribution of new material goods, pictorial representations of science and technology, and in the creation of scientific institutions, empire was a ubiquitous and vexing consideration. Terms like science, civilization, technology, empire, the West, and notions like civic involvement, political involvement, evolution, and social Darwinism, were often understood as "foreign imports," in a nebulous cluster of overlapping associations. These associations clustered around the nucleus of the discourse of national peril, and the mutually reinforcing vocabulary of national salvation. Western science, as much as SF, was rightly understood to be a body of knowledge that helped to produce and was produced by Orientalist discourse. In the words of Qin Shao, I examine the manners in which "in the West science was mainly driven by industrial development, commercial profits, military conquest and intellectual curiosity, [while] in other parts of the world, Western science was 'legitimized' largely by imperialism. It became a measure of one's strength and success in the modern world order" (Qin Shao, 694).

Natural and social sciences were in turn the products of a series of institutional formations that were part and parcel of the imperial project, and these institutions also helped to cement the ontological assertions of Orientalism. As Said notes, modern sciences were among the blades of the ideological arsenal that sprang from the material reality of colonialism.[24]

Overview

Chapter 1, "Genre Trouble," begins with an inquiry into scholarly dating of the emergence of the genre, both in China and the West, examining some key debates and recent developments in academic approaches to sf. Genres are normative heuristic tools, often constructed long after the literary forms that they attempt to define and rarely constitute clearly delineated descriptive categories. To this end, I find many of the questions asked in the chapter headings of Andrew Milner's *Locating Science Fiction* (2012) to be particularly useful in coming to terms with the emergence of sf in late Qing China. In brief, I find Milner's work arguing that sf is a selective tradition, defining a whole field of cultural products best defined by their shared tropes and topoi rather than their formal qualities, to be useful in understanding the constituent elements of early Chinese sf.[25] The question "Where Was Science Fiction?" is answered, as in Milner, in turning toward world systems theory and the work of Immanuel Wallerstein and Franco Moretti; but I also find Tani Barlow, Meng Yue, Dipesh Chakrabarty, and a number of others who have oriented China's recent history in terms of a dynamic global political economy to be informative in specifying where *Chinese* science fiction originated. I find Milner's response to the question "When Was Science Fiction?"—that in the nineteenth century "the Industrial Revolution decisively and definitively redefined science into an intensely practical activity inextricably productive of new technologies, in the everyday rather than the Heideggerian sense" (Milner 2012, 139)—and John Rieder's analysis of the relationship between industrial modernity, colonialism, and early science fiction to be similarly applicable to the emergence of the genre in China, even though attitudes toward science and technology were markedly different. Finally, I also follow Milner's "The Uses of Science Fiction" as it examines the ways in which SF has been "politically or morally effective" and, to this end, how it is "socially useful" (Milner 2012, 18) in the Chinese case. The features, functions, and forms identified in sketching the limits of a genre are subject to shifting ideological and aesthetic trends. Exploring the intersections between genres and the material and social circumstances that produced them has the potential to contribute to the question of canon formation in the national and transnational perspective.

In their essay "There Is No Such Thing as Science Fiction," Sheryl Vint and Mark Bould likewise argue that SF has never been a single, clearly delineated body of work but is instead the result of various cultural forces by which the meaning of SF is constantly subject to negotiation. However, they trenchantly note that it is impossible to come to a full understanding of SF "without simultaneously acknowledging its erasures of women and indigenous people and its suppression of the human costs of colonization" (Vint and Bould, 48). Recent work by Istvan Csicsery-Ronay (2003), Patricia Kerslake (2007), and John Rieder (2008) elucidates the relationship between SF and imperial discourse, and these works are especially informative when applied to the case of early Chinese SF, given its emergence in the context of colonial modernity. SF is one of many genres for which specific definitions are elusive, despite readers' and critics' certitude that they know it when they see it. SF encompasses a wide range of literary forms; while features such as technology as a central device to the development and resolution of plot are common, I contend that they are not necessary and sufficient conditions. It is for this reason that I argue in favor of a functional definition of the genre, one that reads SF as intimately concerned with the ideologies and discourses of empire. Drawing upon this work, I propose that Chinese SF be examined through the same lens. In so doing, this work contributes to the critique of colonial modernity writ large, adds nuance to a promising avenue of inquiry for SF studies, and seeks to understand how Orientalist discourse is apprehended from the perspective of the other.

Chapter 2, "Lu Xun, Science, Fiction," demonstrates how Lu Xun's essays on science and SF, and his translations of Jules Verne, serve as a useful point of departure in understanding intellectual approaches to scientific knowledge, the written word, and the role of SF in the wide spectrum of experimental genres popularized during the late Qing. I argue that Lu Xun's early work can be understood in part in terms of the "knowledge industry," as an effort to write an encyclopedic history of Western thought. Historical developments in the knowledge industry that soon followed illustrate the ways in which Lu Xun was representative of China's cultural zeitgeist. Like previous literary historians, I share the attitude that Lu Xun is one of the most significant Chinese authors of the twentieth century, if not the most important, and that his work is representative of a number of key transitions and literary themes of modern Chinese literature. However, it is imperative that this understanding of Lu Xun expand its focus in two principal ways. First, I demonstrate that Lu Xun's critique of China's national character, and many of the most vivid metaphors of this critique, can be identified as already prevalent in the work of other prominent late Qing writers. This is by no means intended to diminish the status of Lu Xun; rather, in understanding the ways in which he was working with a set of tropes that could already be seen in wide circulation in popular media, we may come to view Lu Xun as having aggregated and articulated a series of concerns that were already prominent in the popular imagination. As such, Lu Xun's status as the representative of a generation is reinforced, rather than diminished. Second, I show that Lu Xun's work prior to the publication of "Diary of a Madman" (*Kuangren riji*) in 1918, especially his early essays on science and evolution, is also vitally important and deserves greater attention. This body of work helps us both to uncover the labor pains associated with the emergence of vernacular literature, and to understand more clearly the relationship between science and the intellectual formulations of twentieth-century China.

Chapter 3, "Wu Jianren and Late Qing SF," presents an extended, close reading of Wu Jianren's *New Story of the Stone* (*Xin shitou ji*). While this work was not the first work of SF to be produced by a Chinese author, it is both one of the most comprehensive visions of late Qing society and one of the most complete visions of a Chinese utopia. Furthermore, as it is one of the most widely read and analyzed texts of the late Qing, a rereading of *New Stone* permits me to frame my analysis of the thematic content of late Qing SF in the context of a familiar work. I argue that both the first half of the novel, which takes place in Shanghai at the turn of the century, and the second half of the novel are marked by a sense of estrangement that has been identified as a key component of SF. One prominent theme of the novel is the pervasive sense of crisis and the inability to imagine lasting solutions to China's semicolonial subjugation. Another leitmotif is a confrontation with China's own past and its mythical tradition, and I examine the implications of an encounter with the alien other when that beast is one's own tradition. The tropes relevant to Lu Xun's work both before and after the publication of *A Call to Arms* (*Nahan*, 1922) and those that appear in *New Stone* serve as the critical and theoretical foundation that I deploy in my analysis of subsequent works of Chinese SF throughout the twentieth century. This sense of crisis, the confrontation with the past, and the prefiguration of many of Lu Xun's most damning images of Chinese society are features of *New Stone* that appear regularly throughout the entire body of early twentieth-century SF from China.

Chapter 4, "SF for the Nation," examines the leitmotif of colonial incursion in Huangjiang Diaosou's *Tales of the Moon Colony* (*Yueqiu zhimindi xiaoshuo*), and the relationship between early Chinese SF and canonical modern Chinese literature. The anxieties associated with utopianism, nationalism, and Occidentalism visible in early Chinese SF prefigure a number of tropes of canonical Chinese fiction and Lu Xun's metaphors of a sick national body and a cannibalistic society.

The most prominent tropes of this early work remain relevant to the modern literary canon, demonstrating that while SF has waxed and waned in popularity, its thematic concerns and imagery remain central to modern Chinese literature.

In chapter 5, "Making Room for Science," through an examination of Xu Nianci's "New Tales of Mr. Braggadocio" ("Xin faluo xiansheng tan," 1904), I demonstrate how late Qing intellectuals envisioned the usurpation of scientific knowledge, and what limitations on overturning Western epistemologies emerged in his work. As a sequel to a translation of a translation, the story is a case study in the linguistic negotiations central to Lydia Liu's *Translingual Practice*. The story depicts the contested intellectual ground of the late Qing as a case of double consciousness through which the narrator's body and soul explore alternate versions of evolution and scientific knowledge. Thematically and linguistically, the text offers up a number of potential points of resistance to Western epistemology, attempting to fit scientific knowledge within the ken of Daoist cosmology. Especially prominent in "Mr. Braggadocio" is the degree to which the narrator's resistance of Western science contrasts with his ready appropriation of the tenets of capitalist accumulation of wealth, as his success in perfecting the techniques of "brain electricity" ultimately lead to a global economic collapse and to the author's own demise.

In chapter 6, "Lao She's City of Cats," I examine the ways in which the concerns of late Qing SF authors continued to be relevant in SF writing of the Republican period. In the wake of World War I and in the buildup to the second Sino-Japanese War, Lao She's allegory for Chinese society set on a Martian landscape reiterates many of the themes explored in earlier chapters but with an even greater sense of urgency and futility. Lao She addressed a now decades-long sense of crisis with the familiar metaphors of physical illness and failed cures. Like its late Qing counterparts, Lao She's narrative is an allegorical presentation of China's tradition and attempts to come to terms with Western epistemology. This allegorical vision is enabled through the device of the (crashed) spaceship, allowing the narrator to see China at an estranged distance. Paralleling Wu Jianren, the story paints Chinese tradition with a revealing and deeply critical ethnographic brush, depicting almost every cultural institution as a resounding failure. At the same time, the story presents attempts to adapt new ideas and technologies as an equally resounding failure.

Chapter 7, "Whither SF / Wither SF," diverges from the analysis of works of fiction in earlier chapters in order to argue that adequately periodizing and theorizing Chinese SF necessitates accounting for the relationship between the genre and preexisting literary forms. A vexing problem for scholars of Chinese SF is the fact that the genre has weathered a number of high and low tides, and that many of the lowest tides for Chinese SF have come during moments of revolutionary utopian political change. Previous studies have attempted to show the relationship between SF and premodern fantastic tropes but have largely ignored the question of literary form. In my examination of scientific images appearing in the late Qing pictorial *Dianshizhai huabao*, I argue that accounts of science both real and fictional drew on premodern genres from the *biji* and *zhiguai* tradition. I examine the ways in which left-wing intellectuals of the May Fourth and New Culture Movements were engaged in a reassessment of the goals, means, and content of scientific popularization. In the popular science publications of the period, and in contemporaneous critical examinations of such writing, emphasis shifted from natural to social sciences, and from the production and publication of specialized expertise to the dissemination of more readily accessible explanations of the science of everyday life. Just like their late Qing predecessors, writers of the twenties and thirties were ambivalent about the resurrection of old forms and literary styles. Leftist advocates of popular education in the social sciences championed repurposing the *xiaopin* essay, arguing that a formerly elite genre of private appreciation could be adopted to serve the purpose of popular education. The utopian focus of nonfiction popular science writing from this period stands in stark contrast to Lao She's *Cat Country*.

1

GENRE TROUBLE

DEFINING SCIENCE FICTION

 The following chapter presents a summary of recent trends in the field of SF studies and offers some initial observations on their germaneness to early Chinese SF. These observations are developed more thoroughly in the close readings and historical accounts that follow in chapters 2 through 6. I do not intend to force Chinese SF at the turn of the twentieth century into a universalizing theoretical framework, nor am I making an Orientalist argument positing the exceptionality of "SF with Chinese characteristics." Rather, what follows is meant to demonstrate that Chinese cultural studies and SF studies have much to offer each other. Though the readings of Chinese SF that emerge from these theoretical foundations often deviate from them in significant ways, I find these areas of disciplinary convergence and divergence to be useful points of departure both in coming to terms with the local emergence of Chinese SF and in contributing to the understanding of SF as a global phenomenon.

In the words of James Gunn, "The most important, and most divisive, issue in SF is definition" (Gunn and Candelaria, 5), an opinion reflected in a number of recent studies of the genre (Vint and Bould; Milner 2012; Latham 2014; Gunn, Barr, and Candelaria; Luckhurst). Darko Suvin's *Metamorphoses of Science Fiction: On the Poetics and History of a Literary Genre* (1979) remains one of the most repeated and widely accepted definitions of the genre. Suvin's linear history of the genre and its constituent elements, and his definition of SF as "a literary genre whose necessary and sufficient conditions are the presence and interaction of estrangement and cognition, and whose main formal device is an imaginative framework alternative to the author's empirical environment" (Suvin, 7), have been fundamental in part because they served as the conceptual framework for the journal *Science Fiction Studies*, which he helped to cofound in 1973 (Luckhurst, 7). Andrew Milner notes that Suvin's work is the "core critical approach specific to the genre, against which almost everything else has been obliged to define itself," and that Suvin's work plays a significant role in theoretical interventions on the genre written by Carl Freedman (2000) and Fredric Jameson (2005) (Milner 2012, 1–2). John Rieder's history of the study of the genre, "On Defining SF, or Not: Genre Theory, SF and History," indicates this as well (Rieder 2010, 192).

Many Chinese-language studies of SF follow in making recourse to Suvin's definition, occasionally pointing to premodern utopias or fables of technology as local predecessors of the genre (Lin Jianqun; Rao Zhonghua; Wu Yan; Wang Jianyun and Chen Jieshi). In practical terms, if one were to ask a store clerk to point to the SF section in a bookstore in Shanghai, she would be likely to find herself in familiar but not entirely identical territory, owing to the contingencies of local historical and social conditions. SF works in China are often sandwiched in the children's section, and this is reflected in the ages of those browsing the shelves. Implicit in the suggestion that they are for children is that they are marginalia—horror, fantasy, and mystery are often nearby, but SF rarely finds its way onto "literature" (*wenxue*) shelves. Chinese SF marketing, like that of its Western counterpart, often emphasizes newness: one is unlikely to find a reprint of a Qing-era SF novel, save for commemorative editions.[1] The SF shelves in a bookstore in China are also very likely to emphasize translated works. This is a reflection both of the perceived exoticism of the genre and of the market forces that push many forms of contemporary genre fiction off bookshelves and onto the Internet. The apparent familiarity of the above generalizations regarding critical trends and market forces influencing the study of Chinese SF makes it all the more important to be cognizant of what is at stake when—to mangle Damon Knight—we point to a work and say, "This is Chinese science fiction."[2]

The Cultural Field

Recent reformulations of genre theory have turned to an understanding of SF as a historically and culturally contingent category: a "selective tradition" (Milner 2012, 202) characterized by shifting and contentious formulations resulting from various critical claims and modes. These studies have in various ways moved away from attempts to define a fixed object of study, in favor of framing SF as a mutable category acknowledging a wide range of media and practices of production and consumption (Vint and Bould; Gunn, Barr, and Candelaria; Milner 2012; Rieder 2010). These definitions draw particularly on Rick Altman's "A Semantic/Syntactic Approach to Film Genre" (1984, 1999) and Raymond Williams's sociological analysis of cultural production (1979, 1980) in understanding SF as a historically situated and socially conditioned constellation of forces of production and consumption. Henry Jenkins's *Convergence Culture* (2006), which demonstrates how narrative content pollinates "across multiple media platforms," and Marc Steinberg's development of this concept as "media convergence," similarly contribute to an understanding of the ways in which narrative topoi function as the product of global networks of production and distribution. Reading literature in general and SF in particular as a conglomeration of socially embedded media, modes, and practices centered on a thematic core has two advantages. First, it strikes a balance between close and distant reading, allowing the critic to see specific texts in terms of their cultural milieu. Second, it allows critics to elucidate connections between narrative conventions that appear throughout a variety of media.

Veronica Hollinger historicizes the emergent understanding of SF as a "mode" rather than a genre, offering that "mode implies not a kind but a method, a way of getting something done. In [the case of William Gibson], in a way of thinking and speaking about contemporary reality so that SF becomes integrated with other discourses about late-capitalist global-techno-culture" (Hollinger 2014, 140). Borrowing Raymond Williams's concept of a "structure of feeling" and analysis of the cultural apparatus, Andrew Milner argues that SF should be understood as (a) a form conditioned by relations between social modes, and (b) specifiable material practices within which those relations are enacted (Milner 2012). In a similar vein, John Rieder has argued that SF might be understood in terms of Wittgenstein's concept of "family resemblance" and Deleuze and Guattari's notion of the rhizomatic assemblage to describe genres in general and SF in particular as a gradually articulated, nebulous assemblage of texts that cannot be reduced to a single historical progenitor or formal type (Rieder 2010). This and other rubrics understand SF variously as a convergence of media, genres, forms, or modes, emphasizing its diffusion and diversity of the objects and modes of cultural production. These works span literary production, fan clubs and other practices of audience participation, film, radio, music, poetry, role-playing games, newspaper comic strips, comic books, and toys. These cultural apparatuses bleed over into political culture at the level of space programs and military defense, emerging religious practices (e.g., scientology), and practices of display evident in museums and world expos (Luckhurst, 10; Telotte, 162–182; Milner 2012, 7). Alongside the expansion of media practices included under the umbrella of SF is an expansion of the analytical frame beyond national borders in recognition of the intensification of global exchange in the culture industry.

Milner argues that SF can be visualized as a distribution of tropes across the media landscape using Bourdieu's notion of the field of literary and cultural production (Bourdieu 1993). Bourdieu maps literary production as a continuum of profitability vs. artistic license on its horizontal axis, high vs. low cultural status on its vertical axis, and diagonally in terms of its political conservatism. Milner suggests that SF in various media can be identified throughout the field. Having placed SF within the cultural field in general, Milner goes on to argue that a more or less isomorphic map may be used more specifically to illustrate the relationships between various mediated iterations of SF narratives and subgenres (e.g., cyberpunk fiction, art-house cinema, SF criticism) (2011, 394–396; 2012, 42–47).

Critics of modern Chinese literature (see edited collection, Hockx 1999) have shown how Bourdieu's cultural field can also be used productively in understanding modern Chinese literary production, leading Michel Hockx to suggest that a map of the Chinese field of cultural production include a third axis that accounts for the political capital of a work. Hockx also notes that a China-specific map of mutual relations between "institutions of material and symbolic production" would necessarily entail certain reconfigurations given the different cultural landscape and different historical trajectories (17–19). In like manner, Paola Iovene's *Tales of Futures Past* (2014) understands modern Chinese literature as an assemblage of texts, social practices, editorial strategies, and experiences of reading (13–14). In sum, recent reconfigurations of genre theory have led to an approach regarding SF as a selective tradition best understood as a mode of reading and interpretation. At the same time, scholars of modern Chinese culture have applied these same observations of cultural production and genre to understanding their area of research. Without attempting to completely reconfigure the above observations in service of constructing a "cultural SF field with Chinese characteristics," it should be noted that late Qing literature was in many ways distinguished by an increasingly central role for fiction (as opposed to poetry) and a contestation of whether the classical language or the modern vernacular best suited the mode. To borrow a scientific (or SF) metaphor, we might add to our three-dimensional figure—depicting symbolic, political, and economic capital—a fourth dimension, permitting us to see the ways that individual elements of the cultural field shifted over time.

Almost immediately after the first Sino-Japanese War, fiction came to be understood as a key battleground in the quest for reform (Huters 1988, 262). For a number of late Qing intellectuals, the vernacular novel was a new form that incorporated a wide variety of new ideas and narrative techniques, a form that could reach a broader audience and make that audience aware of the severity of the crisis China faced (Huters 2005, 100–120).[3] SF was understood as one of a number of genres that, through the literary form of the new novel, could help to espouse lasting social change. This was in part a consequence of the wide range of issues that authors sought to address in their work. Characters travel both domestically and abroad, encounter natural, supernatural, and technological anomalies, have extended dialogues on political thought (that more closely resemble manifestos than fiction), meet great philosophers of Eastern and Western traditions, and often participate in any of the above activities in a dream. Fiction monthlies often included extended treatises on the history of civilization, or the rise of the Western world. Many instances of these works were loose translations of unattributed Western and Japanese works. The generic and epistemological pluralism seen in the pages of late Qing fiction is a reflection of the social and cultural hybridity of China's burgeoning urban, semicolonial centers, and of the multitudinous problems and solutions that late Qing intellectuals grappled with in their writings.

The turmoil engendered by the presence of foreign material and intellectual culture widened the cracks in the foundations of Chinese society through which new ideas flooded in. Culturally hybrid spaces such as Shanghai gave birth to a new worldview that attempted to reconcile radically different approaches to the pursuit of knowledge and government. Literature was no exception. The late Qing intellectual "atmosphere of crisis and utopian hope" (Huters 2005, 132) heralded the introduction of new literary forms and genres. The enthusiasm for the "new novel" represents a rare point of unity in the otherwise politically fractious intellectual atmosphere of early twentieth-century China. Probably the clearest justification for the new focus of the novel was the idea that the form could accommodate two urgent requirements: a larger audience for writing, and the potential to effectively represent to this larger audience the full dimensions of the crisis China faced (Huters 2005, 24–25; 1988, 261). This vision of literary purpose would be adopted by May Fourth literati, and its echoes continue to reverberate in the contemporary period.

Geographically, Milner also considers the applicability of world systems theory in understanding the development of sf, applying Franco Moretti's concept of core, periphery, and semi-periphery developed in "Conjectures on World Literature" and *Atlas of the European Novel* to the development of sf. Milner argues that "what is true for the novel in general is also true for sf. Conceived in England and France, at the core of the nineteenth-century world literary system (Shelley, Bulwer-Lytton and, above all, Verne and Wells), it continued in both countries throughout the twentieth and into the twenty-first centuries" (Milner 2012, 165). Milner describes a largely European semi-periphery, arguing that the United States and Japan transformed from semi-peripheral to core SF countries during the twentieth century. The global periphery of Milner's selective tradition consists of those countries that predominately translated works from core countries into their target languages, and which did not contribute to the global tradition. This parallels the emergence of Sinophone studies, a mode of analysis that understands Chinese-language cultural production as the product of core-periphery relationships betwixt and between a number of local and global empires (Shih 2007; Shih, Bernards, and Tsai 2013).

These approaches help demonstrate that SF is much more than any single Platonic prototype, neatly bound within the borders of a national literary tradition. All reflect a turn toward a historical approach to genre that understands the literary field as the product of global relations of economic and political power. John Rieder observes that "sf's identity is a differentially articulated position in an historical and mutable field of genres," and that furthermore SF fits into an "economy of genres." In other words, SF is a gradual accretion of texts that make use of, rather than belong to, a genre (Rieder 2010, 197–199). In this light, it is most useful to ask what SF was at a given historical moment and geographical location, and what critical, social, or political purposes it served, rather than to seek universalizing definitions.

Milner identifies imperialism as one of the constituent elements of SF but ultimately concludes that social transformations wrought by technological innovation and the dialectic of enlightenment and romanticism are the most salient topoi of SF as a global genre. However, in the case of late Qing China, I argue that Orientalism and imperialism were indeed the most conspicuous themes. For this reason, before we are able to move on to an examination of the ways in which China's semicolonial status shaped the emergence and thematic content of early Chinese SF, the various media and narrative modes that were particular to the emergence of the genre in China, and an analysis of the texts themselves, it is necessary to explicate the relationship between SF and imperialism.

Imperialism and SF

The historical conditions outlined in the introduction apply equally to the literary field of the nineteenth and twentieth century. Fictional depictions of exploration in the work of authors like H. Rider Haggard brought the imaginary horizons of imperial expansion home for readers, inspiring new generations of young imperial subjects to join in the effort (Katz, 1–3, 108–112). Romantic genres like adventure and SF were central to this self-reinforcing impetus to expansion, catalysts fueled by and that in turn helped to fuel the growing sphere of imperial influence. Dreams of material and intellectual rewards of conquest provided ample source material for authors of a number of genres. In turn, this imagination paved the way for and fueled the desire for continued efforts of exploration and conquest. The imaginary horizons of the twentieth century were heavily influenced by the exchanges between Europe and Asia. These exchanges were source material for early European SF, which in turn helped to broaden the literary and intellectual horizons of East Asian countries like China and Japan.

Quoting William Blake in *Culture and Imperialism*, Edward Said noted that "empire follows art, and not vice versa as Englishmen suppose" (Said 1993, 13).[4] Empire is as dependent on the intellectual rationalization that sustains its mission as it is upon the military force necessary to carry out the act of physical conquest. Framed in terms of enlightenment, emancipation, and benevolent paternalism, the justifications for going to war and for continued occupation are as involved as the actual moment of conquest itself. Indeed, this rationalization, however untenable, is dependent on masking military conquest with the façade of moral good and humanitarian aid. Or, as Michael Hardt and Antonio Negri put it, "Empire is formed not on the basis of force itself, but on the capacity to present force as being in the service of right and peace" (Hardt and Negri, 15).

Recent work in the vein of Said's critique of Orientalism has shown that SF was one of many genres that paved the way for empire by creating the conditions for its popular imagination. The wish-fulfillment narratives of science and adventure fiction served as primers describing how young men of ambition might contribute to and partake in the spoils of conquest. The imaginary horizons of imperial expansion were brought to the minds of readers of romantic genres of adventure and SF in the work of authors like H. Rider Haggard and Daniel Defoe, inspiring new generations of young imperial subjects to join in the effort. Images of men of action—explorers, engineers, soldiers, and sailors—were intended to be the role models of a new generation of imperial actors (Richards, 1–6; Mathison, 173–174). In Meiji Japan, translations of science fiction and adventure novels served as tools for establishing an imaginary horizon that valorized the mission of exploration and conquest, priming young men for their participation in what would eventually become Japan's own effort at imperial expansion, the "Greater East Asia Co-prosperity Sphere."

The global relations that led to the emergence of SF mirror those that swung late nineteenth-century China from an empire at the center of Asian trade and tribute to a semicolonial outpost at the margins of European empire. Istvan Csicsery-Ronay suggests that three factors were critical to the emergence of SF: "the technological expansion that drove real imperialism, the need felt by national audiences for literary-cultural mediation as their societies were transformed from historical nations into hegemons, and the fantastic model of achieved techno-scientific Empire" (Csicsery-Ronay 2003, 231).

These three factors reiterate Said's vision of the novel writ large as a literary form functionally tied to the comprehension of expanding networks of global trade and domination, spurred on and enabled by industrial production in the context of the genre of SF in particular. Csicsery-Ronay identifies a positive correlation between SF and imperialism, recognizing Britain, France, Germany, the former Soviet Union, Japan, and the United States as the primary producers and consumers of SF, arguing that SF has been driven by a desire for "transformation of imperialism into Empire" (232). The geopolitical imagination of SF is intimately concerned with the imagination of a historical teleology leading to an all-encompassing world order.[5] As empire is the imaginary political horizon of SF, Orientalism is a major influence on its discursive content. John Rieder's *Colonialism and the Emergence of Science Fiction* (2008) adds to this critique an explanation of the historical conditions that tied Orientalism to sf. Colonial expansion and the simultaneous establishment of European capitalism on a global scale were driving forces in the emergence of the genre. Orientalist discourse strove to define inequalities often produced by the colonial project as the natural outcome of preexisting difference; sf served at turns to reinforce these notions, and at others to subvert them.

> Two aspects of the construction of a world-embracing capitalist economy are particularly relevant to the relation between colonialism and the emergence of science fiction. The first is the realignment of local identities that accompanied the restructuring of the world economy. . . . What the dominant ideology recognized as the relation between civilization and savagery, and between modernity and its past, can be read at least in part as a misrecognition of the corrosive effects of capitalist social relations on the traditional cultures of colonized populations and territories. Understanding the non-Western world as an earlier stage of Western social development, in this line of interpretation, serves the apologetic function of naturalizing the relation of the industrialized economic core to the colonial periphery and rendering its effects as the working out of an inexorable, inevitable historical process. But the scientific study of other cultures—what Derrida calls the decentering of Europe as the culture of reference—is intimately bound up with the same economic process. I therefore will be arguing both that the ideological misrecognition of the effects of economic and political inequality has a strong presence in the ideas about progress and modernity that circulate throughout early science fiction, and also that early science fiction often works against such ethnocentrism. (Rieder 2008, 26)

In many cases, colonialism did not merely recognize inequalities in technological, economic, or social development; it actively produced and benefited from those inequalities.[6] The visibility of these inequalities in turn led to the establishment of both discourses that naturalized and discourses that called into question the centrality of European cultural systems.

Second, in the creation of a "world-embracing capitalist economy," Rieder emphasizes the emergence of a reading public interested in the "vicarious enjoyment of colonial spoils, as attested to in Victorian England by the popularity of travel accounts and adventure stories. . . . The early science fiction reading audience—middle class, educated, and provided with leisure—seems to be one well placed to put into action the consumerism at the heart of modern mass culture" (2008, 27–28). The material transformations of the industrial revolution heralded a new age of mass production and mass consumption and helped to create an audience for sf. Roger Luckhurst enumerates a similar set of conditions to those identified by Rieder: a growing population of readers with at least a primary education; the replacement of popular literary forms like the penny dreadful and the dime novel with new serial formats that demanded formal innovation; a growing class of individuals who had received technical education and training, whose education made them more likely to "confront traditional loci of cultural authority"; and the immediate visibility of cultural transformations brought about by the increasing role of mechanical production in daily life (Luckhurst, 16–17). The industrial economy demanded a segment of the workforce endowed with some level of scientific and technological proficiency. These individuals would have made an apt audience for sf, with its strong emphasis on technological innovation. The industrial revolution also saw a shift away from extensive labor and toward intensive, more productive labor and limited work hours, creating spaces of leisure time to be filled in part by reading. The birth of a consumer industry seeking to capitalize on the free time of individuals with disposable income presents a convergence of market forces productive of both a readership and a widening array of genres for their consumption.

Finally, Rieder argues that the economic boom of the 1850s–1870s, followed by an economic downturn during the latter part of the same century, represented the establishment of capitalism as the global economic system, and increasing competition for land, labor, and capital between industrialized nations. This resulted in "the imperial competition that gave birth to the first modern arms race" (Rieder 2008, 28). "Three masses of modernity" converge in sf—mass production, mass consumption, and mass annihilation. If mass production and mass consumption are productive of readership of sf, mass annihilation and imperialism are among the anxieties at its narrative core. Again, in Istvan Csicsery-Ronay's history of the relationship between sf and other genres, he argues that "sf's characteristic mutations of the adventure forms reflect the discourse of a transnational global regime of technoscientific rationalization that followed the collapse of the European imperialist project. sf narrative accordingly has become the leading mediating institution for the utopian construction of technoscientific Empire. And for resistance to it" (Csicsery-Ronay 2003, 8).

In *Culture and Imperialism*, Edward Said demonstrates the degree to which even narratives that were critical of the excesses and abuses of the imperial mission were marked by a failure to imagine a world free of imperial expansion and domination. As tragic as were the incursion, extraterritorial governance, and virtual (and real) enslavement of indigenous peoples, together with the extraction of native resources for the benefit of the metropole, the discourse of social Darwinism and of the native incapacity for autonomy nevertheless went hand in hand with the assumption that self-governance was an impossibility. In his reading of Conrad's *Heart of Darkness*, Said writes, "As a creature of his time, Conrad could not grant the natives their freedom, despite his severe critique of the imperialism that enslaved them" (Said 1993, 30). The imperial imagination proved to be such a compelling notion that many authors were not able to conceive of the absence of empire, despite growing awareness of its abuses.

Another facet of the universalizing impulse of imperial discourse, Said's "universalizing historicism"—the Orientalist notion that history possessed a "coherent unity" and that spatial difference was equivalent to temporal difference—has been used to explain the widely held impression that different places occupied different points in a universal time line, and that Europe was at the vanguard of history's inexorable forward march. This mode of historiographical thinking also serves to freeze oriental societies in time, substituting culture for history (Said 1986, 211, 230–234; Dirlik, 96–98). Couched in terms of empirically observable truth and mathematical predictability, time asserts itself as a measuring stick of evolution, and Europe as the geographical vanguard of evolutionary progress. Hegelian Asiatic despotism marks China and the East as spatial and temporal laggards. For authors of Chinese SF, a crucial concern was the question of whether identifying cultural equivalencies, asserting cultural superiority, or arriving at cultural compromise could be possible in the context of a universal historical trajectory defined by Western civilization.

Rieder's "world-embracing capitalist economy" came into being in concert with what we might call the "three masses of modernity"—mass consumption, mass production, and mass destruction. These were precisely the material conditions that produced Tani Barlow's colonial modernity, and that led to the polyphonous responses emergent in late Qing society and letters. The naturalization of inequity, an emerging culture of leisure and entertainment spurred on by mass production and mass consumption, and the threat of mass annihilation brought on by an emerging arms race in the competition to seize colonial holdings are as central to the development of Chinese SF and to its thematic concerns as they were to the development of European SF. SF and translations of Western science emerged in the popular presses of early twentieth-century Shanghai and in the publishing ventures that were undertaken in Japan.[7] This publication was one aspect of a vibrant, burgeoning publishing industry, often alongside other more canonically recognized genres and discourses. As an instance of translingual practice, social Darwinism was unmoored from Thomas Huxley's critical reading of its implications (perhaps not surprisingly, given China's semicolonial plight), transmogrified into a system of moral and social valuation, and understood as a road map to emergent global relations of power.

Patricia Kerslake identifies a parallel between the function of the other as delineated in Said's critique of colonial epistemologies and the function of the other in SF's visions of the alien. A leitmotif of SF is the exoticism of the unknown and the expansionist drive, in part for its own sake, but also in the interest of defining the self in opposition to the other: "Where postcolonial theory challenges the silencing and marginalization of the Other, SF takes the stance that such marginalization is a key element of self-identification" (Kerslake, 10–11). Self-identification in SF comes alongside the triumph over and silencing of the alien other, an affirmation of the superiority of humanity. Kerslake identifies an evolution of SF from a genre in which "marginalization is a key element of self-identification," into a "legitimate cultural discourse that has brought "serious social expositions of contemporary society" (11, 14–15). To this end, Kerslake suggests that Said's work offers academic legitimacy to SF studies, through which the relationship between extraterrestrials can be explored in a familiar critical vocabulary, stating that "given a residual academic reluctance to engage with SF, it is necessary to extrapolate certain contemporary theories and exchange the term 'East' for 'extraterrestrial,' so that the principles thus debated become productive in a genre which in itself has been marginalized" (14–15).

Kerslake notes that in canonical SF, the silencing of an alien antagonist is often deployed as a means of subverting the legitimacy of European civilization/humanism as the universal subject. Rieder, Kerslake, and Milner all argue that SF does indeed have the potential to subvert ethnocentrism. Kerslake frames the duality of ethnocentrism and subversion in terms of a forbidden "political pornography" or an increasingly meaningful, if ironic, literary experiment (Kerslake, 29). Milner argues that Said's relatively terse analysis of Jules Verne (Said 1993, 187), Gayatri Spivak's more detailed deconstruction of the function of colonial consciousness in Mary Shelley's *Frankenstein* (Spivak 1988, 1999), and Rieder and Csicsery-Ronay's analyses of SF and empire all overstate the thematic centrality of Orientalism in the genre. Milner contends that "the genre was at once ideological, in the pejorative sense, and yet also critical" (Milner 2012, 159). This approach understands genre in terms of its contradictions—identifying in SF the potential to subvert Orientalist discourse despite the fact that it borrows the same language and is embedded in its cultural milieu. In warning against seeing Orientalism as the single necessary and sufficient condition of SF, Milner goes on to argue that "the novel in general and SF in particular are equally unthinkable without capitalist relations of production, or without patriarchal gender relations, or without systematic heterosexism. Which is why Marxist, feminist, and queer readings are readily available, not only for *Frankenstein*, but for SF texts more generally" (Milner 2012, 160). Acknowledging the pitfalls of identifying industrial modernity or Orientalism as the sole identifying feature of the genre on a global scale, I argue that the emergence of Chinese SF cannot be adequately understood without coming to terms with the degree to which late Qing authors framed their predicament in exactly those terms. In the words of Wu Yan, "Colonialism is not the only problem for SF, but it is the most important question."[8]

Colonial modernity, Shanghai's semi-peripheral position in the world economy, and the peripheral role of Chinese SF at the turn of the twentieth century meant that the contradictions of Chinese SF developed differently from the American and European counterparts at the heart of Milner's and Kerslake's analyses. In their approach to science and to science fiction, Chinese intellectuals were faced with a very different contradiction: even if SF's ideological proximity to Orientalism could be subverted at the discursive level, how could these narrative turns undo the political realities that Orientalism had created? I demonstrate that in the case of Chinese SF, the other that must be silenced is as often China's own indigenous tradition as it is an alien invader. In the same moment that Chinese SF authors attempted to assert the imperial strengths of embattled antiquity, they also struggled to bring other aspects of Chinese antiquity into the interpretive framework of scientific explanation. The impulse to resuscitate antiquity also necessitated choosing which version of antiquity would be restored or reinterpreted, and which would be silenced. Such a response also engendered competing impulses between explanations of science in the context of Chinese tradition and explanations of Chinese tradition in the context of science. This is part and parcel of the schizophrenic response to foreign incursion wherein the binaries of traditional/modern and native/foreign appeared equally nonviable. In Chinese SF, the other is a hydra whose heads are competing versions of tradition and modernity. Time is one aspect through which this study examines the question of narrative and empire from the other side of the colonial equation that the Chinese authors grappled with in attempting to answer the question of whether they themselves could overturn the epistemological realities born of European empire and Western science. Chinese authors were conscious of the contradictions and pitfalls inherent in attempting to use an imperialist genre in the effort to overturn such discourses. As with many Western works of SF that enact critiques of empire, it can be argued that even those authors whose work was highly critical of the world system that empire strove for were unable to envision its absence. At the same time, Chinese SF evinces a competing and contradictory impulse in the often-unconscious desire to expand China's own empire beyond its late Qing borders. Turn-of-the-century Chinese intellectuals often wrote through the lens of a false dichotomy of besieged nation and foreign empire.

Rieder's definition of the functions and emergence of SF has profound implications for the intellectual and literary ground of turn-of-the-twentieth-century Shanghai. Shanghai was one of the locations where the artificial line between civilization and savagery, and between tradition and modernity, was drawn, and where the deleterious effects of colonial capitalism naturalized the difference between conquerors and conquered. It was also a city where the decentering of Europe appeared not as a side effect of an evolving vision of the world, but as an imperative project in the mission of China's own national salvation. Rieder's contention that misrepresentation and misunderstanding of the causes and effects of global disparities in wealth and power are plainly visible in early SF and that SF has the potential to work against such ethnocentrism is of central concern to this study as well. Global disparities in wealth and power, the relations that produced them and the veracity of scientific theories that explain them, are a salient concern of early Chinese SF. The line between civilization and barbarity, and whether this line is drawn by might or right, is a leitmotif in the writing of a number of late Qing SF novels. Furthermore, an explicit point of contention in Chinese discourses on science and in SF was not the question of whether ethnocentrism was a tenable notion, but which ethnic/cultural system deserved to be at the center, and how one could come to be there.

SF against the Empire

In order to assess the particularities of SF in the Chinese context, this study takes late Qing authors such as Lu Xun and Wu Jianren as models for the construction of a local poetics of the tradition. These two authors demonstrate the unique ways in which Kerslake and Rieder's theories of colonialism and imperialism are reflected in Chinese SF. An understanding of the local inflections of these discourses that emerge in analysis of Lu Xun and Wu Jianren will in turn serve as a theoretical springboard for the rest of this work. Lu Xun, positioned between the worlds of medicine and literature, and firmly ensconced in canonical literary historiography as the father of modern Chinese literature, serves as a theoretical linchpin both for understanding attitudes toward science in early twentieth-century China and for understanding the form and function of SF. Wu Jianren, whose multi-genre *New Story of the Stone* contains many of the hallmarks of SF, serves as a second example of local iterations of SF in the late Qing and of the matrix of anxieties that I intend to explore throughout the modern period. In their SF works, both authors evince the utopian "sense of wonder" that Suvin identifies as a hallmark of the genre. This sense of wonder is expressed as a focus on scientific advancement and a deep faith in the transcendental possibilities of technology. This utopian wonder is tempered by a profound ambivalence, which I understand in terms of Lu Xun's iconic iron house metaphor—while both men produced fiction aimed at awakening China's benighted populace, inky shadows of doubt loom large in their work. Both express concern with China's incorporation of Western epistemologies and the process of reconciling these fields of knowledge with Chinese philosophical and political traditions. In many cases, this incorporation is an out-and-out physical confrontation, reflective of the influence of colonialism and imperialism.

For Chinese writers of SF, the question that emerged and that they openly grappled with in their writing was whether a genre that they clearly understood to be imbricated with Orientalism and scientism could be turned against its wielders. While SF was used in attempts to unmask, resist, and subvert Orientalism, such efforts often proved to be futile. On other occasions, these narratives repeated the discourse of imperial domination, finding their own fictional others to depict. Just as often, these narratives were characterized by a dialectic of native tradition and modernity, meaning that the confrontation was not between China and another civilization but between China and its own past.

Furthermore, in Chinese SF, China's cultural totems become representatives of the totality of its history. This reappropriation of Orientalist depictions of China as frozen in history is fraught with uncertainty regarding the power of native tradition and its relationship to Western epistemology. In works like *Tales of the Moon Colony*, "New Tales of Mr. Braggadocio," *The New Era* (*Xin jiyuan*, 1906), and *New China* (*Xin zhongguo*, 1910), time is central to anxieties of social and moral decay, to the reordering of the modern world and the decentering of China, and to the relationship between the power to name the year and the relationship between East and West. In other words, can we set our clocks to an hour other than Greenwich Mean Time, and can we set our calendars to a year other than the Gregorian year? If not or if so, what are the implications of both?

In the case of China, I demonstrate what fraught territory such discourse could be, as late Qing and early Republican intellectuals sought both to overturn the balance of power between China, Japan, and Europe, and to express their own desires for supranational hegemony. In most instances, Chinese SF is concerned with the confrontation between an imperial aggressor and a unified Chinese national body. While this is a false equivalency—the Qing Manchu rulers and the Republican government alike could be understood as imperial systems—the dominant perception was one of a confrontation between European empire and Chinese nation. These narratives reveal a kaleidoscopic response to empire that is seldom as simple as dialectical inversion of its discourses.

This existential crisis shared many of the traits of double consciousness as described by Frantz Fanon and W. E. B. Du Bois,[9] causing authors and intellectuals to see themselves from the perspective of both the oppressed and the oppressor, to desire an end of imperial expansion and in the same moment seek to reclaim and reinvigorate China's own imperial mission. However, this response was more multifaceted than the simple binary opposition of master and slave. The sum total of this series of false dichotomies—empire-nation, self-other, modernity-tradition, science-humanism, and so on—is a kaleidoscopic response, fraught with ambivalence. One dialectical encounter becomes many, and no clear synthesis emerges. Conrad's failure of imagination was one in which he could not conceive of a world absent of empire; for late Qing writers of SF, the failure of imagination entailed the inability to imagine a world absent of European empire. The narrative failure to figure alternatives becomes a de facto assertion of the supremacy of the status quo.

At the beginning of the twentieth century, China resembled the European sphere in the material conditions that Rieder identifies as having given birth to the readership for SF. China was unique in this regard in being the subject, rather than the beneficiary, of colonial and imperial incursion. The anxieties accompanying science also took on "Chinese characteristics"—as not merely anxieties about the destructive potential of science, but also anxieties regarding the inherent foreignness of science—and also differentiate China from the European context in question in Kerslake's and Rieder's analyses. Finally, I would like to argue that China exhibited local specificities in its confrontation with the other—its having emerged as the one of the others of Orientalist discourse did not entail a simple inversion of the European formulation of self and other. My analysis will demonstrate that Chinese SF is as enmeshed in dealing with the country's own indigenous traditions as it is in the confrontation with foreign powers or alien invaders. That is, the alien other that Chinese SF confronts is China itself.

2

LU XUN,
SCIENCE, FICTION
SCIENCE FICTION
AND THE CANON

Lu Xun's preface to *A Call to Arms* relates his apoplexy upon viewing the image of a Chinese man being executed in Japanese-occupied Manchuria and the apathetic countenances of the surrounding crowd, and how this moment in a lecture hall in Sendai in 1905 led him to abandon the study of medicine and turn toward the "spiritual cure" of literature. This moment is ripe material for scholars of Chinese literature and film in search of a single traumatic rupture to represent the inception of modern Chinese literature.[1] His father's succumbing to tuberculosis had led Lu Xun to Japan to study medicine, where he was then exposed to what he determined to be China's spiritual illness. The young man determined that he could do more to save China with the spiritual elixir of the written word than with the curative properties of medicine. Over the course of the twentieth century, he became the emblem of the era, the patron saint of modern Chinese literature. Part of the universe that Lu Xun wanted to bring home was science, and he saw fiction as an apt vehicle for its introduction. Many years before the seminal preface to *A Call to Arms*, the young Lu Xun's translation and writing represent a liminal moment in which his commitment to science began to shift to literature. Lu Xun is an instructive figure for understanding attitudes toward science in early twentieth-century China, for examining the form and function of late Qing SF, and for understanding the relationship between the genre and canonical literature.

Many of the themes identifiable in Chinese SF are central to modern Chinese literature as a whole. Lu Xun's most prominent themes, especially the vision of a sick society and "crisis of figuration" (Huters 2005, 254–279) expressed most forcefully in his short stories "Diary of a Madman" and "Medicine" ("Yao," 1919, *LXQJ*, 1:463–472), are emblematic of the pervasiveness of pharmacological metaphor in popular literature at large. Prior to Lu Xun's adoption of these metaphors, the "sick man of Asia" (*dongya bingfu*) was already a prominent trope in a number of late Qing works, including SF.[2] The anxieties and motifs crystallized in Lu Xun's oeuvre were visible prior to the literary revolution of 1917–1919 and became pervasive in the wake of his lionization as the father of modern Chinese literature.

Lu Xun's essays on science and SF, and his translations of Jules Verne (1903), serve as a useful point of departure in understanding late Qing approaches to scientific knowledge and the emergent role of SF in the multi-genre fiction of the late Qing.[3] Lu Xun's characteristic ambivalence, visible even in his early essays on science and his translations of SF, would become a defining feature of early Chinese SF at large.

Lu Xun heralded the translation of SF, arguing in the preface to his translation of Verne's *De la terre à la lune* that Chinese SF, while "as rare as unicorn horns," possessed the potential to educate the public in the otherwise tedious subject of science, and he encouraged concerted efforts in translation of science fiction (Wu and Murphy, xiii). In the same year, Bao Tianxiao,[4] in his preface to *Tie Shijie* (lit. "Iron world"), the translation of Verne's *Les cinq cents millions de la Bégum*, wrote, "Science fiction is the vanguard of the civilized world," adding that "there are those in the world who don't like to study, but there are none who don't appreciate SF, thus it is an adroit mechanism of importing civilized thought, and its seeds quickly bear fruit."[5] Haitian Duxiaozi (b. ?) wrote in a similar vein, noting the existence "in our country today, [of] the tide of imported Western knowledge, and books volume upon volume to fill a library to the rafters. To get twice the result with half the effort, what might we choose to make popular throughout the land? I implore you to begin with science fiction."[6] Lu Xun and his contemporaries saw in SF the opportunity to disseminate empirical knowledge through the media of popular culture. To this end, Liang Qichao and Xu Nianci produced translations of SF, while the Confucian utopia presented in Kang Youwei's[7] *Book of the Great Unity* (*Datong shu*, 1901) evinced the clear influence of Edward Bellamy's *Looking Backward* (Chen and Xia 1997, 47–48), demonstrating the central role that SF and the utopian imagination played in the formation of modern Chinese literature. This vision of literary purpose would be adopted by May Fourth literati, and its echoes continue to reverberate in the contemporary period. One of these demands was the popularization of scientific knowledge.

The Language of Science and the Language of Fiction

"Science" (*kexue*) was part of the problematic glossary of related and conflated terms associated with what Lydia Liu has termed the "translingual practice" of the late Qing. Much like the concept of modernity, which is firmly rooted in a Weberian/Marxist model that privileges the development of European institutions and economic systems as a teleological historical standard and allows little room for alternatives, the term "science" is rarely associated with its original meaning as simple "knowledge" and is instead tied to the European Enlightenment's scientific method and a limited field of knowledge production. Likewise, the term "civilization" (*wenming*) was transplanted from Japanese, its meaning often conflated with notions of modernity and Westernization. This is demonstrated trenchantly in Lu Xun's early essay "On Imbalanced Cultural Development" ("Wenhua pianzhi lun," 1907), when he asks, "Shall we be instructed to abandon all our past institutions along with the accomplishments of the olden days, and speak only of Western culture as 'civilization'?" (*LXQJ*, 1:47). Wang Hui has shown how understandings of science were further clouded by association with classical Chinese terms. This confusion of terminologies produced a specific and highly paradoxical form of knowledge, one that suggested familiarity through adoption of classical Chinese vocabulary but was often understood to be entirely non-Chinese.[8]

Like the hegemonic narrative of Said's "universalizing historicism," civilization was also a concept associated with the imagination of a single historical trajectory and a universal valuation of cultural worth.

The West was understood to be at the leading edge of evolutionary time: the geographical home of civilization. Logically, if the vanguard of evolution and modernity was in the West, if science was the property of the West, and if civilization was the culmination of Western cultural and scientific achievement on a universal evolutionary scale, then science had to be an indispensable component of civilizational achievement. Theodore Huters and Marsten Anderson have argued that in the literary realm of the late Qing, "modernism" and "realism" were closely associated with one another (Anderson, 27–37; Huters 1993, 147–173). To modernize meant both to cast off the past and the static indigenous tradition that was modernity's other, and to adopt realist modes of narrative representation in writing. Understood as the most viable alternative to a failing imperial system, material modernization and the adoption of realistic narrative modes to promote modernization were also more or less synonymous with Westernization. Science was thus also closely moored to notions of civilization, modernism, and realism.[9]

During the late Qing, definitions of science began to shift toward a sense of objective understanding of the material world. Although precise dating of the first usage of the term *kexue* is clouded by Kang You-wei's penchant for forging memorials, it is clear that use of this term as a translation for "science" did not fully solidify until the early twentieth century, most likely in the year 1911, with the fall of the Qing dynasty (Wang Hui, 15).[10] Not originally a Chinese term, *kexue* was a Japanese import: a product of Japan's Meiji Restoration, and another example of translingual practice. It was during this period that the term *kexue*, and its associations with categorizing knowledge, began to come into widespread usage. *Kexue*, though more closely associated with notions of "observation and factual experiment" (Wang Hui, 18), continued to be associated with positivism and an overarching cosmic order. While Yan Fu's 1898 translation of *Evolution and Ethics* used the term *gezhi*, by 1902, in his translation of Adam Smith's *Wealth of Nations*, he used *kexue* (Qiu Ruohong, 65).

Proponents of Western fields of knowledge like Yan Fu[11] saw sociology as the "science of sciences," offering the ability to unveil the inherent interrelation between natural and social order (Schwarz, 187). "Science was the expression and result of the spirit of positivism, as well as the manifestation of the universal principle and primary driving force known as *tianyan*. As the universal principle, *tianyan* not only revealed the pictures and vistas of the changing world but also determined the criterion of action and direction of value for people" (Wang Hui, 27–28).

As the understanding of science continued to develop, and as its importance continued to ascend in the intellectual hierarchy, science in the Chinese context gradually unmoored itself from its neo-Confucian framework. While the modern scientific lexicon was eventually disambiguated from its neo-Confucian counterpart, the ethical and moral implications of science continued to be foregrounded in intellectual debates and fictional treatment. Science, especially sociology, was seen as a tool for the understanding and reconfiguring of the social order in the interests of nation building. Yan Fu's view of the importance of sociology continued to emphasize the consonance between the natural and the human order, a notion that has long been a central feature of Chinese philosophical thinking.

Despite an ongoing ambivalence about the relationship between Eastern and Western epistemologies, a key shift in attitudes toward science and technology did take place in the wake of the first Sino-Japanese War. Benjamin Schwarz has noted the fact that in translating Thomas Huxley's work on social Darwinism, Yan Fu misapprehended the text's critical stance and, perhaps not surprisingly given China's semicolonial plight, reconfigured a critique of social Darwinism into a system of moral and social valuation (Schwarz, 45–48). The perception that the law of survival of the fittest applied to societies and nations hung over late Qing intellectual life like a sword of Damocles. Yan Fu's translation of Huxley's *Evolution and Ethics* brought Darwinian thinking to China in a form that had already undergone profound reinterpretations. The translator's unique understanding of Huxley's criticism of the social implications of evolution was informed by the apparent reality of social Darwinism under the conditions of colonial rule. What was originally intended to be a criticism of the tenets of social Darwinism was easily understood in East Asia as a matter of historical and empirical fact. At the same time, this tangential offshoot of the main body of evolutionary thinking was identified as its most salient aspect. This is reflected in the writings of late Qing intellectuals like Yan Fu, Liang Qichao, and Kang Youwei, to whom the concept of evolution is most often framed in terms of social Darwinism and racial extinction. Liang Qichao's writing in *Xinmin congbao* reflected a pervasive sense that "naked aggression, once thought barbaric, was now presented as a law of civilization supported by European and American science" (Secord, 48). Many Chinese intellectuals shared H. G. Wells's anxiety that while evolutionary time implied linear motion, the forward progression of time could be reversed, with human intervention playing a key role in the direction a given society was to travel (Pusey 1983, 57–64; Murthy, 79–80).[12]

Translating Jules Verne

Tracing the complicated trajectory that brought Jules Verne's *De la terre à la lune* (*From the Earth to the Moon*) to China presents the scholar of Chinese literature with an interesting case study in Lydia Liu's "translingual practice," as the text was creatively reinterpreted through the process of translation. At the same time, this act of translation demonstrates how a French SF text was incorporated into the Chinese literary field. The novel was translated from the French original into English, made its way to Japan (most likely) via an American translation, where it was then translated into Japanese by Inoue Tsutomu (1850–1928) as *Getsukai ryokō*, and was then rendered into Chinese by Lu Xun as *Yuejie lüxing* (1903).[13] It is unclear which English version Inoue was working with, but it is likely that his translation came from a less-than-accurate version of the original. One glaring inaccuracy is the fact that Lu Xun mistook Jules Verne to be English, an error replicated from Inoue's translation. It is difficult to say with certainty whether either translator was aware of the satirical nature of the novel. Verne himself harbored serious doubts about the efficacy of science and the promise of the future (Smyth, 118–119), but Meiji and Chinese authors writing in a similar vein often adopted such militaristic discourse with a sense of enjoyment, and adventure.

Reinterpretation, rather than translation, is a more appropriate term for Lu Xun's efforts in bringing *From the Earth to the Moon* to a Chinese audience, and Lu Xun himself admitted as much. The specific choices made in reformatting Verne's work illustrate the transformations that took place when foreign novels were rendered into Chinese, and what methods translators employed when they sought to make their work palatable to a local audience. In a letter to Yang Jiyun about his 1903 translation of Verne's *Voyage au centre de la terre* (1864), *Di di lüxing*, he wrote, "though I referred to it as a translation, it was actually a reinterpretation" (sui shuo yi, qishi nai gaizuo) (*LXQJ*, 12: 93).[14] In rendering into Chinese Inoue Tsutomu's translation, which was relatively faithful to the format of the original, Lu Xun reduced it from twenty-eight chapters to fourteen. He also edited out a great deal of the content, especially sections devoted to the descriptions of new inventions and the science behind them. Most visible, however, was his adoption of the traditional "chapter fiction" form of the *zhang-hui xiaoshuo*.[15]

Lu Xun's own introduction to the text further illustrates the vagaries of translating science and SF during the late Qing and the practical difficulties of introducing SF to the Chinese cultural field. "At first I had intended to use only the vernacular language in order to reduce the burden upon my readers, but exclusive use of the vernacular proved to be both troublesome and superfluous. Because of this, I have also made use of classical language in order to save paper ("Lessons," 22).

The cultural crisis brought about by China's ignominious defeat in the first Sino-Japanese War catalyzed calls for language reform on the part of reformers dissatisfied with the examination system, but it would take more than two decades until the adoption of a vernacular register was institutionalized. The literary revolution, inaugurated by Hu Shi in 1917 (Hu Shi, 5–16),[16] came only after a long period of grappling with the classical language and its many different registers (Huters 1988; Kaske 2008). Lu Xun and many of his contemporaries remained more comfortable with classical written forms, especially the *guwen* style,[17] contrary to the post–May Fourth narrative that understands this as "perversely obscurantist," and indeed "the most significant prose produced after 1900 within the [*tongcheng*] school was *guwen* translations of Western works" (Huters 1988, 249, 252). While many late Qing authors envisioned the vernacular language in a position of high symbolic, political, and economic capital, the cultural field they were trying to supplant continued to influence their work.

Lu Xun and many of his contemporaries understood a broad range of historical developments to be the product of evolutionary processes, and writing was no exception. For example, while Liu Shipei (1884–1919) argued that the next step in the development of literary expression was the adoption of colloquial language, he still understood the maintenance of a classical register to be a key component to preserving a sense of national spirit (Huters 1988, 260). Theodore Huters describes the author's style in "On the Power of Mara Poetry" ("Moluo shi li shuo") as "Mimic[king] the elaborate archaisms of Zhang Binglin even as its cosmopolitan polemic points directly at the May Fourth movement that was still ten years away" (Huters 1988, 271). In both language and content, Lu Xun's early work is rife with the sort of contradictions that characterized the intellectual atmosphere of the late Qing. Andrew Jones has observed that the poignancy of the iron house metaphor is its polysemy, presenting "ethical, philosophical, and political questions in narrative form, materializing in a confined textual space complex and often mutually contradictory ideas, desires and anxieties" (Jones 2011, 34). Many of these contradictions were present in nascent form in Lu Xun's earliest writings on science and literature.

Lu Xun's early essays are representative of a late Qing literary trend that favored the use of an archaic grammar and vocabulary blended with the vocabulary of scientific modernity to form a linguistic bricolage. The translingual practice of science translation produced a hybrid discourse composed of an emerging taxonomical vocabulary of biological and physical sciences, with the rhetorical and grammatical range of neo-Confucian *guwen* explication. The *zhanghui xiaoshuo* also included classical poetic forms in its linguistic repertoire. The end of chapter 5 of Lu Xun's adaptation of *De la terre à la lune* features the following poetic coda, which frames the translation of Verne in terms of Zhuangzian philosophy: "*Jiujiu* cries the cicada / knowing not spring and autumn; Great men of reason wander freely about the cosmos" (Lu Xun, *Yuejie lüxing*, 66).[18] The Zhuangzian worldview, with its emphasis on the ineffability of the universe and the limits of human knowledge, was deployed as a heuristic framework in order to suggest the potential to contain science within a broader Chinese epistemological perspective. Lu Xun's translations and scientific writings at turns place Verne's work in the cultural field using Ming-Qing fictional forms, while simultaneously deploying the political and symbolic capital of Confucian disputation and Daoist philosophy as heuristic tools.

Borrowing from Stephen Prothero's work on the creolization of religious practice, John Warne Monroe has suggested that nineteenth-century French efforts to create "sciences of God" could be understood in terms of the creolization of language. In these religious systems, "a 'grammar' of deep structures can be separated from a 'vocabulary' of specific practices, doctrines, and institutional arrangements" (Monroe, 7–8). A similar practice characterized the Chinese iteration of colonial modernity, as attempts were made to Sinify Western science on both the discursive and philosophical levels. Although Lu Xun is deeply critical of *Yangwu*-inspired appeals to the inherent Chineseness of foreign science and technology, the new body of foreign knowledge had to be understood in Chinese terms. Notwithstanding the fact that such modes of Sinification were often expedient and occasionally intellectually necessary, they could not fully quell the deep-seated sense of cultural eclipse and decline. This led in part to an approach to cultural appropriation that emphasized selective and conscious adoption of material, intellectual, and spiritual aspects of European culture.

Repeatedly throughout his early essays, Lu Xun argues that the adoption of material culture, no matter how useful, must be accompanied by the adoption of a scientific understanding of nature. The author is deeply critical of what he views as an excessively materialistic and instrumentalist bent in Chinese culture, the same sort identified by Wang Hui in "The Fate of 'Mr. Science' in China."

Consider these achievements: in what way could they have been aiming for concrete benefits? And yet the safety lamp, the steam engine, and improved techniques for mining were all invented. The eyes and ears of society were opened wide with amazement at such things, and daily praises were sung for their immediate rewards, but people continued, as always, to regard men of science with indifference. This is a prime case of taking effects for causes, no different from trying to urge a horse forward by pulling back on its reins; how could they possibly get the desired result? (*LXQJ*, 1:33; Cheng Min, 11–12; Lu Xun, "Lessons," 94)

For Lu Xun and many of his contemporaries, the exploratory spirit of science, a commitment to resistance of cultural oppression and to the liberating power of arts and literature, were as important as the material results of science and technology. To this end, many of these early essays evince a Nietzschean turn,[19] emphasizing the importance of idealism and individualism, while voicing deep suspicion of democracy and majority rule. Lu Xun's histories of science, evolution, and culture all laud the originators of a given idea as much as the idea itself. In this respect, his early work differs markedly from that of his contemporaries, whose fictional prescriptions for China's technological renewal often focused on the establishment of institutional bodies and systems of knowledge production.[20]

The preface to Verne's *De la terre à la lune* begins with the idea that human beings have asserted dominion over nature and that the world has been made smaller by speedy transportation. Humans used to look upon nature with awe and believe that the seas and mountains could not be traversed.

But then mastery of iron and steam brought forth trains and ships that traveled at lightning speed, man's dominion [over nature] grows day by day, and nature's potency is diminished, the five continents exchanging civilization as if housed in a single room: this is what today's world has become. But the heavens are not benevolent, placing limits on this joy. Though mountains and rivers have lost their strength, gravity and atmospheric pressure still bind mankind, creating a barrier to communication with extraterrestrials that is difficult to surpass. In the mire of an opaque prison, blocked ears and befogged eyes conspire to fool mankind, daily singing nature's praises. This is precisely what nature enjoys, and it is the shame of mankind . . . but later we will colonize the stars, and travel to the moon will seem familiar and natural to even a peddler's son. (*LXQJ*, 10:163)[21]

The ambivalence of this passage foreshadows Lu Xun's seminal iron house metaphor, in which he describes the Chinese people as unaware of their confinement to a prison from which there is no escape. While Lu Xun argues that SF is a necessary instrument for the dissemination of modern knowledge and the reform of superstitious and primitive thought, his calls for progress are tempered by the perceived backwardness of the Chinese people, whom he refers to as the "benighted clan of the Yellow emperor" (*mingming huangzu*) (Jones 2011, 48).[22]

Lu Xun's Evolutionary Epics

This translation of Jules Verne was soon followed by a series of five essays on cultural and intellectual history published between 1907 and 1908, all aimed at identifying European strengths and critiquing perceived cultural weaknesses on the Chinese side. The first was an evolutionary epic,[23] titled "The History of Man" ("Ren zhi lishi," 1907). The evolutionary epic is a style of writing that takes a familiar object or organism and explains how evolutionary principles contributed to its development. The form "became one of the most important narrative formats in the second half of the nineteenth century [in England and America]. It derived its scientific legitimacy from the concept of evolution as a gradual, lawful, and progressive development in the natural world. It assumed epic status by moving through vast expanses of time, by ranging across a series of scientific disciplines, or even by presenting heroes who performed deeds of great valor" (Lightman, 220). These works were an attempt at evolutionary engineering, aimed at passing on the heroic spirit of the luminaries described.

The second essay, "Lessons from the History of Science" ("Kexue shi jiao pian," 1907), chronicles the history of scientific endeavor at large in the same evolutionary terms (*LXQJ*, 1:8–24, 25–43). Three essays on literature and culture, titled "On Imbalanced Cultural Development" ("Wenhua pianzhi lun," 1907; *LXQJ*, 45–65), "On the Power of Mara Poetry" ("Moluo shi li shuo," 1907; *LXQJ*, 1:65–120), and "Toward a Refutation of Malevolent Voices" ("Po'esheng lun," 1908; *LXQJ*, 8:25–40), soon followed.[24] All five of these essays are haunted by the specter of an evanescent utopian past, a neo-Confucian vision of evolution seen as a process of social decline that could not be reversed (Huters 1988, 270; Metzger, 258–260). "The History of Man," subtitled "a study of Haeckel's scholarship on phylogeny," both chronicles the course of evolution from single-celled organisms through human beings and traces the history of evolutionary study, beginning with the Greek philosopher Thales and finishing with a summary of the work of Charles Darwin and Ernst Haeckel. The study takes Haeckel's work as the authoritative voice on evolutionary theory but also presents a summary of Linnaeus's *Systema Naturae* and binomial nomenclature, Cuvier's work on the fossil record, Lamarck's theories of the differentiation of species, and Darwin's theories of adaptation and selection. A substantial portion of the text is devoted to an explication of Haeckel's biogenetic law, the theory that a human embryo repeats the key stages of evolutionary development from a single-celled organism, through fish, and eventually to primates and *Homo sapiens* ("ontogeny recapitulates phylogeny").[25]

Like his introduction to *De la terre à la lune*, Lu Xun's "Lessons from the History of Science" begins with a utopian description of man's mastery of nature, arguing that scientific knowledge has brought humanity into an age in which physical space is easily transcended, famine reduced, and the social benefits of education are pervasive. He goes on to trace the history of scientific knowledge to ancient Greece, praising Pythagoras, Plato, Aristotle, and others for their spirit of exploration. Paralleling the classicism evident in Lu Xun's language is the pervasive sense that Greek philosophy represented a prelapsarian phase in the development of science. He describes the Dark Ages as a time when the knowledge and spirit of these Greek proto-scientists was lost, and the scientific revolution that was set off by Copernicus as a case of "returning to the past" (*Fugu*) ("Kexue shi jiaopian," 1907, *LXQJ*, 1:30). Lu Xun persists in having recourse to the models of Confucian antiquity and its accompanying historiographical mode, paradoxically using it as a frame for understanding Western history in evolutionary terms.

Bernard Lightman compares the sweeping treatments of evolutionary history in "Lessons from the History of Science" and "The History of Man" to the textual equivalent of a panorama, arguing that the form "resonated with important developments within nineteenth-century visual culture, especially when evolution was put on display or when it supplied the guiding theme in a heavily illustrated book" (Lightman, 222). All five essays describe the development of European science, literature, and culture in evolutionary terms, contrasted with China's inevitable decline. These evolutionary tableaus match the visual layout of evolutionary illustrations and the spatial layout of the museum, moving methodically from ancient times to the present moment. The format of these works is comparable to that of late nineteenth-century visual and institutional representations of evolutionary progress, and so was their mission.[26]

"On Imbalanced Cultural Development" repeats this pattern with a panoramic presentation of Western European social and philosophical history. Likewise, in "On the Power of Mara Poetry," European literature is presented in evolutionary terms. Both essays evince a strong social Darwinist strain as well. In "On the Power of Mara Poetry," he writes, "Human undertakings are also thus: disputes over the basic essentials of life—food, clothing, housing—as well as feuding between states have been phenomena so clear and obvious that they can no longer be evaded or concealed. If two men were to share the same compartment, where they had to struggle for air, eventually the one with the stronger respiratory system would emerge the victor" (*LXQJ*, 1:68; Kowallis). This passage is notable for the expression of two pervasive themes of the early twentieth century: the notion that social Darwinism was a defining feature of evolutionary process, and the trope of society as a suffocating chamber. Andrew Jones, citing the historical anachronism of "social Darwinism" as a term that was not used by

Haeckel or Spencer to refer to their own theories, and which "gestures toward a coherent entity that never existed on the ground," instead uses the term "evolutionary thinking" to characterize late nineteenth- and early twentieth-century discourses of national progress or decay. "At a fundamental level, evolutionary thinking involves understanding and narrating the social and cultural realms in terms derived from evolutionary biology. Crucial to this sort of thinking is a reliance on the developmental narratives in which human history is figured in terms of natural history, and individuals as much as nations are assumed to move along a continuum from the 'savage' to the 'civilized'" (Jones 2011, 29). Evolutionary thinking was one of the most prominent modes of explanation for China's historical circumstances and developmental trajectory (34).[27]

In Lu Xun's treatment of evolution, the failure to evolve is a looming threat to social well-being, one echoed in many of the works considered later in this study. At its most extreme, this manifests as outright devolution, a trait shared with Western SF authors like H. G. Wells. Roger Luckhurst identifies Wells's "commitment to evolutionism" as "utopian hope [that was] also always haunted by the devolutionary decline—[it] produced a tradition that has a direct line of descent in English SF down to the present day" (Luckhurst, 46). As I demonstrate in the coming chapters, this trait of Wells, arguably just as salient in the early writing of Lu Xun, became a prominent feature of Chinese SF in the period of its emergence as well.

Lu Xun's translations of Verne, and his early writings on the history of science and Western civilization, overlap with many of the thematic and formal concerns of the late Qing cultural field. Lu Xun's diagnosis of collective, institutional decline was soon met with collective, institutional solutions both fictional and of the brick-and-mortar variety. Reform-minded individuals sought to establish the symbolic and political capital of science in general and Darwinian thinking in particular. Many of these motifs were central to an emergent SF literary field and would go on to germinate in the canonical literary field of twentieth-century China.

3

WU JIANREN
AND LATE QING SF
JIA BAOYU GOES TO
SHANGHAI

Wu Jianren's 1905 "sequel" to the Chinese classic *Story of the Stone* (*Hong lou meng*/ *Shitou ji*), *The New Story of the Stone* (*Xin shitou ji*) is missing one of the key identifying characteristics of sf—the genre label itself on the story as it originally appeared; instead it bore the imprimatur "social fiction" (*shehui xiaoshuo*).[1] In terms of the literary field, *New Stone* overlaps with a number of other narrative modes. The author's introduction acknowledges that it is one sequel among many aimed at commercial profit. Stylistically, Wu adopts the form of chapter fiction, but also incorporates many aspects of the travel narrative. Nevertheless, I argue that the novel's thematic focus on a xenophobic confrontation with a foreign invader and a hydra-headed tradition, and the subsequent construction of a utopian China whose territory and history have transcended foreign incursion, are sufficient elements to define the novel as such. Wu Jianren's *New Stone* is not the first work of native Chinese sf, but its vision of the political and intellectual crisis of the late Qing and its presentation of a Chinese utopia are so thoroughgoing that the work can be understood as an encyclopedia of late Qing sf tropes distilling many aspects of the cultural field of late Qing sf. As in the case of Lu Xun's translations and nonfiction writing on science, Wu Jianren expresses concern with China's incorporation of Western epistemologies and the process of reconciling these fields of knowledge with Chinese philosophical and political traditions. In many cases, this incorporation is an out-and-out physical confrontation, reflective of the influence of colonialism and imperialism.

The sf utopia that is constructed in the second half of the novel is emblematic of its Eastern and Western contemporaries, and the late Qing intellectual crisis of national renewal. Categorizing this or any work of late Qing fiction as sf is often burdened both by the variety of theoretical considerations explored in chapter 1 and by the fact that many late Qing novels would be best described as multi-genre. Nevertheless, both the first half of the novel, which takes place in the new urban spaces of China in the early twentieth century, and the second half, which takes place in the utopian Realm of Civilization (*wenming jingjie*), bear many of the formal and functional markers of the genre. In the second half of the novel, we see many of the material tropes of the genre: flying machines, spectacular weapons, submarines, futuristic foods and medicines, and a general sense of the transcendence of the issues that so plagued Jia Baoyu in the first half of the novel. It is tempting to identify the first half of the novel as not-sf, because it is grounded firmly in the social and technological context that it was written in. To a twenty-first-century reader, Baoyu's amazement and misgivings at the marvels of early twentieth-century science and technology and his response to foreign occupation seem quaint and outdated. However, the first half of the novel, like the second, is marked by the sense of defamiliarization that Darko Suvin contends is one of the hallmarks of sf. From matchbooks and newspapers to the rules governing commercial insurance and boat captains, Baoyu regards much of what he encounters with a sense of wonder, skepticism, and anxiety. This sense of wonder tinged with anxiety that pervades the first half of the novel gives way to wonder and wholehearted acceptance in the second half of the novel when the native Chinese origins of the new technologies and social configurations are confirmed. Even in the sf utopia of the second half of the novel, I identify a pervasive sense of futility in the attempts to imagine and narrate a solution to the epistemological crisis of late Qing China. This sense of futility seems on the one hand foreign to a genre and a text that intersects with utopian narrative in so many ways, and on the other hand quite familiar in the context of canonical Chinese literature. In my analysis of the theme of the confrontation with an alien other (identified in both sf at large, and in

New Stone), this chapter poses questions concerning the ways in which the motif of imperial domination is locally inflected in the context of the late Qing and the problems associated with the attempt to use a genre implicated in the imperial project as a means of subverting that same discourse.

Although Wu Jianren was much more conservative than Lu Xun in his political leanings, as is apparent in *New Stone*, there are some remarkable similarities between the thematic issues addressed by both authors and in the degree to which both failed to come to a workable solution, even in narrative form. In the fiction of Wu Jianren, we see another predecessor to Lu Xun's iron house. Lu Xun's narrators openly lament their inability to reshape the world around them or even to ameliorate a measure of its suffering; in Wu Jianren's novel, the cure is effected but remains invisible and available only to a certain class of people. Jia Baoyu disappears from the topsy-turvy and often dangerous circumstances of the late Qing to emerge mysteriously in an alternate version of China that has been able to revive its Confucian cultural and spiritual essence. This utopian stronghold can only be imagined through the repression of the traumatic circumstances of the first half of the novel. While Lu Xun's intellectual narrators verbally agonize over their impotence, Wu Jianren's narrative conjures a utopian fantasy where the pressures of foreign incursion, social inequality, and political instability have already vanished; but it cannot conjure the moment of the cure itself. Both Lu Xun in his introduction to *A Call to Arms*, and Jia Baoyu in *New Stone*, stand outside the iron house, at a distance from China's ills, and incapable of ministering cures.

Despite this sense of futility, Wu Jianren prefigures or fictionalizes a number of contemporary social trends and desires in his novel, participating in an imagined foundation of scientific institutions prior or simultaneous to their creation. Wu's novel is a strikingly comprehensive vision of the failings of the late Qing state, and of utopian yearnings with Confucian characteristics. In one of China's first SF novels, we see a crystallization of the anxieties that faced late Qing intellectuals. *New Stone* brings the principal character of *Hong lou meng*, Jia Baoyu, back to life in China of the early twentieth century. First finding his way from a small temple outside Shanghai, then making his way into Shanghai, up the Yangzi River, to Beijing and eventually mystically transported to the utopian "Realm of Civilization," Baoyu is shocked and awed by the ubiquity of foreign technologies in late Qing China. He rapidly becomes cognizant of the widespread adaptation of foreign technologies, whether they signaled the cosmopolitanism of elites or were the barely visible implements of everyday convenience that had been adopted for far more practical reasons.

It is initially perplexing that Wu has chosen to revive Jia Baoyu as the hero of *New Stone*. In his last incarnation, to the dismay of his father, Baoyu was far more interested in writing poetry and keeping up his romantic interests than in learning the Confucian classics. Named for the leftover fragment of stone cast aside when the goddess Nüwa repaired the pillars of heaven, Baoyu is dedicated to learning the emptiness of earthly existence, not to rectifying the universal order.[2] It is difficult to imagine him in the role he assumes in *New Story of the Stone*, strongly dedicated to practical knowledge and to national concerns, as he shares little in common with his past self. Baoyu's place in the novel is precisely the degree to which he is out of place. Cast into the cultural hodgepodge of Shanghai, Baoyu has not had the chance to acculturate himself to its raucous diversity. Thus, he does not take for granted any of the new media or technologies he encounters. By the time that we see Jia Baoyu reborn in late Qing China, many of the anxieties he experiences had become quotidian throughout much of coastal China. Another way in which Baoyu does not belong is in his assiduousness in attempting to come to terms with the differences between Chinese and Western civilization. His position as an outsider allows Baoyu to occupy the role of the ethnographic observer. His culture shock when faced with semicolonial Shanghai allows him to see China through foreign eyes. From this remove, Baoyu is aided in his ethnographic study by Xue Pan and Wu Bohui,[3] two cultural insiders who help him to comprehend the new social milieu. In this pseudo-ethnographic study, Baoyu becomes cognizant of the overdetermined crisis of internal decay and foreign incursion. Baoyu, like Lu Xun nineteen years later, is an educated observer standing outside the iron house, blessed with the ability to comprehend the crisis at hand in part because of his distanced perspective.

Xue Pan, the ne'er-do-well, semiliterate son of a gentry family and cousin of Baoyu,[4] has also been reincarnated in late Qing Shanghai. For Xue Pan, and for many of his real-life counterparts, the burgeoning industrial port of Shanghai was a place of opportunity, despite, or even because of, the colonial presence. For the vast majority of individuals living farther inland, the foreign presence in China's port regions did little to change the struggles and concerns of daily existence. It was the educated elite who understood themselves to have the greatest stake in China's fate, and who possessed the capacity to become involved in the public debate on the situation. "Liang Zhangju, critic of imported goods in the early nineteenth century, thus observed: 'People frequently change their minds as soon as they see a new object. If one person admires something, soon everyone else will take to it. At first an object is valued by a high official or a noble lord, eventually passing down to their servants, and further to courtesans and concubines" (Dikötter 2006, 9). Contrary to Liang's comments, Dikötter denies the thesis that the main mode of the adoption of objects and practices was through their acceptance at the higher echelons of society as luxury items, which eventually trickled down the social ladder, instead arguing that the more quotidian the object was, the more rapidly it was imported and imitated and markers of how "foreign" it was were effaced (Dikötter 2006, 31). Dikötter posits that in China it was most often political elites who came to identify "foreign" with "imperialist" in the initial years of the twentieth century. Owing in no small part to a more pragmatic focus on the necessities of day-to-day existence, those outside the sphere of elite culture did not record their own personal reactions to things foreign, but we can assume that both elites and the common folk were often faced with an imperative to discriminate between adoption (out of necessity) of things foreign, and the rhetoric of opposition to imperialist incursion. Understanding Jia Baoyu's and Xue Pan's relationship to colonial Shanghai also benefits from imagining the cultural sphere in three dimensions, considering economic and political status alongside their cultural status. Xue Pan is economically well-endowed but culturally impoverished and only politically engaged to the extent that he sees an immediate personal benefit—an uneducated, dissolute murderer with money. On the other hand, the text reimagines Baoyu as an individual in possession of symbolic and economic capital, and the political will to resist colonization.

Xue Pan is much more enthusiastic than Baoyu about the adoption of foreign goods, especially creature comforts and signs of wealth like whiskey and cigars, or toys like watches and a phonograph. To borrow a turn of phrase from Leo Ou-fan Lee, Wu Jianren's Xue Pan is written in the moralizing vein of "such figures, who moving in the twilight zone between East and West, mixed with greedy merchants, status hungry *nouveau riches*, and decadent scions of rural landlords who migrated into the cities for fun and pleasure" (Lee, 151). For China's new consumer class, Western science and technology offered material objects whose purpose and benefit were very clear. The material necessities and comforts of day-to-day existence could conflict with ideological allegiances to one's nation or sense of social justice. The gulf between Xue Pan and Baoyu, and Xue Pan's own erratic behavior, dramatize the degree to which the foreignness of new goods in late Qing China was met with the same schizophrenia that characterized *Yangwu* thinking.

While Baoyu's companion and cultural informant Xue Pan has fewer problems adjusting to this situation, Baoyu himself is apoplectic. So many foreign objects could be found in late Qing China that for Xue Pan, as for the majority of other citizens, the label "foreign" began to lose its significance as a sign of actual difference. Frank Dikötter has observed that when these foreign technologies were still visibly foreign, they were signs of the modernity of their consumers, and "new commodities rapidly became part of the texture of everyday life, from electric fans and photographic equipment in the palace to rubber galoshes and enamel wash-basins in the farmhouse."[5] The Shanghai that Baoyu is reincarnated in is a consumer-oriented urban society in which identity was intimately connected to purchases made in the marketplace. A rapidly emerging gulf between Baoyu and Xue Pan is the latter's uncritical acceptance of luxury goods as a sign of his own social status. The image of outright universal xenophobic rejection of things foreign oversimplifies the complexity of the introduction of new material goods to China, and ignores how quickly (if perhaps still vexingly) the "foreign" could be incorporated into the "everyday," especially in cases where objects were affordable and useful. The presence of foreign goods, and the prestige of those goods, were often fraught with ambivalence.

Roughly half a century before Baoyu was reincarnated in Shanghai, many of the accoutrements of everyday life, both those produced locally and imported goods, were associated with their foreignness, which often stood in for quality. Baoyu's encounter with the menagerie of foreign goods, practices, and ideas prevalent in semicolonial China is a fictional account of what many late Qing literati recorded in their own personal writings:

> Chen Zuolin [1837–1920] noted how many goods in demand during the Daoguang era were foreign: "Multi-storied buildings are called foreign houses, decorated sedan chairs are called foreign sedans; there are foreign crepes and foreign hats, while hanging lamps are called foreign lamps; chafing dishes [*huoguo*] are called foreign pans, the slender ones which are ideal for soy sauce being called foreign autumn oil pans. Bright colourings are called foreign red or foreign blue. There is nowhere on either side of the Yangzi where foreign is not considered superior." (Dikötter 2006, 27)

Such commentary elides the degree to which economic nationalism often came into conflict with one's consumerism. Patriotic sentiment, resentment for manufacturers, and one's sense of social justice do not always match up with one's conspicuous consumption. Baoyu immediately comprehends that you are what you buy, but his position in the novel is one that defines him as uniquely cognizant of the implications of global capital. Conscious consumerism is a process of negotiation between ideology and the pocketbook, but this in itself is both a material and intellectual luxury that many do not have. Xue Pan is much more conscious of how he can make himself comfortable than he is of the implications of listening to a foreign phonograph. He later goes on to join the Boxer Rebellion, and in his discussion of the rebellion with

Baoyu he demonstrates that he is essentially oblivious of any of the issues involved in considerations of economic nationalism. Xue Pan's attitude is one of opportunism, seeking whatever advantages he might be able to gain. The mere fact of wide adoption of foreign goods elides the degree to which such decisions may have been made with ambivalence, if their provenance was considered at all.

Dikötter argues that "material modernity was not a set of givens imposed by foreigners but a repertoire of new opportunities, a kit of tools which could be flexibly appropriated in a variety of imaginative ways. The global, in this process of cultural bricolage, was modified just as much as the local at the points of contact between the two: enculturation rather than acculturation accounts for the broad cultural and material changes which marked the republican era in China" (Dikötter 2006, 7).[6] The decision to purchase and/or make use of new goods was by no means as simple as the question of whether such goods were of foreign or domestic origin.[7] Economic nationalism demonstrates that in many cases, the objection was not so much to the objects themselves as it was to their provenance, and that patriotic sentiment might not overcome the perceived utility of an imported good. In the wake of the first Sino-Japanese War, reformers such as Zheng Guanying (1894–1922) argued for "imitation" or "modeling" (*fang zao*) as ways to promote the cause of import substitution. In his *Warnings to a Prosperous Age*, Zheng argued that import substitution was key in waging economic warfare (*shang zhan*) against European powers. The ways in which material and intellectual culture were displayed also became a key concern.

Thinking outside the Iron House

Two transportations to an impossible elsewhere occur in the story: first, when Baoyu wakes up in late Qing China, and then when he is transported to the Realm of Civilization. Indeed, while his new surroundings are culturally and linguistically "Chinese," they are clearly distinct from the physical space of China itself. There is no geographic match with China, nor is there any indication that Baoyu has been transplanted to a different time period. Baoyu's tour guide in the

Realm of Civilization, Lao Shaonian,[8] is also aware of the situation in Shanghai, but mentions no personal experience of the situation. The threat of foreign incursion all but disappears as Baoyu and his companions traverse the globe by airship and submarine. The Realm of Civilization is a return to the social utopia of Confucian antiquity; it is at the same time a technological leap beyond the levels of any other contemporary civilization.[9]

Baoyu embarks on a quest for the solution to China's semicolonial misery, but this leads him into peril time and again, and he is nearly killed a number of times. He first comes into physical peril when he becomes involved in the Boxer Rebellion: he is almost trampled by a mob, and later, after criticizing the son of an official, is nearly smothered to death. Jia Baoyu escapes from a scene of cultural and political turmoil that Andrew Jones characterizes as "oddly reminiscent of Lu Xun's parable [of the iron house]" (Jones 2011, 55). Finally, in an attempted robbery by an innkeeper, Baoyu is saved from larceny and possible bodily harm only by uncovering the plot and lying in wait for his would-be assailants with a gun. Upon leaving the inn, Baoyu and his servant Beiming—who has also been mysteriously reborn, initially in the form of a wooden statue in the same monastery where Baoyu awakened—are attacked by robbers on the road, and Beiming is hit by an arrow and transubstantiated back into a wooden statue. The robbers take him for a Bodhisattva, and Baoyu chases them off, pretending to be a spirit. This crisis is a vivid example of what Theodore Huters has identified as a pattern of "failures to construct a narrative world their characters can comfortably inhabit," adding that "in fact all the work of the late Qing that has critical approbation appears to belong in this category" (Huters 2005, 152). Perilous might better define the world that Baoyu inhabits in *New Stone*.

Despite his doubts about the overwhelming presence of foreign technologies, individuals, and social structures, it is China's own moral crisis and Baoyu's countrymen that constitute an immediate physical threat to his safety. It is a foreign soldier and Baoyu's own knowledge of English that save Baoyu when he is caught up in a mob during the Boxer Rebellion. Baoyu's peril is the peril of the nation: an overdetermined crisis that is more the result of an internal deterioration of moral order than the threat of foreign invaders. China's internal failures continue to pile one upon another, and, to paraphrase Vladimir Nizhny, the narrative bursts. Faced once again with a society that is falling into chaos, the story itself becomes unsustainable—the only possible outcome appears to be Baoyu's death at the hands of robbers or millenarian madmen. He suddenly finds himself walking down the path that leads him to the Realm of Civilization, a utopian space that both is and is not China. As is often the case for utopias, the world emerges fully formed, and the program of its creation—the path through which a benighted Qing society would reach such a state—is left to the imagination of the reader.

In shifting the narrative of the novel to this imagined realm, Wu Jianren avoids addressing how the absolute failure of the Confucian moral code and the political and legal institutions that it had so profoundly influenced, and the social decay that pervades the first half of the novel, could possibly be reconciled with the Confucian renewal presented in the second half of the novel. The Realm of Civilization is apparently entirely removed from the traumas of semicolonialism and modernity and the failings of the beleaguered Qing state and social structure. Only the privileged intellectual is granted the opportunity to stand outside the iron house,[10] while the majority of China's population is condemned to suffocate inside.

In figure 3.1, we see the division between utopia and the late Qing dystopia visually presented as a gateway between the two realms. The figurative fence at the border ensures that only those worthy of utopia's graces will gain access. When Jia Baoyu enters the Realm of Civilization, he is subjected to a "character scan" (*yan xingzhi*). Apparently similar to a modern-day MRI, this is a device that helps the denizens of this Chinese utopia determine who shall gain entry to their world. Ill-suited people are turned away, some are "cured," and some allowed in without further delay. This is a vision of a society that has been healed, partly by doctors and partly through cultural restoration, but the healing process is one of extracting China's negative elements. This utopia exists in a historical setting where the social crisis that brought the first

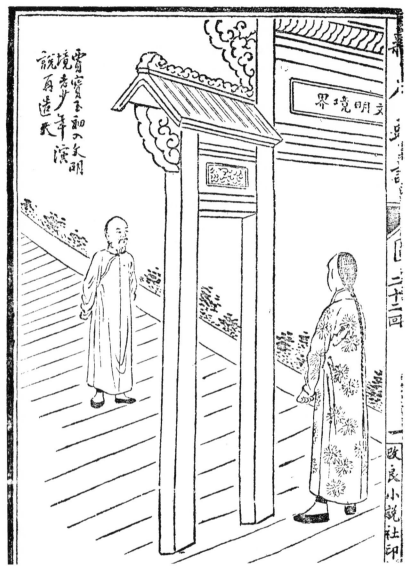

Figure 3.1 Jia Baoyu meets Lao Shaonian at the gateway to the Realm of Civilization. The couplet reads: "Baoyu first enters the 'Realm of Civilization.' Lao Shaonian elaborates on 'Heaven Remade.'"

Wu Jianren, *Xin shitou ji*. In *Zhongguo jidai xiaoshuo daxi*, ed. Wang Jiquan et al. (Nanchang: Jiangxi renmin chubanshe, 1988), frontispiece.

half of the novel crashing in on itself has been entirely avoided through the assiduous elimination of "uncivilized" elements. Having passed an examination of his character, Baoyu asks Lao Shaonian about the process by which one gains admittance to this utopia. Lao Shaonian explains: "If they are civilized, then we ask them to stay here; if the exam reveals some degree of uncivilized nature, then we send them to the Rectification Station and once the doctors have fixed them, they are welcomed in. But, there are those who are completely uncivilized, and can't be helped, they are turned back" (Wu Jianren, *Xin shitou ji* [hereafter *XSTJ*], 280). To this, Baoyu responds by inquiring why this process of moral rectification is not carried out on the rest of the world, and Lao Shaonian replies, "That's easier said than done, most people nowadays are completely uncivilized, we might have miraculous means but it can't take care of that. The only thing for it is to wait for them to die" (282). Utopias are dependent on their isolation from the rest of the world, and the perfection of the Realm of Civilization in no way signals the salvation of China at large. Baoyu is diagnosed with a minor stomach problem but comes out as "glittering" (*jingying*) on the character scan. The partition between the Realm of Civilization and the deteriorating nation-state portrayed in the first half of the novel is made possible by a nearly omnipotent *pharmakon* of Chinese medicine combined with modern technology.

A striking similarity with one of the most prominent tropes in the work of Lu Xun emerges here: the metaphor of sick body and sick society in need of spiritual redemption. Rather than a desperate call for a cure, as in "Medicine," ("Yao," *LXQJ*, 1:463–472) or "Diary of a Madman," Wu Jianren's novel presents a vision of a cured society.[11] This doppelganger of China is a world in which the traumas of semicolonial domination and epistemological crisis have been erased. However, we must keep in mind that while the Realm of Civilization is ethnically Chinese, it is entirely separate from the Chinese nation-state, and the denizens of the Realm of Civilization are cognizant of China's plight.

Aside from the ultimate impossibility of sustaining an imagined utopia that leads to the novel's fantastic dream-sequence conclusion, there are many indications in the novel that the national crisis of the real China remains unsolved. Jia Baoyu has found his escape from the iron house, but its walls still stand. Indeed, Baoyu later learns that Xue Pan has made three attempts to be admitted to the Realm of Civilization, and at each repeated attempt he was found to have grown progressively less acceptable for entry. Lao Shaonian upends a Mencian description of an ideal ruler's visible virtue in describing Xue Pan's moral deficiency, which "hung clearly on his countenance and weighed heavily upon his back" (*XSTJ*, 286).[12] If Xue Pan's fate is any indication of that of his compatriots, it seems that the vast majority of China's citizenry will not be saved.

The Realm of Civilization is a utopia in both senses of the word. It is a place of modernist transcendence: the weather and seasons are subject to human control; its weaponry is superior but unnecessary because all threats foreign and domestic have long since been silenced; reverence and adherence to the teachings of Confucius have led to the withering away of law and religion and rendered the country's benevolent constitutional monarchy obsolete; the words "theft" (*zei*), "robbery," (*dao*), and "rape" (*jian*) have been forgotten along with the acts that they describe;[13] technologies of travel through air and sea have been perfected; technology also allows human beings to see through distance, metals, darkness, and water with equal clarity; the quotidian concerns for famine and illness have likewise been eliminated through a rationalized and technologized system of alimentation and medicine;[14] the lost classics of Confucian tradition and the newest research are both shelved side by side in a massive national library. In short no ill—social, political, economic, or otherwise—remains unsolved.

The Realm of Civilization is also a utopia in the sense that it is literally "no place." According to Baoyu's travel guide—Lao Shaonian's description—the territory of this nation-state geographically demonstrates the nation's modernist rationality in the form of a perfect grid seemingly superimposed on the territory of the Qing Empire. However, Wu Jianren also makes it clear that Baoyu is not in China anymore. The novel leaves unanswered the question of precisely how the achievements of the civilized realm came to be. Baoyu is a witness to the achievements, but not to the process that brings about the superiority of the civilized realm, or of the China of the final dream sequence of the novel (Huters 2005, 170). As is often the case for SF with utopian elements, though one is presented with a society that has achieved transcendence, the reader is not privy to the achievement of that transcendence.[15] We must suspend the disbelief generated by the depiction of moral and social crisis throughout the first half of the novel in order to have faith in the possibility of the existence of this utopia.

Back to the Future: Modernity and Estrangement

In the first half of *New Stone*, the narrative explores the conflict with the imperial European (rather than extraterrestrial) other through the eyes of Jia Baoyu, suddenly awakened to the anxieties of China's semi-colonial situation in the face of European military and technological might. Instead of encountering the inhuman, Baoyu and his comrades come face to face with a terrestrial iteration of anti-cultural forces in the form of an alien epistemology and a dazzling array of new technologies, foods and beverages, and cultural norms, all brought to him through colonial modernity. After a series of repeated failures that reveal China's weakness in the face of foreign incursion and make the internal crisis the nation faces regardless of colonial aggression just as clear, the second half of the novel propels itself into a utopian fantasy, playing out the silencing and conquest of the other that reaffirms indigenous cultural values and that Kerslake argues is at the heart of SF. So complete is the silencing of the alien other in the second half of the novel that the issue almost disappears entirely, only occasionally entering into the conversation of Baoyu and his new travel guide, Lao Shaonian.

Although the second half of the novel is populated with the fictional objects of SF—flying ships, submarines, nourishing elixirs, and weapons of dominion over humanity and nature—the first half of the novel is equally dominated by a sense of Suvinian wonder, though it exhibits a much stronger technophobic tendency. From the moment Baoyu awakens outside Shanghai, he is awed by the real objects that he sees around him. From matches to newspapers, foreign foods, to the system of riverboat pilots and insurance policies, the objects of everyday use are those confronted with the greatest sense of wonder. These objects are also marked by the clearest sense of cultural conflict and exposition. On Baoyu's boat ride to Shanghai, he is introduced to foreign foods and ways of eating. Most foreign food names are transliterated, giving a sense of defamiliarization, and more insistently marking these objects as foreign. Baoyu's trip to visit the Jiangnan Arsenal signals the beginning of a deeper interest in foreign learning, but again this is purely for the sake of economic nationalism. In his tour of the arsenal (figure 3.2), Baoyu makes clear that the ultimate goal would be local production of the knowledge that is translated at the arsenal, and local invention and manufacture of the goods available there as well.

When Baoyu has the opportunity to sample foreign alcohol, he takes on a similar tone, highly suspicious and often outright dismissive of the foreign goods he consumes. Wu Jianren turns on its head Darko Suvin's structuralist definition of SF as relying upon an imaginative framework alternative to the author's empirical environment. The *novum* that seizes Baoyu with the greatest sense of estrangement is the quotidian environment of semicolonial China, while there is little indication that the Realm of Civilization is estranging at all. Whereas the technological and social feats of the second half of the novel are marked as somehow inherently Chinese and nonthreatening, every object encountered in the first half of the novel is a source of suspicion and subject to Baoyu's reproach.

These suspicions are entirely wiped out when Baoyu is introduced to the Realm of Civilization. There, food has been incorporated into a technologized and rationalized system. At a central processing plant, nutrients are extracted from raw foods and reduced to clear liquids, which are personalized based on individual health requirements and sent to their intended recipients through a system of pipes. Especially in the increasingly consumer-oriented sphere of twentieth-century global culture, food (along with language) is one of the cornerstones of essentialist versions of national character. Western foods and beverages, instruments for eating, and techniques of the body required for such consumption are identified as a threat. On the other hand, in the Realm of Civilization, where science decocted tradition into a trans-

論文野方及園林
考工執編游向廠

Figure 3.2 Jia Baoyu pays a visit to the Jiangnan Arsenal in Shanghai. The couplet reads:
"Debating civilized and barbaric leads to talk of gardens. Investigating technology
on a factory tour."
Wu Jianren, *Xin shitou ji*. In *Zhongguo jidai xiaoshuo daxi*, ed. Wang Jiquan et al.
(Nanchang: Jiangxi renmin chubanshe, 1988), frontispiece.

parent, tasteless, and impersonal instrument of efficiency, no threat is seen. Baoyu expresses less consternation about this shift, apparently because of its inherent "Chineseness." "All in all, these episodes in the civilized realm represent the ultimate wish fulfillment of *'Zhongxue wei ti, xixue wei yong'* (Chinese learning as the essence, Western learning as the application), that slogan so thoroughly imbricated in the late Qing intellectual life" (Huters 2005, 167). When technological achievements are the product of Chinese inventors and craftsmen, put to use in affirming native dominance, their appropriateness is no longer a matter of contention.

Confronted with objects like a phonograph (figure 3.3), Baoyu is dismissive—these objects are entertaining but surely have no real value. The presence of the West is an almost entirely material presence—for the most part, it is foreign objects, rather than foreign people, that he comes into contact with. Baoyu's personal encounter with the foreign in the first half of the novel is limited to directions from a soldier of the European force that invaded Beijing during the Boxer Rebellion. Baoyu's new knowledge of foreign language and the soldier's knowledge of Beijing save Baoyu from being overrun by an angry mob. The foreign presence, more material and economic than personal, of the first half of the novel is all but erased in the civilized realm. Baoyu and his companions are never challenged by having to confront the outside world.

Neither aliens nor robots nor foreign aggressors lead to the narrative collapse through which Baoyu is mysteriously transplanted to the Realm of Civilization. Additionally, in the civilized realm, neither robots, aliens, nor foreign aggressors must be brought under the control of imperial force. The other that Baoyu and the civilized realm are struggling to come to grips with is China's own cultural heritage. The novel details a concerted attempt to identify which aspects of cultural heritage can be revived, and to find ways to make this heritage work in the new age. On the one hand, Baoyu is witness to a resuscitated Confucian antiquity. On the other hand, he and his companions struggle with the mythical bestiary that defines China through its radical difference and distance from China as both a geographical and cultural center. The untamed wilds of the *Shanhai jing* and the *Zhuangzi* are

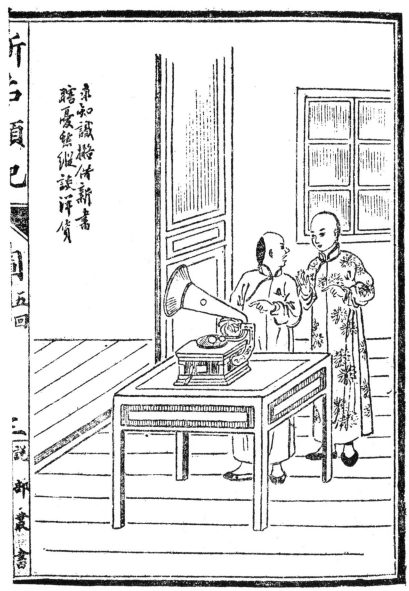

Figure 3.3 Jia Baoyu questions the utility of a phonograph machine. The couplet reads: "Seeking knowledge by borrowing new books. Overcome with worry in a conversation about foreign goods."
Wu Jianren, *Xin shitou ji*. In *Zhongguo jindai xiaoshuo daxi*, ed. Wang Jiquan et al. (Nanchang: Jiangxi renmin chubanshe, 1988), frontispiece.

geographical and zoological metaphors for the difference between the untamed creatures and spaces beyond the central plains and the socially tamed space of the Confucian world order.

The Museum in the Realm of Civilization

In the Realm of Civilization, Baoyu and company are constantly coming into violent conflict with China's mythical past. The *peng* is one discovery among many made by Baoyu and his cohorts in the second half of the novel that they choose to kill and bring back for preservation in a museum. Over a period of days, they chase the enormous bird, firing at it from the decks of a flying ship with an arsenal of machine guns, until their endless stream of bullets finally sends the symbol of an ever-changing and unknowable natural world crashing to the ground. They land their ships to find that they have pursued the beast all the way to Africa, attach the bird to the flying ship via a system of cables, and eventually succeed in coaxing the engines of their vehicle into returning them to the civilized world. Upon their return to the Realm of Civilization, the enormous bird is preserved by a taxidermist and put on display in a huge museum that serves as a comprehensive intellectual repository of China's real and imagined past. Baoyu is rewarded for his bravery, while Zhuangzi's vivid metaphor of transformation and the incomplete nature of human knowledge dies alongside the bird. The mythical past becomes an artifact, both through its incorporation into the imperial project of the museum and the imposition of order through the domestication of the unknown.[16] To borrow Stephen Owen's terminology in his assessment of the reinvention of China's literary history undertaken under the banner of the May Fourth Movement, Baoyu and his friends seek to "embalm" myth and the past, making it "the possession of Chinese culture, rather than its medium" (Owen, 167–190). In other words, the *peng* stops being part of a master narrative about the limits of human cognition, as it is absorbed into the master narrative of the nation-state's claim to systematic knowledge of the natural world; a metaphor for understanding the sublime and ineffable quality of the universe is repurposed as a symbol of sovereign power and a tool of cultural education. The image of Chinese culture as material substance that could be taken away like so much porcelain was not an unfounded anxiety.

This anxiety reveals itself in a strange manner, especially in the illustrations appended to the text. Comparing this taxonomizing effort to the work of Captain Nemo in Jules Verne's *Twenty Thousand Leagues under the Sea*, Andrew Jones notes that nearly half the narrative in the second half of the novel is dedicated to air and sea expeditions devoted to killing, capturing, and collecting a series of specimens (Jones 2011, 47–58). The majority of the illustrations featured in the 1908 reprint from the second half of the novel depict Jia Baoyu shouldering a rifle to take aim at one or another of the denizens of China's mythical bestiary. In figure 3.4, we see the episode of their hunt for the *peng*.

Milner's identification of SF as simultaneously ideological and critical is useful here. The second half of the novel vacillates between an ideological, self-Orientalizing mission that repeats the abuses of colonialism and a critical unraveling of the European world order. Baoyu's safari can also be explained in terms of economic capital as a less critically engaged and more market-oriented form: one that offers readers the thrill of flight, the danger of the hunt, and a sense of sublime wonder in the form of fantastic creatures. Jia Baoyu hunting the *peng* is less a sign of the confrontation with the imperial other than it is a dramatization of the Confucian acculturation of Daoist anti-culture. Baoyu and Lao Shaonian make the *peng* fit into the museum, and in so doing, Daoist cosmology is subsumed under imperialism with Chinese characteristics—a repetition of the European conquest and knowledge industry that Baoyu was so suspicious of, covered in the veil of a Confucian moral and social code.

Another way of reading this, also related to the notion of the expanse of empire, is as an expression of the anxiety of cultural loss. If the untamable wilds of Daoist cosmology could become the property of Confucian tradition, they could just as easily become the property of another tradition entirely. That is to say, if the *peng* can fit into a museum, an urgent question becomes whose museum it will wind up

Figure 3.4 Jia Baoyu takes aim at the *peng* during a ride on a flying ship. The couplet reads: "By lamplight the honored guest chats about government. Aboard a hunting ship man battles flying beast."

Wu Jianren, *Xin shitou ji*. In *Zhongguo jidai xiaoshuo daxi*, ed. Wang Jiquan et al. (Nanchang: Jiangxi renmin chubanshe, 1988), frontispiece.

in. As possessions rather than evolving fabular signifiers, culture can become the property of whoever has the power to seize it. Beyond the walls of the Realm of Civilization, and off the pages of *New Stone*, it was clear that if Baoyu and Lao Shaonian did not lay claim to the *peng*, someone else would. In other words, this episode can be read as illustrative of two competing anxieties: the anxiety of the untamable universe asserted in Daoist cosmology, and the anxiety of cultural loss. The Confucian acculturation of Daoist myth is impelled at least in part by the fear that if the *peng* does not wind up in the museum in the Realm of Civilization, it may very well end up in the British Museum, signaling the intellectual authority of another tradition entirely. As Benedict Anderson has argued, the museum, alongside colonial institutions like the map and the census, was another undertaking that helped develop "the way in which the colonial state imagined its dominion—the nature of human beings it ruled, the geography of its domain, and the legitimacy of its ancestry" (Anderson 2006, 164). Bridging the gulf between the ideological and material aspects of empire were the institutions that rendered empire visible to its subjects. Thus, Baoyu's safari in the Realm of Civilization can be read both as an internal contestation of Confucian and Daoist epistemology, and as a contestation of colonial domination spurred on by the prospect of the Occident's claim to the Orient as a field of knowledge. The architectural design of the museum figured historical and evolutionary trajectories through its spatial organization, while the spectator's examination of the museum acted as a civilizing force, imbricating the viewing subject into the taxonomic schema of the museum itself. Hunting down and bringing home the mythical bestiary of China's past is a leitmotif of the novel, as Baoyu and Lao Shaonian embark on a global safari, first in the air, then underneath the ocean in a submarine resembling a whale. During his undersea journey, Baoyu rescues two of his shipmates from a group of mermen.[17] Following the rescue, in their discussion of the undersea wonders encountered in the area, Baoyu is informed that it is unnecessary to collect them because these items are already cataloged in a museum. He does have the opportunity to kill, capture, or collect a number of other creatures and minerals and to confirm the existence of a number of locations mentioned in the *Shanhai jing*, though. In figure 3.5, we see Baoyu in a familiar posture, rifle shouldered as he stands on the deck of Lao Shaonian's submarine, taking aim at a "seahorse" (*haima*). Not depicted in the image itself, but predicted in the poetic introduction to the chapter, is Baoyu's next encounter, a violent confrontation with the *shu* fish (*shu yu*) from the *Shanhai jing* (*Classic of Mountains and Seas*, c. fourth century BCE).

Soon after, Baoyu and Lao Shaonian encounter a particularly strange creature, which we learn is nothing other than the *shu* fish itself. Lao Shaonian is able to quote the passage from the *Shanhai jing* from memory to guide his companions in understanding what is before them.[18] Not only does the fish's existence verify that the creatures described in the *Shanhai jing* actually existed; we also learn that the places described in the work existed as well. After hunting down the fish and returning it to their submarine, Lao Shaonian launches into a tirade against the detractors of China's mythical tradition:

> "What I hate most are those who call themselves 'renaissance man' and can't keep from talking about everything in the 'five continents' and 'ten-thousand nations' at the slightest provocation. They say they know everything about astronomy and geography without having the slightest bit of personal experience. Having read a couple of books in translation, they decide to go and wipe out their motherland's heritage of ancient texts in its entirety, casting it off like so much foolish talk. This *shu* fish I've caught today is perfect for taking the *Shanhai jing* and stuffing the mouths of those 'renaissance men.'"
>
> Baoyu asked, "but the *Shanhai jing* talks about 'Mount *Dai*'s waters of *Peng*' and 'Lake *Bi*,' what could these places be?" The navigator chimed in: "by now we've already been cruising in the South Pacific for some time." Lao Shaonian replied: "why ask what those places are, do you mean to say that fish couldn't have swum here? Besides, plenty of place names have changed over time!" (337)

In the form of the *peng* and mermen, China's mythical past appears as a greater threat than that of foreign incursion. The vision of the colo-

Figure 3.5 Jia Baoyu and company shoot at mythical creatures from the *Shanhai jing* during a naval adventure. The couplet reads: "Coming upon a barren island, shots fired at sea horses. Deep beneath the seas, electricity is used in a battle with a whale." Wu Jianren, *Xin shitou ji*. In *Zhongguo jidai xiaoshuo daxi*, ed. Wang Jiquan et al. (Nanchang: Jiangxi renmin chubanshe, 1988), frontispiece.

nial other is entirely absent from the second half of the novel, replaced by mythical beasts that threaten to eat Baoyu and his companions. These beasts are literally killed and cataloged, metaphorically silenced by being put on display in a museum. The *peng* is the embodiment of the sublime, ineffable metamorphosis; a metaphor for a universe that can never be fully apprehended both because it is more expansive than the human mind can grasp, and because it is in constant flux. The *Shanhai jing* is a chronicle of the untamed wilderness beyond civilization's reach. The order of the domestic realm is reasserted through the depiction of its inverted other. Both books depict spheres of knowledge beyond the scope of "China." In a museum, explained neatly with a 250-word label, these creatures lose their metaphorical power.

At the same time, this episode can also be read in terms of the colluding missions of empire and science. We might also read these episodes in terms of the expansion of empire as a parallel mission of territorial conquest and scientific observation. We see Baoyu and Lao Shaonian engaged in exactly the sort of exploratory and experimental activity that went hand in hand with the European seafaring voyages of the seventeenth and eighteenth centuries. These years, "for all their wars and colonial rivalries, were a golden age of collective observation and verification. . . . [Sea and land expeditions] typically also took the occasion to carry out geodetic, hydrographic, and cartographic surveys; to catalogue and collect flora and fauna; to make ethnographic observations; and to gather such other information as an intelligent curiosity might discover" (Landes, 159–160). I would argue that while Landes understands such endeavors to be fortunate, laudable, and ancillary to colonial rivalry, they are indeed part of an effort to stake a claim to territory, both physical and intellectual.

Fa-ti Fan pointedly articulates the stakes inherent in the real-life categorizing effort contemporaneous to the novel:

In the imperial context, the activities of natural history—mapping, collecting, ordering, classifying, naming, and so on—represented more than matter-of-fact scientific research. It also reflected an aggressive expansion of cognitive territory defined in particular cultural terms. The "discovery" of a new bird or plant—classifying it, placing it in the Linnean or other universal taxonomy, describing it in strict scientific Latin, representing it in Western pictorial conventions and techniques, turning living samples of it into material embodiments of abstract scientific concepts and specialized terminology, configuring its global distribution in rigorously defined diagrams—privileged a specific way of defining nature, facts, and knowledge. In the nineteenth century, scientific expeditions, whose core concepts and activities involved collecting, measuring, mapping, and traveling, and whose ultimate goal was to write the natural history of the globe with exhaustive comprehensiveness and precision, originated in part from a view of geography and nature coupled with European expansion and from an assumption of the right of "objective" European scientists to travel and observe other continents of the world. (Fa-ti Fan, 89)

The anxiety that the flora and fauna of the Chinese world will be classified by, and thus become the possession of, European empire, I argue, drives Baoyu and Lao Shaonian to expand their menagerie of curiosities, and this too must be seen as an act of colonial expansion. What is vexing about this endeavor, and the way in which it challenges Kerslake's and Rieder's assumptions about SF and colonial discourse, is the fact that these efforts are turned inward on China. Why is Baoyu collecting things that he and Lao Shaonian identify as already inherently Chinese, rather than collecting things that are either up for grabs, or the property of the Western world?

Kerslake's identification of the crisis of confrontation with an alien outsider as a form of silencing is applicable to SF that appears to silence cultural insiders as well. In the case of *New Stone*, a crisis of indigenous epistemology, and the specter of cultural loss, are the driving anxieties of the narrative. Lao Shaonian's silencing takes a circuitous route: only in rebuking Chinese scholars who would impugn China's literary traditions, who must in turn be parroting the words of foreign scholars, does this serve as a silencing of the other. To this extent, the safari constitutes a double silencing: bringing both mythical tradition and indigenous scholars who impugn the veracity of such texts under the ontological control of the museum; silencing Daoist tradition while establishing the geographic and taxonomic veracity of the *Shanhai jing.*

Alongside its silencing mission, the museum in the Realm of Civilization is a new place, imbuing new meanings in the artifacts on display. Rather than privately owned symbols of invisible monarchical power, these objects are on public display as the shared heritage of a social body. Wu Jianren's imaginary museum represents a shift, from elite collection to public display of monarchal power. This shift signaled a transformation in which the "categorical structuring of goods eases the transition from private to public collection, from commodity to museum artifact, from symbol of the private collector to symbol of the corporate body. Acting civilized or being part of a civilization requires that these things be transferred into the public domain" (Claypool, 580). It is not merely the fact of their existence, but the mode of display that imbues these objects with cultural meaning, and the changing contexts of display reflect new ways of imagining the relationship between cultural artifacts and the social sphere.

The museum in the Realm of Civilization lays claim to the remembrance and resuscitation of a bygone utopian age in its vast and complete collection of Confucian classics, including works that were thought to be lost entirely. Placed on display in the reliquary, Zhuang-zi's *peng* is torn from its role as a fabular marker of the sublime vastness of the universe and is made part of a system of Confucian-colonial order. The museum in the Realm of Civilization goes a step beyond winning the struggle for cultural survival, recuperating that which had been thought lost as part of the dominant moral-philosophical system.[19] *New Stone* portrays a situation in which the natural world has been brought under control, demonstrating the technological and moral superiority of the Realm of Civilization. Just like its real-world counterparts, Wu Jianren's fictional museum was "a site in which order could be brought out of chaos" (Claypool, 570).

Domestication of the Unknown—
Museums, Exhibitions, and Empire

The imaginary museum in the Realm of Civilization paralleled a budding, real-world Chinese knowledge industry, built in imitation of its Victorian counterparts, often at institutions like the Jiangnan Arsenal, which were staffed by British Protestant missionaries (Jones 2011, 42–43).[20] The museum was one of a number of emerging social institutions aimed at displaying scientific wealth and mapping evolutionary schemas, institutions that emerged almost simultaneously in media representation and in the form of brick-and-mortar construction.

In Europe, symbols of private secular power like the *studioli*, which had affirmed the renaissance princes' sovereignty and the fact that knowledge of the world was reserved to such sovereigns, were reconfigured from spaces of private viewing into places of public display and moral education. In the words of Giuseppe Olmi, the *studiolo* was an assembly of cupboards around a central viewing point, representing "an attempt to reappropriate and reassemble all reality in miniature, to constitute a place from the centre of which the prince could symbolically reclaim dominion over the entire natural and artificial world" (quoted in Bennett, 36). One key institutional project of the emergence of the modern European nation-state was the reversal of this architectural layout, transforming the hidden space from which regimes of power displayed the objects of personal dominion into a public space where the objects within became totems of the national imagination. A similar change took place in China, whereby museums shifted from the imperial collections of emperors to public displays.[21]

Two museums established in colonial Shanghai served the dual function of laying claim to fields of knowledge and inculcating modern values in the citizenry. The first was the Siccawei Museum (Ziran lishi bowuyuan, or the *Musée de Zikawei*), a museum established by a Jesuit priest on the outskirts of the French Concession in 1868. The second was a museum established by members of the Royal Asiatic Society, many of whom had close contacts with Father Pierre Heude (1836–1902), the founder of the Siccawei Museum. The Shanghai Museum (Shanghai bowuyuan) on Museum Road (originally Yuanmingyuan lu, then Bowuyuan lu), was established in a building given to the society by the British government in 1874, meaning that the earliest museums in semicolonial Shanghai were the product of Fa-ti Fan's "scientific imperialism." The quest to be the first to identify and name flora and fauna, and to incorporate them into a Western taxonomic schema was visible at the museum. While the Jesuit-run Siccawei Museum sought to reestablish the intellectual legitimacy of the Jesuit order both in China and within the Catholic Church, the Shanghai Museum was meant to demonstrate Britain's intellectual superiority. Specimens were displayed with the names of their European and American "discoverers" attached to them, signaling the deterritorialization of China's biological and zoological heritage (Claypool, 574–593). According to the Royal Asiatic Society, "In the extremely probable case of any new species turning up . . . the collector of each new one will obtain the necessary credit for it" (curator's report, *Journal of the Royal Asiatic Society* 9 [1875]: xiii, quoted in Claypool, 592). Through the specimens' newly formalized Latin names, a degree of newness, of the "modern," was imparted on the natural world (Bennett, 593). As observed previously, the mark of modernity was a double-edged sword that also often signaled the potential for incompatibility with native epistemology and the loss of cultural heritage.

By 1905, this anxiety had led Zhang Jian (1853–1956) to found China's first Chinese-owned museum, the Nantong Museum in Nantong, Jiangsu (approximately sixty miles southwest of Shanghai). "Zhang's acute sensitivity toward cultural loss and the possibilities for cultural maintenance was heightened by knowledge of the colonial museums in Shanghai—one established by the French Jesuits, the other by the British Royal Asiatic Society—which attempted to collect natural specimens indigenous to China and frame them as part of the European world" (Claypool, 570). The Nantong Museum was designed in imitation of the museums in Shanghai, both in its architecture and in the bilingual Chinese-English labeling of specimens. The museum functioned as a site for the affirmation of moral and cosmological meaning and political relevance as much as it was a site for the dissemination of science.

[Chinese observers] positioned it in grand narratives about nation, world, and often about the place of Chinese things, if not the Chinese nation, in the world. These things were not limited to art and archaeological artifacts (*qi*), as we might assume; they included natural specimens (*wu*), from sawdust-stuffed ospreys to peonies and nephrite hardstones. The museum exhibited the civilizing strength and wealth of a state by demonstrating its ability to explore the globe and extract specimens and objects from existing networks of material and historical relations. The larger, older, and more exotic the thing, the better. (Claypool, 569)

The arrangement of Zhang's museum "sustained the fiction that [it] constituted a coherent representation of China. Western science, which Zhang promoted as part of the educational mission of the museum, served to inject objects not in the science category—art and historical artifacts—with 'objective' factual content. It also suggested a Darwinian evolutionary progression from the past to the present, a present that was going to win the struggle for survival" (Claypool, 590).

This organizational principle paralleled that of European museums in their civilizing mission. Objects were "arranged in a manner to make intelligible a scientific view of the world." That is to say, the laws of nature were reflected in the ordered system of display in the museum, and the evolutionary development of nature and the arts was reproduced in the spatial configuration of the museum. Walking through a museum is a performative act, tracing evolutionary history (Bennett, 2, 185). The museum both made visible the progress of civilization and acted as a civilizing force, inculcating in the museumgoer a sense of proper social deportment in such a setting, and demonstrating to him or her the evolutionary order of the world. Qin Shao adds that the mission of the museum as a display of national strength was a familiar concept in the sphere of Chinese notions of statecraft, noting that "it was a small leap from mastering the art of ancient ceremonies to learning the visual spectacle of modern exhibitions." Zhang argued forcefully and sought support from the Qing court for his efforts, but he was unsuccessful, owing to the immobility and fiscal insolvency of the declining state apparatus (Qin Shao, 687–691). Nevertheless, Chinese rulers and intellectuals quickly grasped the significance of exhibitionary culture as a vehicle for displaying the vitality of the state in the modern international sphere.

Zhang Jian's museum was at once a rationally ordered space dedicated to the creation of national subjects, but like the knowledge texts of Lu Xun, it also framed the institution in terms of Confucian antiquity. Parallels were drawn between the modern, Western, scientific sense of knowing the world and notions of study and knowledge of natural phenomena as they appear in Confucian philosophy. For example, two wooden panels that hung from the balcony of the south building were inscribed with a couplet: "Constructed as a village school to teach and to more fully know the names of bird and beast, grass and tree" (*she wei xiang xuexiao yi jiao, duo shi niao shou cao mu zhi ming*). These two phrases consisted of a paraphrase of a passage from Mencius (*She wei xiang xu xueexiao yi jiao*) and a quotation from the *Analects* (*Duo shi niao shou cao mu zhi ming*). The first line of the couplet alludes to Mencius's criticism of King Hui of Liang in an episode that emphasizes the Mencian conception of the ideal state (Claypool, 576), while the second line evokes Confucius's exhortation that students memorize the *Shijing*, the knowledge text of Zhou dynasty disputation.[22] Though the museum itself was deeply implicated in the new world of knowledge and new notions of time, the couplet is suggestive of another moment of contestation, where at best the museum is subordinated to the Confucian tradition of knowing the world through naming (Qin Shao, 689), or at worst Confucianism demonstrates its viability within the new epistemological framework of evolutionary science. By the 1920s, Nantong had become "a model of modernity and local self-government and attracted a large number of visitors" (Qin Shao, 689), demonstrating the vital role of exhibitionary culture both in promoting modern institutions of statecraft and in staking a claim for traditional epistemological frames.

It is tempting to read the events of the second half of the *New Story of the Stone* as an ironic commentary on the adoption of Western science and technology. At one point in their safari, Baoyu jokes to Lao Shaonian, "One medal [for bravery in hunting a *peng*] isn't enough; are you looking to get a second one?" They both get a chuckle out of this but continue their hunt basically uninterrupted (*XSTJ*, 328). Later, Dongfang Fa makes essentially the same remark to Baoyu, quipping: "Catching one *peng* isn't enough; are you planning on catching a second?" (368) Aside from these brief moments of commentary, there is little suggestion that what occurs in the second half of the novel should be read as satire. While it is difficult to imagine that Wu Jianren lacked the intellectual capacity to see the irony in Baoyu's "civilized safari," it is also important to keep in mind the paradox facing all his contemporaries and the difficulty of producing lasting solutions to China's semi-colonial plight. As the novel makes abundantly clear, China's survival as a nation would be possible only in the context of a radical shift in politics, society, and epistemology. And how could China remain China in the context of such a radical shift? Though the explanation that there simply was no adequate solution for this problem, and that the absence of viable solutions manifests itself in narrative inconsistency, seems in the end dissatisfying, it is also the most likely one.

In this chapter, I have addressed some of the theoretical issues associated with SF and their relevance to *New Stone*. In exploring some of the common formal features of SF that are apparent in the novel, I have attempted to explain why this novel might be identified as a work of SF, despite the likely objections of its author, and I have identified the importance of exploring this work in such light. One important theme that emerges is the confrontation with domestic turmoil in the form of admitting the true nature of China's crisis. China's internal problems are the most pressing issue in the first half of the novel, and the techno-utopia of the second half cannot solve all these problems. The silencing of the tradition that occupies much of the second half of the narrative entails both a silencing of those who doubt the veracity of Chinese myth and fantasy, and the internal silencing of a conclusive and authoritative exegetical stamp. The paradox of reform is inescapable: in order to survive, China must destroy itself. What cannot be addressed in direct terms—the impossibility of imagining satisfying and lasting solutions to the crisis of colonial intrusion—is addressed in the form of narrative collapse.

For Lu Xun and for Wu Jianren, there is no way to imagine a space beyond the walls of the iron house. Two stereotypically utopian literary works—a late Qing SF adventure, and the emblem of May Fourth iconoclasm—produced very dystopian narratives. Beyond helping us to understand the literary and social field of the late Qing, this should also expand our understanding of SF. SF is in many respects a product of imperial imagination. Chinese SF is strongly informed by China's own traditions of fantasy and myth. Already in late Qing SF, one obvious concern is the position of tradition in modern Chinese society. Another concern is the threat of foreign incursion; but neither of these can be dealt with conclusively. It would appear that the utopian hopes of SF are balanced by anxieties over the death of tradition, fear of the other, and fear of the unintended consequences of technology. On the theoretical level, critical studies should take this into account both in terms of its influence on authors and its influence upon the growing field of academic criticism. If SF's arrival in China was delayed by some time, it quickly took on local inflections and adapted itself to reflect the concerns of Chinese authors.

4

SF FOR THE NATION

TALES OF THE MOON COLONY

AND THE EMERGENCE OF

CHINESE SCIENCE FICTION

 Published serially in the fiction monthly *Xiuxiang xiaoshuo* between 1904 and 1905, Huangjiang Diaosou's (b. ?) *Tales of the Moon Colony* (*Yueqiu zhimindi xiaoshuo*) is the first native Chinese work labeled as science fiction. Through a close reading of this uncompleted novel, this chapter examines the anxieties associated with utopianism, nationalism, and Occidentalism that revealed themselves in early Chinese SF.[1] While the text depicts a world in which Asian scientists and explorers successfully vie with their European counterparts for hegemony over their common Southeast Asian others, the novel ultimately foretells a universal order marked by concentric circles of colonial domination—Asia over Southeast Asia, Europe over Asia, the moon over planet Earth, outer planets over the moon, etc. Colonial incursion is a leitmotif, and while technological superiority justifies violence visited upon terrestrial others, there will always be other extraterrestrial groups who can use their own superior civilization as justification for similar domination. The novel shares with Wu Jianren's *New Stone* the prefiguration of a number of tropes of canonical Chinese fiction, and with the seminal author Lu Xun (1881–1936) the metaphors of China as the "sick man of Asia" and of Chinese society as cannibalistic.

As observed in the previous chapters, the problem of social Darwinism was apprehended not as a theoretical conundrum but as a very real threat to the continued existence of the nation-state. The dialectic opposition of the West as modern, scientific, and civilized and the East as traditional, unscientific, and uncivilized gave rise to a world in which the Orient became the fruit of Western conquest. In producing knowledge about the East, the European imperial project had a profound impact on the material and intellectual history of early twentieth-century Asia. Because Asia is literally created by this encounter, Occidentalism—or a reversal of colonial and imperial discourse in which the Orient produces knowledge about the Occident—becomes unattainable. In response to Edward Said's contention that "the answer to Orientalism is not Occidentalism" (Said, 1986, 328), it might also be observed that in many cases in late Qing fiction, Occidentalism was impossible to achieve. *Tales of the Moon Colony* represents one such instance of this conundrum.

In Huangjiang Diaosou's *Tales of the Moon Colony*, simultaneous confrontations between China and Europe, and China and its own past, give voice to a conflict far more complex than the dialectical opposition of Occident and Orient. This conflict is explicitly stated in the characters' discussion of colonial logic, and in their overt critique of the deleterious effects of Chinese culture and literature, but it also appears in the shift to the Gregorian calendar and the recognition of deep time in the discourse of social Darwinism. A simple reversal of Orientalism—Occidentalism—did not emerge as a counter-discourse.

The incomplete novel is loosely centered on the character Long Menghua (lit. "the dragon [who] dreams of China"); I say "loosely" because Menghua spends most of the narrative in an infirmary recovering from a series of illnesses. The plot presents a series of encounters that result from the ongoing search for Long Menghua's missing wife and son conducted by Tamatarō and the other fugitives aboard his hot-air balloon. Having killed a man to avenge his father, Menghua flees to Southeast Asia. En route, he becomes separated from his wife, née Feng, when their ship sinks off the coast of Malaysia. He is saved and brought to the town of Sungai Buloh, where he meets a number of other Chinese refugees and befriends a Japanese man named Fujita Tamatarō (Ch. Tengtian Yutailang). The group climbs aboard Tamatarō's hot-air balloon and sets off to find Long Menghua's wife, who they later learn has been rescued by an Englishman named Masuya.

Menghua is one of many people in the story who have been forced to flee China as a result of persecution and various miscarriages of justice. He and Tamatarō travel around the globe in the hot-air balloon, in search of territory for future colonization. Menghua spends much of the novel in the grips of a self-recrimination, self-pity, and melancholia and is often asleep or drunk, while Tamatarō is scientific and rational (he built the hot-air balloon) and quite efficacious in his encounters with the outside world. Tso-Wei Hsieh identifies Tamatarō as a rational and active foil to Long Menghua, who represents Chinese sentimentality and confusion (Tso-Wei Hsieh, 197–198). While in New York, Long Menghua is arrested for not carrying a passport and thrown in jail. While the story imagines pan-Asian technological superiority in the form of Tamatarō's hot-air balloon, Menghua's global citizenship is second class at best. The international shame of the Chinese Exclusion Act of 1882, which effectively banned Chinese immigration to the United States for more than twenty years, is compounded by domestic corruption in the form of an ambassador who is out carousing with prostitutes when Menghua's friends seek his aid. The strongest Chinese characters in the novel are the women: Menghua's and Tamatarō's wives are both literate, do not have bound feet, and dress in Western clothing. Tamatarō's wife, Pu Yuhuan, has invented a light-emitting coat that she wears when accompanying the other characters on their adventures, and she often serves as a translator. Tamatarō's own personal efficacy is expressed most clearly in his miraculous and well-equipped hot-air balloon, which is outfitted with an array of modern amenities, including an exercise room, bedrooms, a dining room, a hospital, and a conference hall. In a reversal of Europe's technological superiority, Tamatarō even informs his companions that the English are trying to copy his invention.

The marriage between Tamatarō and Pu Yuhuan and the alliance between Tamatarō and the Chinese exiles elides a much more complex relationship and an open wound in Chinese history that is rarely directly addressed in the narrative. Menghua's detention in New York makes clear that there are differences in the international rights enjoyed by Chinese and Japanese citizens, and the corrupt and ineffective Chinese embassy's failure to come to Menghua's aid reveals this to be a sign of systemic dysfunction. Tamatarō hatches a plan to break

Menghua out of jail, the first of a series of rescues he is compelled to perform. Tamatarō's heroic role hints at the paradoxical reality that although Japan had begun to move down a path toward regional hegemony, it was the nearest neighbor able to offer China scientific training and expertise, and China's strongest proponents for industrial modernity and governmental reform were exiles in Japan.

Tales of the Moon Colony occupies the space between the travel narrative and the imperial encounter with the other characteristic of SF. The balloon serves both as a techno-utopian enclave and as a vehicle for visiting a series of allegorical tableaux where the boundaries between civilization and barbarity are explored. The characters travel between Southeast Asia, London, New York, Transvaal (modern-day South Africa), India, and a series of imaginary islands in the Indian Ocean. Eventually, they find Long Menghua's wife, but the story ends before Tamatarō can successfully manufacture a balloon capable of going to the moon, which he plans to model on those used by the people from the moon.

John Rieder's observation that colonial expansion and the establishment of global capitalism were driving forces in the emergence of SF, and that the discourse of modernity naturalized the difference between center and periphery as the result of different stages of development, is visible in *Tales of the Moon Colony*. Social Darwinian science fiction posited the West and modernity as the future, identifying the periphery with the past. This in turn led to the false identification of asymmetric colonial power structures as the outcome of an inevitable historical process. Early SF played a key role in affirming the dialectical opposition of colony to metropole, progress to backwardness, and civilization to barbarity. Rieder goes on to posit that early SF worked in opposition to such ethnocentric misrepresentations and misunderstandings as well (Rieder 2008, 26). In the case of *Tales of the Moon Colony*, this discourse becomes fraught with ambivalence, torn between affirming the superiority of pan-Asian civilization represented by Tamatarō and his balloon and reaffirming the weakness of East and Southeast Asia through the sickly Long Menghua and the benighted islands the explorers visit.

The islands in the Indian Ocean are inhabited by natives whose allegorical relationship to China is at times so transparent that one would hesitate to call them allegories at all. These exploratory visits also see the travelers offering their audience a chance at what Rieder refers to as the "vicarious enjoyment of colonial spoils, as attested to in Victorian England by the popularity of travel accounts and adventure stories" (2008, 27). The travelers take golden tables from troglodyte tribes who bind their women's hands and feet; they collect jadeite stones, identify new species, and kill giant pythons. When they descend from the heavens, the tribal chieftain of another island takes them to be gods.

The Critical Gaze

Many of these islands are vignettes of Chinese intellectual and social life. The practice of foot binding is a particular concern. On the island of Yulinguo, the women's hands are bound so that "their arms resembled stalks of threshed grain, and their fingers a clutch of orchids, they were considered to be the great beauties of this country" (Huangjiang Diaosou, 94). On the Isle of Le'erlaifu, the inhabitants are descendants of the Chinese who have become "pedantic scholars" (*fu ru*),[2] having confined their scholarly outlook to the Song neo-Confucian commentaries of the brothers Cheng Yi (1033–1107) and Cheng Hao (1032–1085) and Zhu Xi. The inhabitants of Le'erlaifu fled Taiwan at the fall of the Song dynasty (960–1279) and eventually wiped out the indigenous population that had been living on the island upon their arrival. The island is described as resembling an iron barrel, impenetrable on all sides so that "not even birds could fly over it" (Huangjiang Diaosou, 92). The island distills late Qing intellectual life into a geographic prison from which there is no escape and into which no new ideas will penetrate. Huangjiang Diaosou's image of Chinese civilization as an iron barrel is uncannily similar to Lu Xun's depiction of China's citizens as sleepers in an iron house (examined in chapter 2) and echoed in the Wu Jianren's *New Stone* (examined in chapter 3). Far from marginal, the themes at the heart of early Chinese science fiction parallel many of the core themes of modern Chinese literature.

Tales of the Moon Colony is also in dialogue with a number of familiar tropes of the modern Chinese canon, including the association between the health of the human body and that of the body politic. Long Menghua is sickly and subject to erratic emotional states, regularly succumbing to a series of illnesses from which he must be resuscitated by a series of doctors. Like Lu Xun, the doctors in the story are often concluding that the issue is Chinese literature and civilization. Dr. Ha Lao, armed with an X-ray lens (*touguang jing*), determines that Menghua's heart is functioning at only 70 percent capacity, his liver looks like a sponge gourd, and his lungs are withered. After some debate about whether the bungling fraud whose name is a homophone for "Fake Western Doctor" (Jia Xiyi) can be of any help at all, they go to the ship's infirmary, and Ha Lao uses a series of elixirs to cure Menghua— he even closes up his chest using a special medicinal liquid rather than stitches. In the post-operational debriefing, Ha Lao informs the group,

> I believe your heart has been misused since your youth. I've heard someone say China has a writing style called the eight-legged essay [*baguwen*]. After managing to finish writing one of these your heart will slowly shrink and all sorts of bitter and astringent substances will begin to collect in your ventricles. Your gallbladder will also be many times smaller than a normal person's. . . . The first symptom is delirium, and ends in terror-stricken nervousness. . . . In my humble opinion, you had better stop writing *bagu*. (Huangjiang Diaosou, 66)

In what is recognized as the very first native work of Chinese SF, the metaphor of cultural and national health is presented in bodily terms. Though this metaphor is most closely associated in literary historiography with the concerns that permeate Lu Xun's writing, it can be traced back at least as far as the Han dynasty (202 BCE–220 CE) to the writings of Dong Zhongshu (195?–105? BCE).[3] Social critique and the prospects for national salvation are expressed in terms of physical and mental illness, and writing is seen as both a cause and possible cure. As early as 1898, Kang Youwei had called for the elimination of the *bagu* form, associating its elimination with the adoption of science (Qiu

Ruohong, 64–65). This theme appears throughout the novel, tying together the themes of physical health and Chinese letters. Later, Yu Lawu compares Chinese poetry to the practice of foot binding, arguing that this also has contributed to Long Menghua's poor health (Wang Hui, 119). Early Chinese SF is indicative of the degree to which Lu Xun and other May Fourth authors were working with and refining a series of familiar literary devices rather than inventing the tradition anew.

Two more tropes that appear in Lu Xun's writing emerge in the adventurer's trip to Sichang sha'er Island. The people of Sichang sha'er believe that their ruler, a tyrant named King Muhuade, is the descendant of God, and as such he cannot eat normal food or be clothed in normal garb. Instead, he is fed human flesh and clothed in human skin. The common people have all taken to living hidden underground, but the custom of cannibalism has continued for thousands of years. Tamatarō and company bring their balloon to the imperial palace, where they see

> hundreds of people . . . tied up before the palace gates. Some had had their skin peeled off; others had had their hands or feet severed. The atmosphere was cold and wretched. Yu Lawu hurriedly pulled Tamatarō and Pu Yuhuan back aboard the balloon, saying "What use is there in visiting an uncivilized place like this?" He walked over to one side of the balloon and began hurling down chlorine gas bombs with wild abandon. Tamatarō said, "The international community has banned the use of chlorine gas; how can you just set to bombing them like this willy-nilly?" Yu Lawu didn't even respond as he continued dropping bombs. After dropping bombs for quite some time he finally said, "Mr. Tama, you say that chlorine gas shouldn't be used? If we don't use uncivilized weapons in uncivilized places like this, then where shall we use them?" (Huangjiang Diaosou, 108–109)[4]

The inhabitants of the island pre-date by roughly sixteen years Lu Xun's imagery of Chinese culture as cannibalistic ("Diary of a Madman," 1918), while the explorers' response accepts and repeats the logic of colonial violence. This narrative preempts a number of tropes associated with Lu Xun, indicating that the author was deploying an already existing symbolic vocabulary. The prevalence of these tropes in science fiction demonstrates the degree to which the genre reflects the literary concerns of the early twentieth century at large.

Whose Colony Is It Anyway?

Instead of offering a counterpoint to the legitimization of violence visited upon the other, the characters in the story end up adopting the same reasoning in their own colonial mission. In *Empire*, Michael Hardt and Antonio Negri have argued that non-European others were the "signs of primitiveness that represented stages of humanity's evolution toward civilization [and] were thus conceived as present synchronically in the various primitive peoples and cultures spread across the globe" (Hardt and Negri, 126). The denizens of Le'erlaifu represent a stage of primitiveness that is so lost on the evolutionary scale as to be undeserving of the "humane" rules of modern warfare. Two forms of primitiveness and abject difference are at play in this moment: for the rulers of Le'erlaifu, their inhumanity is representative of their hopeless social decay, while the inferiority of the cannibalized is figured through the citizenry's retreat underground. Like the cannibalistic Morlocks in H. G. Wells's *The Time Machine*, their life underground "is a telling measure of how far they have fallen socially" (Alkon, 145–147). This social decay results in a moral calculus through which the social Darwinist biological will to power through consuming the weak is trumped by the ability to destroy both the cannibalistic consumer and the consumed subject from the safety of the bombardier's cockpit. *Tales of the Moon Colony* reduplicates the logic of coevality through the historicization of the various Chinas-in-miniature that are encountered in the Indian Ocean. These evolutionary epics in miniature freeze the islanders as a dialectical negation of Tamatarō and his companions' own level of civilization. The imagery of anthropophagic savagery and of a suffocating social realm sealed off from the outside world in this vignette prefigures two of the most salient images of modern Chinese literature, which appeared in the works of Lu Xun approximately two decades later.

The balloon-goers come to an island plagued by a tradition thousands of years old. This custom is the consumption of human flesh. Here as well we see an even more sinister version of the iron house metaphor—in this case, it is not so much that we might just let some people suffocate in their sleep; it's that the best thing for them might be to be eradicated by chemical warfare. The "just war" exacted upon the rulers and citizens of Sichang sha'er Island is a mercy killing. Salvation is far from universal, and in its early incarnation, Chinese SF was far from utopian.

It becomes clear that while the technological superiority that the travelers aboard the balloon have mastered justifies the violence that they visit upon unknown islands in the Indian Ocean, there will always be another group who can use their own superior civilization as justification for similar domination. Tamatarō reveals that *Tales of the Moon Colony* will not narrate the establishment of a colony of humans on the moon, but the inevitable colonization of Earth by the superior lunarian race. The people on the moon are more "civilized" than the people of Earth, and the inevitable outcome of this higher level of civilization is the establishment of a colony of moon-men on Earth. Tamatarō relates the likelihood of this development to Japan's expansion during the Meiji period (1868–1912), saying,

Luckily, our Meiji emperor became aware of these issues, and all my countrymen strove to be the best. Eventually, they took Taiwan in the south and gained a foothold in Korea to the north, assuming a position as one of the strongest countries in the world. But in the end, even such a position of strength was untenable. The moon is but a minute orb, yet it has developed such a high level of civilization. In a few years, they'll establish a colony here. I fear that the five races of red, black, yellow, white, and brown people are headed for a great calamity indeed. And if this is the case with the moon, then what of Mercury, Venus, Mars, Jupiter, and Saturn? And what of Uranus and Neptune? If there are people in all these places, and all these places have developed their own civilizations, each of which is a thousand times, or ten thousand times, or even infinitely more developed than ours? As they begin to establish contact with us, what could the outcome be? (Huangjiang Diaosou, 198–199)

The colonial situation is mirrored when Yu Lawu gasses the uncivilized denizens of a lost island in the Indian Ocean, and Tamatarō is led to the conclusion that the inevitable outcome is not a reversal of the colonial order, but a repetition of these relations on a greater and greater scale. People from the moon will colonize Earth, people from Mercury will colonize the moon, and so on. The colonial subject will continue to be a colonial subject, and knowledge of the world will continue to be produced by an alien civilization.

Colonial logic is subverted through a reductio ad absurdum argument explaining its logical extension of imperialism on a cosmic scale rather than its inversion. The colonial dialectic insists on the other as an absolute negation, or the reverse of the European, and through this negation the civilized, scientific, rational, and liberated subject is created. In *Tales of the Moon Colony*, the repetition of colonial discursive practice and of colonial incursion suggests a proliferating multiplicity of colonial identities. The dialectic conflict between thesis and antithesis is replaced by concentric rings, or hierarchical ordering of power relationships, where progressively more "civilized" members of one polity prey on those lacking civilization. In the adventurer's dealings with local, transnational, and extraterrestrial relations between individuals, social Darwinism is the rule of thumb. China itself is near the very center of this power schema, one of the weakest agents in the concentric hierarchy of imperial domination. Geographically and politically, China is practically erased from the narrative, a weak state that cannot guarantee the rights of its citizens at home or abroad. Its presence in the narrative is as a spectral space from which most of the characters have made a hasty escape, and as a foil to the relative civilization of Japan and the Western world. China's spectral presence is also felt in the series of mini-China islands dotting the Indian Ocean that the characters visit.

Colony and Time

The story's radical reconfiguration of the geopolitical imagination is accompanied by a shift in the conceptualization of time, bearing further witness to the changes engendered by the encounter between the Orient and the Occident. Ren Dongmei argues that the degree to which perceptions of space and time are reconfigured in *Tales of the Moon Colony* is symptomatic of a major epistemological shift. The characters and the balloon reckon time based on the Western calendar, and they measure their day in the calculated terms of hours and minutes. Day-to-day, experiential time is also shifted from the agricultural generalities of seasons to the industrial specificity of hours and minutes. The characters pay close attention to their daily schedule, noting the hour they sleep, the hour they wake up, the time they plan to arrive in a given place, or the hour they will reconvene to depart from another place. The duration that it takes to complete a given task—flying from one island to another, for example—is also noted in number of hours. This is a thoroughly modernist vision of time and space, where travel between landmarks is not conceptualized in discrete units of distance, but in terms of the time necessary to move between them. The shift in consciousness from measuring space as distance to measuring space as time is often identified as one of the distinguishing characteristics of modernity, one that has a particular resonance in SF.[5] *Longue durée* historical time shifts from the sixty-year cyclical system of the "heavenly stems and earthly branches" (*tiangan dizhi*) to linear time.[6] Ren argues that this shift to linear time not only signals the decentering of the Chinese way of reckoning the past, but that linear time also opens up the horizon of imagining the future (Ren 2008, 192–200). The linear perspective on time and the adoption of the Gregorian calendar cannot be traced to a single moment. Instead, many publications and individuals during the late Qing functioned using both calendars, and in many respects this practice continues today. David Wright identifies this gradual (and still not absolute) transformation as the cumulative effect of a series of crises in foreign and domestic affairs that eventually led intellectuals to the painful conclusion that there was "no cyclical redemption in sight" (Kwong, 171–173). The notion of tripartite time—

overlapping and evolving divisions of past, present, and future—was the product of a crisis of historical consciousness that insisted that this moment was like no other, and that therefore cyclical time could not exist. This crisis of consciousness resulted in a series of attempts to map Chinese history in terms of developmental stages, however crude, on the part of translators and intellectuals like Xue Fucheng (1838–1894), Wang Tao (1828–1897), Zheng Guanying (1842–1922), Liang Qichao, and Kang Youwei. All these were models based upon Darwinian notions of evolutionary progress through *longue dureé* time (Kwong, 174–178). "The displacement of one by the other, in so far as it did occur, was never uncontested or complete" (185). China continues to function on two calendars, making reference both to the lunar calendar and to the Western calendar—celebrating both the lunar Chinese New Year and January first. Historical events that occurred before the adoption of the Western calendar are dated using the *tiangan dizhi* system as often as they are dated using the Gregorian calendar.

Those aboard Tamatarō's balloon and those on the ground occupy separate calendars and separate historical trajectories. The people of Sichang sha'er have been dated from the reign of the first emperor of Japan, Jimmu Tennō (r. 660–585 BCE), while the people of Le'erlaifu trace their lineage to the time of the fall of the Song dynasty, and they are essentially frozen in time, dressing in Song-period scholarly outfits, speaking *guanhua* ("official speech"—that is, the common spoken dialect of the Ming and Qing court), and conducting Song court rituals (Huangjiang Diaosou, 91). The discovery of deep time was in many ways made possible by the colonial era. The ability to navigate led in turn to a race to discovery, which eventually brought Charles Darwin to the Galápagos Islands, where his observation of plant and animal life played a vital role in the development of the theory of evolution. This Darwinian vision of time pervades the novel, freezing the various islands in the Indian Ocean in their own respective evolutionary stages. Darwinian time and the pseudo-Darwinian vision of the "survival of the fittest" are central themes in the *Tales of the Moon Colony*.

This ongoing shift in the perception and method of marking of deep time paralleled a new vision of day-to-day, humanly perceptible time as well. Clock time came to replace subjective time. This epistemological revolution, too, was enabled by colonial modernity. European exploration in search of land, labor, and capital necessitated more accurate methods of navigation. Navigators found themselves in need of precise, mechanical methods of keeping time in order to calculate their longitudinal distance from the Greenwich meridian. In turn, exploration and the extraction of resources helped to encourage the development of the industrial revolution domestically in England and Western Europe, and the industrial mode of production also necessitated more precise measure of time in service of its new, machine-oriented workday. In other words, the way we reckon humanly perceptible time is indebted in great part to the age of marine exploration. Time becomes one of the most salient symbols in the representation of the differences between China and the West.

In *Tales of the Moon Colony*, the reader is left with a work that can be described neither as a complete novel—the narrative ends before Tamatarō's speculations can be borne out—nor as particularly "Chinese," as it takes place entirely outside China and centers on characters who have cast off the material signs of their "Chineseness." Long Menghua and his companions aboard the Japanese-made balloon have relinquished the external markers of their national heritage by cutting off their queues, drinking coffee, and dressing in Western garb.

First, the novel goes to great lengths to delegitimize China as a geographic or moral center. China has lost its status as the Middle Kingdom, and the emerging relationship with the people on the moon suggests a decentering not only of Europe, but of the planet Earth itself. In the recurring vignettes of a failed social and political system, China's moral and intellectual centrality is undermined. As a representation of Japan's technological and military superiority, Tamatarō's balloon seems to imply that China too must embark upon a Meiji-style mission of national renewal. However, the discussion of solutions takes a backseat to a pointed critique of China's cultural shortcomings. The novel shares with its contemporaries a sense that China faced an unprecedented crisis, and a pervasive lack of solutions.

Second, the novel goes to great lengths not only to displace China as a geopolitical center, but also to suggest that Europe as well is not the ultimate center of imperial might, ceding hegemony to extraterrestrial others. In *Tales of the Moon Colony*, the colonial relationship is concentric, as levels of domination extend from Asia to Europe, to the moon and beyond. Rather than challenging the dialectical opposition of colony to metropole, the narrative suggests a constantly shifting relationship between center and periphery, depending upon the breadth of one's vision. The text imagines a universal hierarchy of imperial domination where all civilizations conquer those beneath them, but are in turn subjected to the rule of more civilized peoples above them on the colonial chain of being. Orientalism is repeated along all levels of these concentric circles, not reversed. Where many SF narratives find a way of reaffirming the inviolability of planet Earth and the superiority of a universalized humanity (that is, Western civilization), *Tales of the Moon Colony* suggests a narrative trajectory in which the cosmopolitan metropole will eventually shift to deep space.[7]

Finally, *Tales of the Moon Colony* also depicts the temporal decentering of China. This occurs on three distinct levels, all of which reiterate a major shift in China's position in the world. First, the shift from cyclical time to linear time symbolized a radical shift in Chinese cosmological consciousness. Linear time was associated with the concept of deep time and universal evolutionary processes as well. Second, aside from indicating that traditional Chinese visions of cosmic order were being undone, the notion of linear time also suggests that China might not be at the same evolutionary stage as its European counterparts, a concern prefigured in the introduction of Darwinian thought to China (examined in chapter 2). Third, the shift to clock time means that Long Menghua and Tamatarō are functioning in their day-to-day lives on the universal clock of Greenwich mean time. This was accompanied by a change in the perception of space, through which distance between places was measured in units of time.

This novel set the stage for a remarkably dystopian strain of SF. Many of the themes in the novel appeared throughout turn-of-the-twentieth-century Chinese SF and continue to figure prominently in SF narratives to this day. In their visits to the various allegorical doubles of China in the Indian Ocean, the travelers observe China at various stages of the evolutionary scale but never see the country as having attained the sophistication of the West. Imperial discourse is turned inward, focusing the colonial attentions of the explorers on the backward aspects of Chinese culture they encounter in the Indian Ocean. At the same time, the narrative turns its attention away from one of the most pressing and growing threats to China's sovereignty—Japan's ambition to become the center of its own Asian empire. As mainland China disappears, only to reappear in allegorical miniature in the Indian Ocean, the fraught relationship between Japan and China is glossed over. While the characters openly contemplate the relationship between East and Southeast Asia, between hemispheres, and indeed between Earth and the cosmos, the complexities of northeast Asian relationships and Japan's annexation of Taiwan following the Sino-Japanese War are ignored.

Many of the most salient tropes of twentieth-century Chinese literature—various versions of the "sick man of Asia" and Lu Xun's iron house—appear in *Tales of the Moon Colony*. The intellectual discussion of the need for language reform that led Chinese authors to pen their own works of SF is reflected in the novel as well, both in its overt criticism of classical Chinese education, the examination system and literary Chinese, and in the vernacular register of the novel itself, demonstrating that in the case of early modern Chinese literature, SF played a central role. The ongoing discussion of the relationship between SF and imperialism is especially relevant to understanding the emergence and development of the genre in late Qing China. Such a mode of analysis can help us to more fully comprehend the means through which late Qing intellectuals apprehended the crisis engendered by the incursion of European empire.

5

MAKING ROOM
FOR SCIENCE

MR. BRAGGADOCIO

 "New Tales of Mr. Braggadocio" ("Xin Faluo xiansheng tan"), Xu Nianci's[1] "sequel" to Iwaya Sazanami's[2] "Hora Sensei," was published in 1904 in *Forest of Fiction* (*Xiaoshuo lin*) and features two different moments of Fanonian double consciousness in its opening pages. A prefatory remark in the voice of the author's pseudonym, Juewo ("The Awakened One"), refers to the work as little more than "gossip heard through the bean trellis" (*doupeng xianhua*) and a "ludicrous attempt at imitation" (Xu Nianci 2011, 1; "New Tales of Mr. Braggadocio," 15). This pseudonymous disavowal opens the text up to at least two modes of reading: a work of art that is mere popular entertainment, or a work of art that contains a serious message. This instance of narratological distancing is immediately followed by a series of moments of doubled consciousness in the plot itself. The narrator New Mr. Braggadocio becomes distraught to think that all worldly phenomena can be described in terms of scientific law, and he flees his home. He ascends Mount Everest, whose supposedly 360,000-foot-high summit is so lofty that the gravitational field of Earth is compromised by neighboring planets and stars, causing his corporeal body (*quqiao zhi shen*) and his soul (*linghun zhi shen*) to become separated. Believing he is dead, the narrator becomes despondent, crying for twenty-four hours. Realizing the ability to cry means he must not be dead, he laughs at his own folly for another twenty-four hours. Regaining composure, he undertakes a series of experiments on his corporeal body and his "soul body" from his vantage point atop Mount Everest. Shaoling Ma notes that "what is more fantastical than his out-of-body *and* out-of-spirit experience is the first-person narra-

tion that is simultaneously a third-person reference to his 'selves,' an 'I' as a third-person to himself'" (Ma, 59). Mr. Braggadocio is a figure literally torn between fields of knowledge for whom double consciousness is a leitmotif in terms of narrative style, voice, and plot.

The narrator straddles a number of intellectual realms—Chinese folk beliefs, Christian theology, classical Chinese *wenyan* fiction, Japan's Meiji-era *shōsetsu* fiction, the emergence of children's fiction as a literary category in Japan, Liang Qichao's *Xin xiaoshuo*, social Darwinism, the Daoist antirationalism of the *Zhuangzi*, and scientific rationalism, to name but a few. As a sequel to a loose translation of a Meiji-era Japanese short story by Iwaya Sazanami, which Takeda Masaya has suggested was in turn a loose translation of the Rudolf Erich Raspe's *Baron Munchausen* stories (Takeda 2008, 84–85; 1988, 78–80),[3] the story and its translated prequels bear many of the thematic and historical hallmarks of colonial modernity—globally circulated Baudrillardian homages to translations of translations long divorced from any originary "master text." Though his didactic purpose and desire to write in a vernacular style were in concert with other writers of the *genbun-itchi* (unification of spoken and written language) movement, Sazanami is recognized as the first author of modern Japanese children's literature (initially through translation), placing him at the margins of canonical literature as a writer of adventure who was hoping to appeal to a juvenile audience (Wakabayashi, 228). As an SF sequel to the loosely translated Japanese children's story, Xu Nianci's story attempts to bridge the gap between serious literature and entertainment. The story is disavowed by the narrative voice of an author who wrote elsewhere about the power of the novel to transform society.[4] The narrative itself is more a dialogue with the anxiety engendered by the universality of scientific knowledge than any kind of primer on real scientific discoveries or principles; and those principles that do play a narrative function in the novel are often only vaguely scientific. While they may stand out as either disproven or pure fabrication to a contemporary lay reader, many of the scientific elements of Xu Nianci's story represent relatively recent developments.

Xu Nianci's allegory for the crisis of colonial consciousness dra-

matizes late Qing intellectual ambivalence about the relationship between science, religion, and philosophy. In so doing, the author reveals
a great deal about the tensions between science and indigenous modes
of knowledge. His work first makes a number of gestures to more concrete elements of the colonial effort—the race to discover and map
uncharted territories on the surface of the globe—then projects these
efforts as fantasy into outer space, reflecting the romanticization of
colonial accumulation engendered by the era of European empire that
was so common to Victorian SF, what Giovanni Arrighi and Prasenjit
Duara have referred to as the logics of accumulation and territoriality,
part of the rising tide of global capitalism (Arrighi 1994; Duara 2003).
The main character's success in producing a pseudoscientific discovery
that renders obsolete many of the material trappings of industrial technology results in a paradoxical defeat, suggesting that while modern
science may potentially be resisted, the cycles of production, accumulation, and destruction at the heart of capitalism cannot.

In this chapter I examine a set of interrelated issues. First, drawing
on Lydia Liu's *Translingual Practice*, I examine how "New Tales of Mr.
Braggadocio" reflects processes of cultural exchange that imbricated
"science" and associated terms into the vocabulary of colonial modernity. In this context, science and scientific institutions were translated
into late Qing fiction and culture as tools of social transformation.
These translations drew upon the vocabulary of neo-Confucian positivism, but Daoist language and concepts were also used in attempts
to describe, refute, or enculturate Western science. Through popular
media, late Qing intellectuals pondered whether Daoism or Confucianism could serve as epistemic frames for science, or if the reverse
was true; could science be contextualized and explained by indigenous modes of thought, or was science the ultimate field of knowledge? Second, I examine how the story also reflects on the relationship
between capitalism and modernization, suggesting that while there
were potential avenues for resistance to or the reframing of the philosophical rubric of science, there were no such alternatives to the socio-
political logic of global capital. Finally, I contend that this fictional
failure to resist incorporation into the global economy is symptomatic

of a deep-seated anxiety about the emancipatory potential of a genre closely associated with the colonial effort. Late Qing authors were ambivalent about the question of whether Orientalism could be turned against itself in any of its incarnations. Science, science fiction, and engagement with global capital were seen as necessary components of modernization, but were regarded with suspicion for their complicity in the colonial project.

Fictive Archaism

Linguistically and thematically the story is a case study in Lydia Liu's *Translingual Practice*. Xu Nianci's story, like the work of many of his contemporaries, is a fictional instantiation of the coexistence of vernacular and literary Chinese, and the blending of contemporary scientific vocabulary with *guwen*[5] grammatical and rhetorical structures that is visible in the world of late Qing letters, before its overshadowing in the wake of the New Culture Movement (Ma, 55). "New Tales of Mr. Braggadocio" is written in the style of the Daoist classic the *Zhuangzi*, which we can reasonably date to somewhere around the third century BCE. On a number of occasions, Mr. Braggadocio uses direct quotations of the *Zhuangzi*. The story's appearance in the popular press, and its ostensibly frivolous subject matter, stand in stark contrast to the deliberate archaism of the text and the philosophical tone that it serves to invoke. Even the literary register of Jia Baoyu and Lao Shaonian in the Realm of Civilization in Wu Jianren's *New Story of the Stone* is by comparison relatively familiar to a contemporary reader of *baihua*. Again borrowing from Monroe in his analysis of the creolized religious practice of French spiritualism, wherein a newly emerging (often scientific) "vocabulary" of practices, doctrines, and institutional formations are grafted onto a relatively stable "grammar" of deep structures (Monroe, 7–8), I find that the language of Xu Nianci's SF story, like that of Lu Xun's early nonfiction essays on science, can be explained in such terms as well. The thematic content of the story enacts a similar creolization, taking Daoist philosophy as an ontological "grammar" for understanding the universe, while the structural grammar of the *Zhuangzi* serves as a textual model. These ontological and rhetorical patterns are deployed alongside an array of modern scientific terms as the semantic "vocabulary" of Xu Nianci's unique take on science. Mr. Braggadocio describes two attempts at overturning colonial modernity: by "making room" for the totalizing force of scientific taxonomy within the realm of Daoist philosophy, and by seizing the reins of global capital. The narrative most successfully overturns the realities of colonial modernity in linguistic, rather than narrational, terms.

Istvan Csicsery-Ronay, riffing on Darko Suvin's concept of the *novum*, has argued that the literary texture of SF produces a "chronoclastic" effect, "embody[ing] cultural collisions between the usage of words familiar in the present (a neologism's 'pre-history') and the imaginary, altered linguistic future asserted by the neology." The language of SF is one of futurism and invention, deploying neology to place the reader in an imagined future whose language suggests a teleological history that made such language possible. Fictive neology imagines the existence of the future but also suggests the past that led to the emergence of imagined technologies and social conditions (Csicsery-Ronay 2003, 13–46). Xu Nianci takes a different tack (albeit familiar in the context of the late Qing), opting to present science through the rhetorical structure of a pre-Han model. This form of linguistic invention puts the reader in the position of an imagined past rather than an imagined future history. In the language of the *Zhuangzi*, we see the modern world as Zhuangzi would have seen it. What are the implications of Xu Nianci's deployment of philosophical Daoism as the language of his own fictive neology?

What is indicated when science fiction is written in precisely the opposite linguistic register—fictive archaism, rather than fictive neology? Where Jia Baoyu, in *New Story of the Stone*, attempts to counter the colonial threat by resuscitating Confucian tradition and embalming the unknowable universe of Daoist myth and the unpredictable wilds beyond China's borders of the *Shanhai jing*, Mr. Braggadocio revives Daoist language. This narrative and thematic repurposing of the *Zhuangzi* attempts to place science within the context of Daoist hermeneutics and to assert the precedence of an unknowable universe over the clockwork predictability of scientific ontology. Here again is a

Making Room for Science

reflection of a particular vision of time and historical development that positions utopia in the past rather than the future, further muddying the emerging vision of evolutionary time. This form of linguistic invention puts the reader in the position of an imagined past rather than an imagined future history. Again, in the language of the *Zhuangzi*, the reader is compelled to see the modern world and scientific progress as Zhuangzi would see it.

At the same time, this language again asserts the authority of a very specific form of literary Chinese as the most suitable language for writing about and comprehending the universe and the scientific worldview. Like Lu Xun, who lamented that his translation of Verne's *From the Earth to the Moon* could not achieve sufficient sophistication without recourse to literary Chinese, Xu Nianci also suggests that the best way to speak of the present is through resuscitation of the language of a bygone era. The *Zhuangzi* is a text (or accumulation of texts) that denies the capacity of human reason to understand the true nature of the Dao/universe. To this extent, we could read "Mr. Braggadocio" as antiscientific, or at least antimodern and anti–language reform.

Such deliberate archaism resists linguistic modernism in a manner rarely seen in SF. Csicsery-Ronay has argued that SF relies on neology to create a sense of an imaginary future that is the teleological result of present social conditions. Linguistic estrangement helps contribute to an imaginary social framework through the creation of terms that embody the fusion of a known present with the imagined future that they suggest (Csicsery-Ronay 2003, 13–46). Xu Nianci's own chronoclasm is not a sense of disorientation wherein familiar vocabulary has been repurposed in order to suggest an imaginary history seen from the future; rather the Zhuangzian language of the text disrupts and subverts the linear progression of Darwinian time. This attempt to contradict Darwinian theories of evolution, and in general to subvert science's claims to universality, is borne out thematically in the text as well.

Zhuangzian diction, syntax, and the occasional direct quotation are contrasted with a catalog of modern, translated terms. Many of these are rendered in transliteration only: "telephone" (*delüfeng*) and "Everest" (Aipolaisi) are two examples. Another passage, where the narrator visits the surface of Venus, features an extended treatise on an alternate theory of evolution, peppered with biological terms like "coelenterates" (*qiong chang dongwu*), "echinoderms" (*jipi dongwu*), *and* "mollusks" (*ruanti dongwu*).[6] Along with a prodigious ability to name the world around him in contemporary scientific terms, the author also demonstrates a keen attention to time and the measurement of it, regularly observing the duration and speed of events in the story. In these aspects, the language of the story distances itself from its philosophical model text.

Some of the most important vocabulary in the text can be traced neither to the language of Chinese philosophical antiquity, nor to that of translated scientific modernity. Xu Nianci uses the word *linghun* to mean "soul," stating that "I have no word for it, but it would be referred to in the common language of religion as the 'soul'" (Xu Nianci 2011, 3), calling to mind popular Chinese beliefs in a *hun* and *po* soul. Chinese folk and world religious practice are in no real agreement on how many *hun* and *po* souls one has, what their relationship is to the living body, where they go after death, or whether they live on forever after the death of the body (Harrel 1979). While the usage of "my soul-body" (*yu linghun zhi shen*) to refer to his "soul" and "my corporeal-body" (*yu quqiao zhi shen*) to refer to his body is unique to this text, the story seems to confirm that they conform roughly to *Li ji* associations of the *hun* with vital energy and the ascent to heaven and the *po* with the physical body and a descent into the earth (Brashier, 127–130). Neither of the terms—"soul body" or "corporeal body"—corresponds very well to either the vocabularies of Christian theology or Chinese thanatology. In short, even in a "pure Chinese" context, it is very unclear just what a *linghun* is.

Equally possible is that Xu Nianci is dealing with a Judeo-Christian theological understanding of body and soul. Late nineteenth-century serials like *Chinese Serial* (*Xia'er guanzhen*) and *Shanghae Serial* (*Liuhe congtan*) were among the wide range of missionary publications that offered readers Christian theological discussions of the body-soul duality[7] alongside scientific tracts on subjects like human anatomy, articles on mesmerism, and news pieces about the completion of a transatlantic telegraph cable. Emerging scientific knowledge about the human body was presented alongside theological arguments about the immortal soul, further muddying the dividing line between science and religion or metaphysics. Xu Nianci blurs the distinction between Chinese and Christian spirituality and science by placing the already ambivalent *linghun* in the context of empiricism and scientific knowledge. The *linghun* in the text is indeed a *shen*, or a body endowed with a physical presence that he is able to weigh and quantify. The text's borrowing from Daoist philosophy and Han thanatology sets it apart from the work of other late Qing intellectuals, who framed science in terms of neo-Confucianism, but it shares the tendency to understand science in the context of established ontological categories that implicate science in a broader moral and metaphysical universe. Thus, "New Tales of Mr. Braggadocio" attempts to vitiate science's claims to universal knowledge by subsuming it under the rubric of Daoist cosmology. Under the Daoist rubric of an ineffable universe, the text also subverts Christianity's claims to theological preeminence by blurring the lines between Christian and Chinese folk religious practice. In other words, the *Zhuangzi* is positioned as both a potential conduit for and counter to Western science.

Time, Space, Capital

Mr. Braggadocio's fictional discovery of conditions on Venus that contradict Darwinian theories of evolution, and his mission to uncover evidence subverting science's claims to universality, are contradicted by what he sees in his terrestrial journey. On a corporeal journey to what he first believes to be a facsimile of China at the center of the earth, Mr. Braggadocio encounters an elderly man named Huang Zhongzu (lit. "Yellow Race"), the benevolent overseer of a simulacrum of Mr. Braggadocio's homeland, populated by four hundred million people. Underground, time is refracted: one second equals 216,000 aboveground seconds, allowing Mr. Braggadocio and Huang Zhongzu to see the progress of Darwinian deep time. He calculates: "Reckoning by Huang Zhongzu's clock, one second took two and a half days, and one minute was equal to 150 days. One hour was the equivalent of 25 of our years, and twenty-four hours equal 600 of our years. And thus the oldest people among them live for only four hours. 'The morning mushroom knows nothing of twilight and dawn, the summer cicada knows nothing of spring and autumn.' In apprehension of the universe, so vast the gulf 'twixt thee and I!" (14–15). The passage juxtaposes the rational segmentation of time based on the European horological system with the Daoist vision of ineffable time by making reference to the limited perspective of Zhuangzi's morning mushroom and cicada.[8] Another iteration of Mr. Braggadocio's double consciousness is thus temporal double consciousness—a fastidious attention to the measurement of rational, industrial time is juxtaposed with the language of Daoism as a hermeneutic tool for explicating the mysteries of deep time. Baoyu and Lao Shaonian's safari and taxidermy, which are arguably motivated by the anxiety of the colonial project of claiming ownership and knowledge of the world by cataloging and categorizing, can be contrasted with Mr. Braggadocio's Daoist revivalism, which suggests the ineffability of the universe, even in the face of Western science. Part of this ineffability is the sublime nature of the universe, which astronomy teaches us is spatially bigger than human imagination can comprehend and the discovery of deep time has taught us is temporally beyond the human capacity to comprehend.

Beneath the earth, the slowing of time allows Mr. Braggadocio and Mr. Huang to perceive generations of social transformation aboveground occurring before their very eyes. For China, the clockwork machinery of time ticks inexorably forward, but at a different pace. Coevality is expressed as a geological metaphor—deep beneath the planet's surface, where geologists unearth the past, Mr. Braggadocio discovers the "truth" of China's decay. Social decline is sited underground—the place of both the past and of an undeveloped, troglodyte society, paralleling the inhabitants of the island of Le'erlaifu in Huangjiang Diaosou's *Tales of the Moon Colony* and the Morlocks in H. G. Wells's *The Time Machine* (1885). Despite the fact that time is slowed down in this underground facsimile of China, the future still looms on the horizon as an inevitable catastrophe. This episode, and an earlier failed attempt to awaken his own countrymen "from their muddled dreams, wipe the sleep from their eyes, push them to catch up and create a new civilization," lead him to remark that he would like to cause a holocaust in East Asia, "leaving a new uncharted territory to a future Columbus" (Xu Nianci 1905, 9). Although the text insists on the explanatory superiority of Daoism over science, these assertions are undermined by depictions of a society that is indeed devolving, causing the narrator to imagine himself as the harbinger of a social-Darwinian catharsis. The perceived logic of social Darwinism is presented as one facet of Western science that cannot be overcome.

Social Darwinian racial evolution becomes a visible and actively influenced process as Huang Zhongzu employs a collection of elixirs to alter the behavior of the denizens of underground China. Huang Zhongzu at first appears to be a contemporary, "scientific" iteration of Mencius's proponent of neutral human nature, Gaozi, informing Mr. Braggadocio that the human capacity for good and evil is innate, and the development of one over the other is the result of the environmental conditions one is raised in. As Huang explains how he manipulates human behavior in his laboratory, the vision of human nature has taken on a Xunzian turn, suggesting that the opinion of the Warring States–era philosopher that "man's nature is evil" was correct.[9] The substances associated with good moral qualities are nearly all used up, while those associated with sloth, avarice, and self-interest are still in ample supply and are more efficacious. Showing Mr. Braggadocio a shelf stocked with jars of various liquids, solids, and gasses, Huang Zhongzu informs him,

"This one also brightens and purifies society through the understanding of principles and eschewing hypocrisy. It is a solid, and all of it is contained in this bottle, of which only five ten-thousandths remain." He pointed to a large bottle, saying, "This bottle contains a liquid, of which sixty-five percent remains. It is called *morphine*, the most poisonous of substances. If one is poisoned by it he'll lose all ambition and his flesh will waste away, cutting short his lease on life. I'd hate to be poisoned by it, but many have already come to such an end. This substance [he indicates another bottle] is the desire for money, and this is superstitious faith in spirits. And this gas is unbridled arrogance, while this one is benighted ignorance. This liquid is aimless wandering, and over here we have indecision. This yellow solid is the cause of encephalitis and pneumonia, and this violet colored liquid is desire for fame. All in all, the roots of human good are being eaten away and only 8 or 9 ten-thousandths remain. What hope do I have?" (19)

The lab filled with various substances for the manipulation of human behavior calls into question both Mencius's and Xunzi's shared Confucian vision of human nature perfected through education and moral cultivation, instead replacing human agency with chemical reactions. Alongside *New Story of the Stone* and *Tales of the Moon Colony*, these early appearances of the "sick man of Asia" prefigure the prominence of the trope in Lu Xun's fiction and May Fourth literature.

When Mr. Braggadocio realizes that he himself is one of Huang Zhongzu's doomed progeny, and he is seeing China itself, rather than a subterranean facsimile, his epiphany leads to a narrative rupture similar to Baoyu's transportation into the Realm of Civilization. The narrative leaves behind Mr. Braggadocio's corporeal body and the intractable decay of life on earth that he has discovered, switching to the journey of his soul-body through space. He witnesses a group of Mercurian doctors replacing an old man's cerebral tissue in order to restore his youth. Mr. Braggadocio remarks,

My Lords! I am quite certain that this is their method of making people. The human faculties of life, motion and cognition are all accumulated in the brain. Now, if we were to take out the old and replace it with new cerebral matter, lost teeth would grow anew, hunched backs would straighten, and greying pates return to lustrous black. Aged men awaiting the tolling bells could be reborn as vibrant youth. Alas, I was not able to learn the method of this art. Had I been able to, upon my return home I would have amassed the necessary capital to open a brain-matter renewal company in Shanghai, and the makers of Mr. Ailuo's Brain Tonic [*Ailuo bunao*

zhi] would have had to close their doors at once. All of those outdated, polluted and contemptible customs of this country would be
completely washed clean. (22)

The competition between an ineffable universe and the taxono-
mized universe of the knowledge industry thus comes into conflict
with a third interest: the accumulation of capital. Mr. Braggadocio's
revelatory remark at the end—that he would "wash clean" the intractable customs of his countrymen—is one of the moments in which his
own double consciousness bursts forth in the narrative. Remarks like
these reveal that there is much more at stake than money, and that re-
vitalizing China is more than a matter of displacing the hegemony of
scientific knowledge. As Baoyu discovers in *New Stone*, China still has
its own indigenous problems to deal with as well.

The temptations of capital continue to assert themselves as Mr.
Braggadocio traverses the solar system. In outer space, he demonstrates that, as Viren Murthy has observed in his analysis of Tan Sitong
and Zhang Taiyan's own attempt to address the disparities between
Confucian and evolutionary models of time, "equality, Abstract time,
and evolution are intimately associated with the logic of global capitalism" (Murthy, 50). On the surface of Venus, when he discovers a
trove of precious gems, he quips, "My heart raced as I began to plan
how I would gather them up and steal away to Earth. When compared
to so-called wealthy men, their jaws would drop in as they conceded
the superior vastness of my riches. Unfortunately, I stood there empty-
handed, unable to devise a method to do so" (24).

He discovers that the gems are a form of living mineral, which become superheated if they are shattered, and begins a series of experiments into their nature. His exploration of the gems leads him to a
series of further discoveries, contradicting a number of theories of the
evolution of life on Earth and throughout the universe. First, he sur-
mises that heat was inherent in matter at the creation of the universe,
and that younger planets and earlier stages of matter contain more
potential energy than older ones. Second, he discovers that extinct and
still existing species are able to coexist, disproving theories of evolu-

tion through distinct stages that asserted that some species could no longer exist. Finally, he infers that elements are brought together as a result of the planet's revolutionary motion. All these discoveries fulfill the fantasy that inspired his original flight to the top of Mount Everest desiring to find knowledge beyond the ken of Western science. While Mr. Braggadocio does make inroads in wresting the knowledge industry from its European "owners," he is less successful in overturning another aspect of colonial modernity: the imperatives of global capitalism.

Brain Electricity

After his body and soul are reunited and Mr. Braggadocio has returned to Shanghai,[10] he attends a conference on mesmerism, where he invents the technique of producing and transmitting "brain electricity" (*naodian*). While mesmerism (*cuimianshu*), animal magnetism (*dongwu ciqixue*), and other "spiritual sciences" had been more or less disproven in Europe and the United States by this time,[11] and occupied a liminal position between science and religious practice, these practices were still relatively popular in Japan and continued to gain a foothold in China after Xu Nianci's story was published. Luan Weiping has suggested that Tan Sitong's syncretic concept *ether* (*yitai*)[12] in his *Exposition of Benevolence* (*Renxue*, 1899) and John Fryer's translation of Henry Wood's (1834–1909) *A Method of Avoiding Illness by Controlling the Mind* (*Zhixin mianbing fa*, 1896) were sources of inspiration for Xu Nianci (Luan Weiping, 52). During the same year, the *China Press* (*Dalu bao*) featured a report on a Shanghai conference on mesmerism hosted by a "Mr. Tao" (likely Tao Chengzhang; Luan Weiping, 49). In the decades following the publication of "Mr. Braggadocio," a number of texts on mesmerism made their way into China via translation from Japanese.[13] These texts were produced by a wide range of institutional apparatuses dedicated to mesmerism that sprang up during the second decade of the twentieth century. Many of these societies started in Japan and were soon transplanted to mainland China. These institutions buttressed their teaching efforts with a number of publications on the subject; in total more than eleven publishing compa-

nies produced over forty texts on mesmerism, mentalism, and spiritism between 1916 and 1935 (Li Xin, 13–17). These texts focused on
mesmerism as a rationalized set of bodily practices, giving ordered,
detailed instructions for both the hypnotist and his subject. While
many aspects of mesmerism have been discredited, the core practice
of hypnotism and hypnotic suggestion continues to be an important
aspect of some approaches to contemporary psychotherapeutic practice. In other words, what looks to be half psychological commonplace
and half outright fantasy as we enter the second decade of the twenty-
first century was arguably "hard science fiction" at the end of the nineteenth century.

As a matter of personal discipline, Mr. Braggadocio's perfection
of the techniques of "brain electricity" and his intense focus on mea-
surements of distance, time, and even numbers depict science in the
category Marcel Mauss refers to as "Techniques of the Body" ([1935]
2006)—ritualized and patterned behaviors that the scientist deploys to
gain control of his own body and in turn understand and effect change
in the world. Mr. Braggadocio opens a school in Shanghai, and soon
demand for his six-day training program is so great that he has to open
a series of schools across China and eventually around the globe. These
techniques also resemble a Fordist-Taylorist mode of scientific management of the individual and social body.[14] Brain electricity is neither
the product of an idiosyncratic genius, nor is it the product of a unique
cultural tradition. Instead, mastery of brain electricity derives from
rationalized labor broken down into a series of prescribed, specialized,
and repetitive tasks overseen by the narrator/manager. Mr. Braggadocio's schools follow a similar model, churning out graduates with the
measurable efficiency of an assembly line as soon as unnecessary dis-
tractions have been eliminated.

"Brain electricity" allows the practitioner to produce light and heat
and to send and receive messages, eliminating the need for lightbulbs,
telephone and telegraph, heating devices, and even the newly invented
wireless. A global economic crisis ensues; trains, ships, telecommuni-
cations, lightbulbs, the mining and forestry industries are all rendered
redundant by brain electricity, and they collapse. One-third of the

world's population is left unemployed, and Mr. Braggadocio is forced to go into hiding when an enormous angry mob gathers, threatening his safety. This episode allegorizes science as both a practice of personal discipline and a socioeconomic endeavor.

Ma Shaoling, examining the narrative in terms of the relationship between modern subjectivity and the Marxist conception of social labor, has argued that the story moves from an allegory of primitive accumulation to one that "foresees the future postindustrial or information society in which the technological knowledge of brain electricity creates surpluses in both capital and labor" (Ma, 67). While China's full incorporation into the system of global capital may not have come for another eighty-five years, and in that time the balance of economic and political power would shift dramatically from Western Europe and the United States to the United States almost exclusively, "New Tales of Mr. Braggadocio" makes a daring prediction of the inevitability of this moment. Nearly dismantling international networks of capital, Mr. Braggadocio discovers that he is part of a system whose destruction would spell his own demise.

Another prevalent trope of the story is that of the relationship between exploration and expansion of empire. Mr. Braggadocio's first ascent of Mount Everest is noted only in passing, and his trip to the North Pole is revealed through a coincidental encounter with a diary on the planet Venus, which he hides for the entertainment of a future archaeologist; but both these feats of exploration featured prominently in the nineteenth-century race to map and reach the last "undiscovered" places on the planet's surface. First surveyed by the Great Trigonometrical Survey of India in 1849, Peak xv (known to the people of Nepal as Sagarmatha and to Tibetans as Jomolungma) was calculated three years later by Radhanath Sikhdar to be the tallest in the world, and this was confirmed in 1857. In 1865, Sir Andrew Waugh chose to rename the peak "Mount Everest," in honor of his predecessor, Sir George Everest. Confirmation that this was indeed the world's tallest mountain was soon followed by the decision that it needed to climbed, and after an American explorer claimed to have reached the North Pole with Inuit guides in 1909 and Roald Amundsen reached the South Pole in 1911, Everest came to be known as the "third pole," and one of the most vied-for objectives in geographic exploration. Seven years after S. A. Andrée's real-life failed attempt to reach the North Pole in a hot-air balloon, Mr. Braggadocio beats American explorers to the North Pole by at least five years, and beats Edmund Hillary to the summit of Mount Everest by forty-nine years. The race to reach the North Pole was driven by the desire to find a northern passage for cargo ships.[15] For all Mr. Braggadocio's claims to be working against the logic of science and Western hegemony, only a reading of the text as hyperbolic irony would render his narrative a form of resistance or subversion of the logic of global capitalism. These contradictions lead to a narrative collapse that suggests the difficulty of resistance. The violent response to the economic repercussions of his most successful endeavor underscores the economic imperatives of science.

A series of crises of consciousness lead Mr. Braggadocio on a journey beneath the earth and across the solar system, and result in a series of failures. Many of these failures are characterized by the narrator as the inability to capitalize on what he sees and learns. In other words, as much as Mr. Braggadocio wants to undo the ontological hegemony of science, his real motivation for doing so appears to be personal profit rather than national renewal. While what he sees on Venus and Mercury, and his invention of "brain electricity," do not conform to the logic of Western science, Mr. Braggadocio does his best to see to it that his discoveries do work within the logic of global capitalism. His eventual unsettling of the planet's economic system is a rare narrative feature of Chinese SF—a fictional toppling of the relations of power that produced the context in which the story was written. However, the narrator's plight suggests that such an act would be a form of suicide; he himself is already so deeply woven into the fabric of the global economy that disruption of the system constitutes an inevitable threat to his own well-being.

Careening through space in one body and falling to the center of the earth in another body, he is dual consciousness personified. Mr. Braggadocio's soul, traveling across the solar system, is a projection of the fantasy of scientific and colonial exploration taken to its logical conclusion. Meanwhile, his corporeal body, miles beneath the surface of the earth, turns his gaze back on himself and on his nation, in an act of self-discovery through which he becomes aware of the severity of China's national plight before him in Huang Zhongzu's viewing lens. Again, the figure of the person of knowledge appears, viewing China's social crisis from afar as the people near their impending doom. This time he is in the form of the old man Mr. Braggadocio meets beneath the earth. Unlike Lu Xun outside the iron house, the old man does have the power to intervene, but it is clear that his efforts are destined for failure. Mr. Braggadocio's world is yet another uninhabitable narrative space. The narrative style of the work suggests that the attainment of utopia and true understanding of the universe is a matter of returning to a state of Daoist inaction, but the narrator's actions are anything but an embodiment of quiescence. The outlook on time that is evoked through this language, seen also in *New Stone*, subverts the notion of linear-chronological progress, while the narrator lays claim to the observation of phenomena outside the realm of known scientific laws of planetary and animal evolution. As much as the story does suggest a successful dethroning of Western science, or at least the ability to make new discoveries that overturn previous theories, other iterations of colonial modernity continued to insist upon the primacy of the new world order, and its inescapable logic.

6

LAO SHE'S CITY OF CATS

A SOCIAL-SCIENCE FICTION?

 *Cat Country*, the dystopian Martian travelogue of Lao She (1898–1966),[1] was originally printed serially in the magazine *Xiandai (Les Contemporains)*, between August 1932 and April 1933. The novel represents a brief resuscitation of sf after two decades of near total silence in the genre—the exception that proves the rule in a rapidly shifting cultural field. By the time Lao She penned *Cat Country*, vernacular writing had for the most part won out over classical registers as the ideal vehicle for reform-oriented fiction. In chapter 7, I attempt to demonstrate that the apparent absence of sf between 1910 and 1949 can be explained in part by the genre's sublimation into more quotidian forms of popular science writing. This chapter demonstrates that even as Chinese sf began to disappear on the cultural map, having enjoyed only a very brief ascendancy, the seminal tropes and topoi of late Qing sf continued to resonate, even in the face of a literary revolution.

Cat Country takes up many familiar features and forms in continuing to serve its functional role as an arbiter of the discourses of Orientalism and social Darwinism. From the familiar position of the outsider, enabled by the sf device of the flying machine (albeit one that has crash landed), the narrator makes a detailed observation of the political, familial, and social institutions of Cat Country, sharing the perspective of Tamatarō's companions aboard the hot-air balloon, Jia Baoyu in turn-of-the-twentieth-century China, and Mr. Braggadocio underground as an outside viewer of a cultural vignette. These observations lead to the diagnosis of social and institutional illness, and the prognosis is devastatingly bleak from the outset.

As in the work of his late Qing predecessors, social Darwinism manifests itself in Lao She's novel as a heuristic for understanding what is deemed to be a process of inevitable national extinction, and through the unconscious attitude the narrator adopts in relating to the denizens of Cat Country. Colonial consciousness results in a disjoined, schizophrenic response to the national crisis, both for the narrator and for the cat people. The narrator assumes the role of the colonial overlord, acting as a savior, but willing to revel in his ability to heap verbal and physical abuse upon the cat people. Meanwhile, the cat people are seized by a national schizophrenia. Unable to make use of either foreign epistemology or their own history in a meaningful manner, they simultaneously dismiss and worship the foreign while selling off the material traces of their tradition to the highest foreign bidder as a sign of its indigenous value. Where late Qing sf manages to carve out some space for China's intellectual redemption, be it in the revival of mythical tradition, the wholesale adoption and superior application of Western technology "with Chinese characteristics," or some combination of the two, Lao She condemns all of China's possible responses to the ongoing crisis of foreign invasion and domestic corruption, spanning two political systems and roughly nine decades.

Colonial Modernity c. 1934

Having recently returned to China after a five-year stay in England and a six-month writing and teaching layover in Singapore, depressed at the defeat of Chinese troops following the Manchurian Incident, and wondering why Chinese people on the mainland were not as politically active as overseas Chinese he had met in Singapore, the author found himself in a state of deep concern for the future of his country. On a personal level, Lao She wrote that depression was one of the primary motivators behind his decision to write the novel (Lao She, "Wo zenyang xie," 544–545; Guan Jixin, 167; Zhang Guixing, 1997). Lao She's depression was no doubt attributable in part to the ongoing political crisis that gripped Republican China. The author's suffocating image of Chinese culture has been attributed to the fact that not only had China lost to a foreign enemy, but that its own cultural decay and selfishness were to blame for the national plight (Guan Jixin, 172).

In 1915, Japan's Twenty-One Demands forced Yuan Shikai and the government of the Republic of China to cede control of Manchuria and much of the Chinese economy to the expanding Japanese empire. China had supported Allied forces in World War I, on the condition that colonial concessions to Germany be returned. However, the 1919 Treaty of Versailles eventually resulted in the transfer of German holdings to Japan. While protests on the part of students at Peking University led to the May Fourth Movement, a moment that would be historically recognized as the initial spark for the fire of China's Communist revolution, the short-term outlook was much bleaker. In the meantime, 1916–1928 marked China's Warlord Era, during which control of the "Republic" was indeed the province of local governors, military commanders, and other strongmen, while territories like Tibet and Mongolia, never fully incorporated into the Qing Empire, declared their independence. While the Warlord Era was officially brought to an end with Jiang Jieshi's (Chiang Kai-shek, 1887–1975) Northern Expedition of 1926–1928, the country remained fragmented until the end of the civil war in 1949. The 1931 Manchurian Incident, a conflict manufactured by Japanese forces in Manchuria, led to the occupation of Shenyang in the name of Japan's "self-defense," and Chinese protests of the Japanese occupation were soon met with an attack on Shanghai. China's appeals to the League of Nations led to condemnation of Japan's actions but no intervention on the part of the international community. Viewing resistance to Japan's clearly superior military to be futile, military leaders like Jiang Jieshi opted instead to purge internal opposition prior to any resistance to external aggression (Spence, 310–434).

To a great degree, Lao She's opinions of world affairs were shaped by his deep familiarity with Western literature and culture. He had lived in England for five years, during which time he taught Chinese and studied Western literature and literary criticism; later in his career he published extensive work on these subjects (Song Yongyi, 41). He stands apart from intellectuals like Lu Xun and Liang Qichao for his more direct experience of Western culture, unmediated by Japan, but remains a product of colonial modernity—the uneven exchange of material and intellectual culture brought on by ongoing European and Japanese imperialism and compounded by internal political failures. Lao She also stands out in the context of reform-oriented authors of the 1930s for his not having been directly involved in the May Fourth Movement (Hsia, 166), though he wrote that he was deeply influenced by it. His political education was not as dictated by radical and revolutionary trends as that of many of his contemporaries, since he was in London during the mid-1920s as the leftist mission of May Fourth literature became firmly established. Nevertheless, in terms of his commitment to national renewal through literary education, his work may be seen as a continuation of the efforts initiated with publication of Liang Qichao's *New Literature*.

Lao She has been identified as one of the fiercest critics of Chinese culture outside of Lu Xun (Guan Jixin, 174), and this pessimistic attitude permeates *Cat Country*. Lu Xun and Lao She have also been identified as two of the authors most dedicated to "correcting the national character" (*gaizao guomin xing*), but *Cat Country* reads much more like an extended treatise on the foibles of the national character than it does as a prescription for its remediation (Song Yongyi, 57, 158). Reflecting on this early work, Lao She disavowed the book as a failure. In 1935, in a reflective essay for the magazine *Yuzhou feng*, he wrote that "*Cat Country* was destined to crawl about on the ground like a broken-winged bird," going on to say that he had failed to come up with the proper prescription for China's national salvation. In this essay, he also noted that this "failed" attempt at SF and at satire was inspired in part by H. G. Wells's *The First Man in the Moon* (Lao She, "Wo zenyang xie," 45). Lao She spoke of his own work as a writer, his personal history and his sense of having failed to craft literary solutions for China's social ills, in terms that mirrored Lu Xun's sense of a failed literary purpose. The experience of alienation in a foreign country brought him to a profound crisis about the fate of his home country and the capacities of his countrymen.

Echoing the conclusion to Lu Xun's preface to *A Call to Arms*, where he speaks of having no other option than to continue hoping in the face of an overwhelming sense of defeat, "for hope lies in the future" (LXQJ,

1:437; Lovell, 20), Lao She's narrator continues clinging to hope. Even in his hopefulness he occupies the role of an outsider, viewing the crisis from afar with no sense of personal agency. As foreign invaders overrun the country near the conclusion of *Cat Country*, he remarks, "I was inclined towards optimism and somehow or other felt there was still some hope for Cat Country. (A healthy man usually finds it difficult to understand why a sick one takes such a dim view of things. People should always keep up their hopes—as a matter of fact, hope is really one of mankind's responsibilities; for despair is a sign of self-abandonment while hope is the mother of all endeavor)" (Lao She 2008, 120; *Cat Country* [trans. Lyell], 224; subsequent page citations are from these two sources).[2]

In the writing of both Lu Xun and Lao She, hope, while not entirely absent, is a duty deferred to future generations, an unavailable luxury to those who need it most. Both authors speak in the voice of witnesses to a tragedy who are powerless to intervene and who inevitably question whether intervention has any inherent value at all. A gulf emerges between those who observe and understand the developing predicament, and those who experience it firsthand.

The Colonial Gaze on Mars

Shortly after crash landing his spacecraft on the surface of Mars, the narrator meets his cultural informant Scorpion (Da Xie), a landlord and member of the cat people gentry who owns a plantation of "reverie leaves" (*miye*), an opium-like drug that all the people in Cat Country are addicted to. First Scorpion, and then his pessimistic son, Young Scorpion, lead the narrator on a tour of Cat Country, its ailing and primitive economy, and its various civil and cultural institutions. To this extent, the narrator notes "if I had political questions, I could go to Old Scorpion; if I had questions related to culture, I could go to Young Scorpion" (80; 150). Aside from their differing realms of expertise, Scorpion and Young Scorpion also represent a generational gap in their cultural attitudes. Scorpion, the elder statesman, represents a generation for whom any former idealism has withered away, while Young Scorpion represents a new generation whose idealism is being slowly overcome by pessimism and despair as he comes to realize the impossibility of transformative, positive change.

Almost immediately, the narrator of *Cat Country* determines that he is bearing witness to a civilizational collapse. When Scorpion first leads him into Cat City he remarks, "As soon as I set my eyes on Cat City, for some reason or other, a sentence took form in my mind: *This civilization will soon perish*" (49; 96). Social collapse is a leitmotif in the novel, and the narrator's internal recognition that he is witnessing the end of a civilization becomes a mantra, a reality that he relates to terrestrial history and the legacy of social Darwinism: "I knew that it was possible that a whole civilization or even a whole race might perish, for the history of my own planet, Earth, was not entirely wreathed in roses. And since perusing the history of mankind had been at times enough to make me shed tears, imagine my feelings at the prospect of seeing a civilization breathe its last before my very eyes!" (49; 96–97).

Lao She's novel, written more than two decades after the works of his late Qing predecessors in SF, shares the characterization of social Darwinism as a universal historical force.[3] *Cat Country* depicts an epic tragedy unfolding before the narrator, despite his best efforts to stem the tide. The realities of social Darwinism and the poverty of cat civilization propel the narrator into a crisis of consciousness as he ponders his own role in the fate of the cat people. The narrator's allegorical travelogue of Mars, where he witnesses the extinction of a civilization, is a nihilistic condemnation of China's historical consciousness and of any attempts to resuscitate or reform political and social institutions. Whereas all the late Qing SF writing examined above narrated attempts at transcendence of quotidian social ills, which resulted in deficient or unachieved utopias (often expressed as a collapse of the narrative itself), *Cat Country* is an outright dystopia. The novel is a broad, sweeping critique of China past and present and a damning vision of China's future, as condemnatory of left-wing socialist demagoguery as it is of nationalist fascism.

Through Scorpion and Young Scorpion's guidance, the author witnesses a series of cultural practices and institutions, all of which are described in the same negative terminology that China's harshest critics, both indigenous and foreign, painted China with at the beginning of the twentieth century. Alongside the problem of rampant drug use, the narrator notes that manners and mutual respect are absent to the point that people have lost their dignity; women are a form of property, and prostitution and concubinage are common practice. The cat people regard all things foreign with a sense of suspicion and awe but have failed to adopt any of the technologies or practices that make foreigners strong; and schools, museums, and libraries are an empty farce.[4]

Reverie leaves are a transparent analogue for opium (Raphals, 74), constituting the first symptom of the deteriorating feline society that the narrator is introduced to by Scorpion. Upon sampling the leaves as a palliative for his hunger and thirst, the narrator muses that he feels "benumbed and excited at the same time—the kind of feeling that one gets when slightly high." Once the drug has reached its full effect, he notes that "every last pore in my body felt relaxed and happy enough to laugh, if pores could laugh. I no longer felt the least bit hungry or thirsty, nor did I any longer mind the dirt on my body. The mud, blood, and sweat that clung to my flesh all gave me a delicious feeling, and I felt that I should be perfectly happy if I never took another bath as long as I lived" (19; 36). Reverie leaves signify the narrator's introduction to the poverty of cat civilization, but his introduction to the drug is also the first sign of his own moral decay.

The narrator adopts a colonial attitude toward the people of Cat Country, understanding them in terms that mark their entire society as primitive and barbaric. The narrator learns "Felinese" very quickly, stating that it is even easier to learn than Malayan (21; 40). This offhand remark complicates the binary logic of Orient and Occident, echoing *Tales of the Moon Colony* in suggesting a concentric political and social hierarchy wherein South and Southeast Asia become the Oriental other to a Northeast Asian cultural center. The simplicity of the cat people's language is one of many markers of their inferior cultural status.

Cat Country's inferiority, signified in the inhabitants' poor hygiene, dilapidated housing, and vast social inequality, leads the narrator both to look down upon the cat people and to a mission to save them. This is the Earth Man's Burden—Kipling's "White Man's Burden" in space, where all violence committed in the name of rectifying the colonial subject can be justified, a moment of double consciousness echoing Mr. Braggadocio's desire to cause a holocaust in the interest of establishing a new China. The narrator's introduction to cat society sees him at times distraught over the cat people's treatment of one another. This determination to root out the causes of Cat Country's moral and spiritual decline and to bring a solution leads to the adoption of the narrator's abusive and imperious tone. When Cat Country is invaded by a country of short people, the narrator throws in with Young Scorpion and the ascetic hermit Big Eagle (Da Ying), though all three of them are fully cognizant of the futility of their struggle. Like Joseph Conrad's Kurtz, who has effectively become one of the "savages" whose customs he aims to suppress, the narrator repeatedly asserts his superiority to the cat people, often to his own great benefit.

The narrator's fragmented attitude toward the people of Cat Country parallels the ambivalent sense of envy and disdain with which the cat people regard "Mr. Earth" and other foreigners. The cat people's schizophrenic attitude to foreign and domestic affairs is a self-serving logic by which they insist on their own moral and spiritual superiority, capriciously adopting foreign ideas and practices while others are rejected, with little rhyme or reason, and even less benefit to the country. This psychological response to the foreign is one in which Fanon's and Du Bois's double consciousness is fragmented and multiplied; the dualistic mirroring of the master-slave relationship is tessellated as if viewed through the lens of a kaleidoscope. One of the foundational aspects of self-perception in Cat Country's political schizophrenia is their sense of a long national history.

His willingness to beat or threaten the cat people escalates, until his actions result in the deaths of cat people. On his tour of Cat Country's cultural apparatuses, the narrator finds the schools and museums in a state of total disarray. The teachers, who have not been paid in twenty-five years, make their living through embezzlement. Meanwhile, the students occupy themselves by beating the teachers. When the narrator comes to visit the school, a near-riot erupts, and he fires a shot from his pistol into the air to interrupt the fray. The percussion of the gunshot causes the walls, long having fallen into disrepair as a result of the teachers' and principal's embezzlement, to collapse on the heads of the students and teachers.

> I pulled out my pistol. Actually, they'd have all run away had I just yelled, but I was furious and felt that only a pistol could do justice to such a pack of little beasts. Of course, they really weren't worth wasting a bullet on, but I was beside myself.
>
> I fired once and immediately occasioned a great crash. The concussion collapsed the walls. I had goofed again. I should have known that in Cat City walls cannot stand any sort of a shock after a heavy rain. I had wanted to save the principal, and had only succeeded in crushing him along with his students under the walls. I didn't know what to do. I couldn't simply throw up my hands and run away, for even the would-be assassins were still fellow creatures and therefore deserving of my help. But how could I save them?
>
> I noticed that, fortunately, this wall was made entirely of dirt! It occurred to me that I had been too self-abasing in condemning myself for the principal's death, for this principal was probably a man looking to be killed. Judging from the way the school was put together, one would guess that he had misappropriated the building funds. Perhaps that's why the student had wanted to kill him. (87; 164)

The narrator vacillates between referring to the cat people as people and describing them in more bestial terms, or as "things." While a verbal interruption would suffice, the narrator wants to display and wield a more shocking form of power over the students. The statement that the rioting students attempting to tie up their teacher "weren't worth wasting a bullet" reveals the deepest level of contempt for the people of Cat Country, suggesting that their lives are worth less than the weapons used to take them. His admission that he has made yet another mistake reveals that he does not fully understand Cat Country and that his efforts at civilizing the inhabitants in his image are meeting with failure. Finally, he mollifies himself with the conclusion that the principal was as deserving of death as anyone else lying under the pile of rubble. The allegorical stand-ins for the Chinese people quickly begin to lose their humanity in the eyes of the narrator.

The narrator and the cat people all use the word "person/man" (*ren*) in describing themselves. The cat people and the narrator both acknowledge that while he is descended from apes, their evolutionary-ancestral lineage can be traced to cats. The denizens of Cat City were not always beasts, but they have returned to a state of beastliness, largely as a result of their educational system and their penchant for mistreating one another. The narrator repeatedly refers to the cat people as having lost their "moral dignity" or "human integrity" (*ren ge*), suggesting that they did indeed at one time possess uniquely human characteristics, but that these have been lost. This view, that the inhabitants of Mars are more or less human beings who have, as a result of historical vicissitudes, lost their humanity, is countered by a cat-person from Light Country who insists that failings of national and personal character cannot merely be attributed to environmental conditions (58–59; 110). In either of these evolutionary schemas—devolution and delayed evolution—the narrational ethnography opens a window on a society whose distinction from the world of birds and beasts is narrow indeed.

As observed above in chapter 2, as the first work detailing theories of evolution to be translated into Chinese, Yan Fu's translation of Huxley made social Darwinism appear as the most salient aspect of the Darwinian system. The question of the provenance of animal species and the categorization of *Homo sapiens* in the order of primates were eclipsed by questions of social fitness, notions of phrenological quantification of racial superiority, and the inevitability of racial extinction. In other words, whether humans descended from monkeys was of less concern to Chinese writers than whether one social group would be extinguished by another, and how this might come to pass. This misapprehension carried on into the mid-1930s, making itself visible in the work of Lao She.

Nevertheless, another salient theme in early Chinese SF is the implications of Darwinian evolution in the understanding of human nature. Thematically, this issue emerges in the blurring of lines between human and animal. In the case of Lao She's cat people, this fading distinction is the result of both failed evolutionary processes and educational failures. Young Scorpion's pessimistic tirade on Cat City's educational institutions closes with his cynical observation that "if education can cause people to turn into beasts, you can't say that they haven't achieved any results—hah!" (97; 183). Evolution in Cat Country is turned on its head, and institutional structures are responsible for regression rather than progress.

Cannibals and Self-Criticism

Like Lu Xun's madman, Young Scorpion sees the educational system as little more than a means of perpetuating a cannibalistic culture. Young Scorpion's jeremiad in chapter 18 details the intellectual and fiscal bankruptcy of the educational system, essentially confirming the conclusions the narrator had drawn in his own disastrous visit. He describes the middle schools and colleges as an "utter failure," wherein students graduate on the very first day they are enrolled, all funding has been diverted to corrupt officials, teachers work only in the hopes of advancing up the career ladder to become principals and eventually officials, and all schools are supposedly top-rank. In the last two hundred years, the introduction of "new learning"—the kind of acculturation so championed by Liang Qichao, Xu Nianci, and their contemporaries—has been an equal failure because of the failure to adopt the underlying spirit of foreign knowledge; instead, new ideas fester like a failed skin graft: "During the initial period of borrowing, our people entertained an idle hope. Although they became aware of the folly of thinking that a piece of new flesh cut from another man's body would insure one of eternal life, they still clung to another superstition. For somehow or other, they always felt that as soon as new knowledge arrived—no matter how little—they would immediately become as vigorous and prosperous as the foreigners. In retrospect, I think that we can forgive this arrogant pipe dream" (94; 176).

Lao She's own cannibalistic metaphor begins to develop in the context of another concern that emerged in the early work of Lu Xun—the issue of adopting foreign knowledge without also dedicating oneself to the spirit of exploration and inquiry that leads to such knowledge in the first place. Young Scorpion goes on to explain that the present educational system has amounted to little more than a dual failure to inculcate moral value (one of the few triumphs of the old system) and to produce knowledge relevant to the modern world. William Lyell notes that "disenchantment with educational modernization is a dominant motif in his works" (*Cat Country*, xi).

Education in fields like commerce, engineering, and agriculture are ultimately useless because the entirety of Cat Country's productive forces are devoted to little more than the production and sale of reverie leaves. The schools have been the site of a series of movements echoing the various social movements going on in China (and throughout East Asia) during the first decades of the twentieth century. The supplanting of one movement for another describes a historical trajectory of devolution. Young Scorpion informs the narrator that the "Slandering New Learning Period" has been supplanted by the "Damning New Learning Period" and that "the Damning New Learning Period is not at all far from the Death of the Nation Period." In *Cat Country*, history and evolutionary schema are turned on their heads, as the cat people descend into a progressively less civilized state of being.

The end result of this failure has not only resulted in a loss of moral character, "but back to the cannibalism of antiquity" (96; 133). Once again, the nadir of social and moral turpitude is portrayed in terms of cannibalism. Thirteen years after Lu Xun's "Diary of a Madman," and thirty years after Huangjiang Diaosou's vision of the cannibalistic denizens of Le'erlaifu Island, the pervasiveness of anthropophagy in modern Chinese literature (and in contemporary avant-garde art) suggests a salience in the popular imagination that is more significant than the critique of an isolated historical moment. In his reading of the symbolic valences of cannibalism in contemporary performance art in China, Carlos Rojas has argued that "cannibalism is often viewed as a foundational prohibition on which the social order is grounded."[5] However, for Lu Xun, Huangjiang Diaosou, and Lao She, cannibalism in these three texts is portrayed not as a breakdown of cultural norms and a violation of the moral code, but as a social practice through which Chinese culture is sustained. The anthropophage is not the violator of social order, but its inheritor and conservator.

Mirroring the depiction of cannibalism as a persevering feature of a decadent society is the imagery of female subjugation. During a conversation between the narrator and a group of concubines and prostitutes about the practice of foot binding in China, the prostitutes are all quite enamored with this idea. After explaining that the practice of foot binding has been done away with, the narrator informs his audience that women on earth cover their faces in makeup, comb their hair in various styles, use perfumes and aromatic oils, and wear earrings. In terms of clothing, he opines that suggestive clothing is better than going naked because it is more aesthetically pleasing:

> "It's rather curious, for although they have beautiful clothes, they're always devising ways to expose a little more of their flesh. The charming result of all this is that they're partially hidden and partially exposed at the same time; they're really much more interesting than women like you who go completely nude all the time." I had decided to tease them a bit.
>
> "By going stark naked, you reveal only the beauty of the flesh; and when you come to think of it, one color—even flesh color—gets a bit monotonous after a while." (99; 186–187)

Earth is not necessarily any more moral, and the narrator does not argue that Earth women are treated particularly better than women on Mars. The cultural practices of the "more civilized" society are not superior because of its refusal to treat women as objects, but because of its more aesthetically pleasing and visually diverse system of objectification.

The concubines are titillated by the idea of foot binding and cannot understand why the practice has been done away with. The narrator attempts to mollify them by explaining that bound feet have been replaced by high heels, which he describes as equally grotesque:

"They stopped binding their feet, right? But they all started wearing high-heeled shoes, the tip of the toe was here." I pointed at the tip of my nose, "and the heel is here." I pointed to the top of my head, "it could add five inches to their height. Oh, it's beautiful, and it still manages to twist the bones of the feet out of shape, what's more sometimes they even have to lean against a wall to walk, and also if they broke a heel, they'd have to totter along like cripples." (99–100; 187–188)

The narrator distances himself from his description of women's fashions in Republican China by suggesting that his intention is merely to make his audience envious of the social perceptions of feminine beauty back home. However, his description of feminine adornment is in no way fictitious; this is a faithful representation of women's fashion in the twentieth century, identifying the narrator as a member of a society that has as many foibles as that of the cat people.

Fascinated by the idea of high-heeled shoes, the group of concubines and prostitutes quizzes the narrator about what they are made of. One of them asks, "Can you make shoes of human skin as well as animal hide?" (100; 188). This comment goes completely unaddressed, as the narrator simply thinks to himself that if he knew how to work leather he would be able to make a fortune in Cat Country. Before he has the chance to inform the harem ladies that Earth women actually do have agency, and are active participants in society, he is interrupted by the arrival of a group of scholars. This brief interlude in the narrator's tour of Cat Country's cultural apparatus forgoes the paper-thin veil of allegorical representation in order to argue that women, as symbols of national weakness and the need for reform, are in as dire straits in the real China of Lao She's contemporary moment as they are in the allegorical China on Mars.

The Knowledge Industry on Mars

The mere age of Cat Country is a mantra recited as proof of its cultural superiority. The narrator soon learns that "the cat people *did* have history—twenty thousand years of it!" (21; 41). History in and of itself becomes a justification for the rejection of the new or foreign, regardless of its utility. Scorpion informs the narrator, "There are plenty of foreign goods . . . and they are quite useful, but we have no interest in imitating them; we are the oldest of all countries!" (25; 48). Lao She's novel accuses his countrymen of the same kind of cultural chauvinism that fostered the *Yangwu* movement four decades prior. Like the *Yangwu* movement, this self-deception is for the most part a rhetorical palliative that denies the true social reality.

At the same time that the denizens of Cat Country look down their noses at foreign technologies and learning, they are paradoxically enamored with it. This schizophrenic apprehension of the foreign is also reflected in the naming of foreign countries. The name of one of these countries is "Light Country" or "Brilliant-land" (*Guang guo*), echoing the Chinese names for America and England, transliterations that suggest beauty and flourishing culture (56; 109). Young Scorpion informs the narrator that "my father believes that someone who knows a few words of a foreign language can be considered to understand everything," despite the fact that many returnees from trips to study abroad know almost nothing of the language or culture they have been immersed in and simply continue to live off the largesse of their gentry families (61; 81). When elements of foreign culture are adopted, they take the form of unsuccessful grafts and piecemeal appropriations without a true understanding of their intellectual content. A group of students whom the narrator meets have taken to using Russian-sounding phrases, referring constantly in their speech to "Yayavski," "Hualavski," and "Tongtongvski," all of which he learns are merely nonsense terms; not even the students understand each other in their babbling, pseudo-foreign exchange. Cat Country's political schizophrenia prevents any meaningful dialogue or change from occurring.

Cat Country's political schizophrenia is also marked by convoluted logic through which any personal humiliation is psychologically reframed as bringing shame on others. This logic justifies Scorpion's father's decision to eat reverie leaves: because reverie leaves were originally brought in by foreigners, he claims that eating them is his way of making foreigners lose face. National weakness and self-destruction are cynically presented as acts of resistance. This attitude also pertains to the confused attempts at adopting foreign education and in the handling of Cat Country's museums, whose treasures have slowly been sold off to the highest bidders.

After his visit with the scholars—a philologist, an astronomer, and a historian—who can do little more than bicker over whose field is most significant, the narrator's tour with Young Scorpion takes him to Cat City's museum, a dystopian inversion of Lao Shaonian's museum in the Realm of Civilization. Where Baoyu was treated to a repository of all things Chinese, past and present, neatly preserved and stored safely out of the reach of the imperial conqueror, Cat City's museum is an empty shell, where all the relics have been sold off to foreign countries. The curator, Cat-fuski (Mao fusiji), has given himself a clearly Russian-sounding sobriquet to demonstrate his familiarity with foreign learning, and presides over a series of empty, mud-walled rooms. He leads the narrator around, naming absent objects and their respective values:

> "This is where we store the stone implements that were used ten thousand years ago; they are displayed according to the most modern methods. Look around at your leisure."
>
> I looked all about, but there was nothing there! "Well, here we go again," I thought to myself. Before I had a chance to ask him what the joke was, he pointed to the wall and said, "This is a stone jar, ten thousand years old. It has foreign characters inscribed on it and is worth at least three million National Souls."
>
> So that was it! Now I began to understand. There was a small row of characters inscribed on the wall; what he probably meant was that a stone jar worth three million National Souls at one time *had* been displayed in that location. (107; 202)

Cat-fuski's charade borders on Kafkaesque, as he insists on the existence of objects that have long since been sold into foreign hands. The museum has been reduced to little more than an empty-shelved gift shop, its functions of gathering, ordering, and serving as a center of cultural education now meaningless. Not only has the material evidence of history been carried off, and the order that it represents destroyed, but monetary value has entirely eclipsed the objects' symbolic capital as tangible cultural heritage. The knowledge industry that contributes to the construction of Cat Country's imagined community does so out of objects that have been reduced to exchange value and have in their absence become imaginary.[6]

A visit to the library in Cat City unveils a situation paralleling that of the museum and the school. The book stacks have been entirely sold off, and like the school, the building is a hive of activity, having been converted into a community center where a series of social movements and revolutions are acted out, and where the proponents of "new learning" are housed. Like the teachers, the librarians have been tied up, this time by students who are "making revolution against the library." The library has become a battleground for the fierce proponents of a number of "isms" and "evskys," the various fad revolutions and ideologies that the new scholars become enamored with and enact with violent fervor. Like the vacant bookshelves, the revolution being carried out in the library is intellectually empty, having been reduced to a disagreement over sartorial choices. The "modern scholars," infatuated with foreign learning, assert that wearing shorts is a form of revolutionary work. Meanwhile, the Everybody Sharesky-ites (Dajia fusiji), who will "kill a man without thinking twice about it" (110–111; 209), have decided, along with the "new scholars," that wearing pants is a sign of one's conviction in the progressive cause. Because they believe in communal property, the Everybody Sharesky-ites have demanded that the librarians furnish them with pants, on threat of death. The revolutionaries' plan to convert the space into a hotel in order to bring in new revenue, since income from the sale of books dried up nearly fifteen years ago, completely divorces the library from its original purpose, as it becomes a capitalist enterprise.

It is tempting to read the Everybody Sharesky-ites as analogous with the Communist Party, as Communists are recognized as being in favor of shared property, and the redistribution of property and cultural artifacts serves as a rallying cry for the people in the final moments of the novel, as a protest plays out in front of the crumbling capitol building.

Guan Jixin has argued that Everybody Sharesky is in fact a stand-in for the Guomindang, and that Mazu the Immortal (Mazu daxian) is a stand-in for Karl Marx (Guan Jixin, 174). William Lyell translates Mazu as "Uncle Karl," in agreement with this interpretation. While this argument would save Lao She some face in terms of his image as a loyal Communist, ultimately differentiating the two is a moot point. Both Everybodyevsky and Mazu the Immortal are lost in a meaningless cacophony of sloganeering as the country plummets into chaos. A demagogue emerges from a group of students gathered around a stone at the west end of the city and begins pleading for the destruction of the gentry class and the return of reverie leaves to the common people, saying that the emperor must be captured and handed over to the foreign invaders. His rallying cry culminates in a torrent of gibberish: "Everybody Sharesky is ours, Mazu the Immortal said: the blahblah-poolah is the property of the yaya didang-didangs, the upper and lower classes harrumph harrumph! Let's go to the Imperial Palace!" (139; my translation).

Before the students can work up the courage to attack the emperor, they begin arguing over whether they should kill their own fathers first. The group breaks up into smaller and smaller factions. Eventually, they grow weary of arguing and end up going their separate ways, the revolution having died out. The would-be youthful revolutionaries are incapable of distinguishing between the Communists or Nationalists, and their movement falls first into factionalism before dying an anticlimactic death attributable only to apathy. Lao She's cat people are unable to assemble as a national body under any political rubric.

As Young Scorpion and Big Eagle concoct their plan to sacrifice Big Eagle in a final effort to rally the citizenry, the narrator stops them to ask what benefit this sacrifice will bring. They respond that there will likely be no beneficial outcome of this act; instead, Big Eagle's death is a desperate and final attempt to call the citizens of Cat Country to arms, and one that they understand will most likely result in failure. In all likelihood, both of them will die, and their deaths will be symbolic acts of resistance, which will punish their enemies for having looked down on them. This sacrifice presents the final act of the convoluted logic of political schizophrenia. Young Scorpion and Big Eagle know that they will not emerge as heroes, but at the same time, they are the only individuals willing to make a concerted resistance. "And if not a single person heeds our call to arms? Well, the answer to that is simple enough: Cat Country will have deserved its death and the two of us will have deserved to die too. There's no consideration of sacrifice or glory involved in this" (132; 245). With this, Big Eagle eats a fatal dose of reverie leaves, and his head is displayed in a basket in Cat City. Rather than becoming the symbol of a martyr around which the people of Cat Country can rally, the head becomes a curiosity for the entertainment of the city dwellers. Soon after, Cat City is overrun by an invading army of short people. The last few surviving citizens of Cat Country are rounded up and put into a cage, where they end up clawing one another to death. The narrator notes that six months later he was rescued by a French ship and returned to Earth.

Thus concludes a story that from the very outset was narratively framed as an exercise in witnessing the end of a civilization. Lao She's novel, in the midst of the utopian fervor and leftist passion of the New Culture Movement, is as dark a depiction of China as any work of late Qing SF, if not darker. Where many of Lao She's predecessors struggled with the relationship between tradition and modernity, attempting to salvage usable elements from preexisting and new models both foreign and domestic, Lao She's novel is deeply pessimistic, seeing little hope in the importation of new foreign ideas or in the resuscitation of traditional modes of thinking and social structures. Lao She's work bears a strong resemblance in features, form, and functions to the SF of his predecessors, especially in evincing a strong desire to save China while harboring sincere doubts about the prospects of such a project.

Lisa Raphals has noted that in many respects, *Cat Country* does not fit into any of the subgenres of early twentieth-century Chinese SF identified by David Der-wei Wang and Henry Zhao, setting it apart from works like *New Story of the Stone*, *Tales of the Moon Colony*, and Bihe Guanzhuren's *The New Era*. "It clearly is not a reworking of an earlier Chinese novel, and it is a stretch to call it a science fantasy. While it uses utopian (or rather dystopian) literary motifs, it is not concerned with technological or scientific elements, beyond its *mise-en-scène* of a flight to Mars. The future as such is not an important element in the book. In summary, *Cat Country* is both one of the earlier works that can be called Chinese science fiction and a curious misfit to that title" (Raphals, 79). It is true that the only imaginary technology involved in Lao She's novel are the spaceships that bring the narrator to and take him away from Mars. The plot and its denouement are not driven by techno-scientific invention or the application of the scientific method. However, to say that the story does not feature science misses the deep concern with the institutions of scientific production that featured so prominently in late Qing SF, and early twentieth-century intellectuals' concern with scientific theories of human development.

The narrative is set into motion by allowing the narrator to see his own society at a distance, a trope we have seen in *New Story of the Stone*, "New Tales of Mr. Braggadocio," and *Tales of the Moon Colony*. From this removed perspective, the narrator is aided in his ethnographic study by an informant, who helps him to comprehend the new social milieu. What the narrator comes to see in this ethnographic mapping is an overdetermined crisis of internal decay and external aggression, leading him to a realization of the "reality" of social Darwinism—that the erasure of a civilization is fast approaching on the horizon. This realization inspires a Fanonian double consciousness in the narrator, who is paradoxically dedicated to working out a solution to the crisis at the same time that he is horrified by the cultural body he has dedicated himself to saving. Likewise, the denizens of these allegorical doppelgangers of China approach the confrontation with the West with an attitude of national and political schizophrenia, at once awed by and staunchly refusing to accept the achievements of their colonial overlords. Both social decadence and the chances for survival or salvation are depicted in terms of medicinal metaphors of a sick body and the possible pharmacological and psychological cures. As the informant leads the narrator / main character on a tour of the critical social institutions, including museums, libraries, and schools, the original perception of a crisis of extinction is confirmed. The looming threat of cultural annihilation is also expressed in terms of material loss, through the narrator's anxiety about the cat people's failure to collect or preserve salient elements of historical and cultural value. Whereas the overdetermined crisis of internal social decline and external aggression propels many of the narratives I have already examined into (often unsustainable) utopian fantasy, *Cat Country* makes no such attempt—the narrator simply bears witness to the annihilation of a society. Much like *New Story of the Stone* and *Tales of the Moon Colony*, the critical attitude of *Cat Country* is directed as strongly at traditional Chinese society as it is at colonial incursion. The narrator stands at an oblique angle to all this chaos, unable to minister cures, and pondering whether resistance or sacrifice in the name of the nation-state is of any value at all. In this sense, *Cat Country* occupies an important place in the history of Chinese science fiction, but it also fits squarely among some of the key thematic concerns of modern Chinese literature in general.

7

WHITHER SF /
WITHER SF

AN ALTERNATE HISTORY
OF CHINESE SF

 As the field of Chinese sf studies evolves, the ebb and flow of sf in China continues to be a central question. As early as 1905, essays on the genre attempted to identify premodern adventure and fantasy novels like *Journey to the West* (*Xiyou ji*) and *Flowers in the Mirror* (*Jing huayuan*) as examples of early Chinese sf, and a number of contemporary studies (Takeda and Hayashi 2001; Zhang Zhi 2009; Wu Xianya) make similar claims, including a number of works that might best be described as fantasy in their taxonomy (Wu Yan 2011). Shortly after appearing on the literary scene in the early twentieth century, Chinese sf all but disappeared for more than two decades—very little that could be identified as sf was published between Lu Shi'e's *New China* and Lao She's *Cat Country*.[1] Masaya Takeda's, Zhang Zhi's, and Wu Yan's studies remind us that merely defining the genre is as much a problem in Chinese sf studies as it is in any other national or linguistic context, and that consideration of more "fantastic" elements is especially necessary in the context of the contemporary Chinese word for sf—*kexue huanxiang xiaoshuo* (lit. "science-fantasy fiction"). The translations and novels discussed in the previous chapters were all part of a cultural field that recognized science fiction as a genre. This final chapter is meant to serve as a coda, suggesting how approaching Chinese sf in terms of its relationship to prose forms other than fictional narrative is important in understanding the origins and directions of the genre by examining some of the points of intersection between genres that preceded its appearance and rose to prominence during its absence.

In this chapter, I examine two mediums that featured "scientific" discourses, occurring almost immediately before and immediately after the short-lived high tide of Chinese sf during the late Qing and Republican period, in order to illustrate the manner in which traditional Chinese literary forms commingled with sf. Wei Yang has argued that in the case of Chinese sf cinema, "the genre's function is very different from its Hollywood counterpart," demonstrating how elements of sf narrative are combined with other genre conventions in Chinese sf cinema (Wei Yang 2013). In the cinematic language of Rick Altman (1999), one might posit that Chinese sf cinema incorporates the semantic elements of the genre into the syntactical structures of other genres. The late Qing saw the emergence of popular pictorial journalism, while the latter half of the 1910s saw the emergence of a new style of essay dedicated to popularizing scientific knowledge, the *kexue xiaopin*. The tropes and topoi originally prominently featured in late Qing sf—the popularization of science and the scientific spirit, nation building, the encounter with the other, the relationship between tradition and modernity, and the specter of social Darwinism—saw precursor elements in late Qing visual media. These same tropes and topoi were sublimated into other prose genres and literary forms in the decades before the establishment of the prc when sf "disappeared."

On the surface, these two "new" media forms are quite different—one was a sensationalist commercial enterprise that emphasized the thrill of the spectacle above any faithful representation of concrete reality (Huntington 2003), while the other was a sober, almost entirely textual presentation of scientific fact committed to popularization over the development of expertise. However, both these "new" forms borrowed heavily from preexisting prose conventions in their attempts to reach a broad popular audience. Late Qing pictorials, which rose to prominence in the 1870s, preceded both the definition of the category of *kexue xiaoshuo* and the explosion of fictional genres that accompanied Liang Qichao's call for a new literature of national renewal. In Milner's terms, this would be to say that while the late Qing pictorial occupied a position in the cultural field that shared thematic content with the wider range of modes of media production and consumption that would come to define Chinese SF, the pictorial has not been identified as belonging to the selective tradition. Translations of foreign SF were also few and far between during this period.[2] In the case of *kexue xiaopin*, rising to prominence in the late 1920s and 1930s, the category of SF existed, but few examples from this period are labeled as belonging to the selective tradition. Neither of these genres took the form of narrative prose, the primary focus of this study. Nevertheless, these two media forms are instructive in understanding the relationship between SF and the shifting cultural field of late Qing and Republican China.

Again in terms of Monroe's concept of the creolization of religion, as in the discussion of "New Tales of Mr. Braggadocio" in chapter 5, both late Qing pictorial journalism and Republican period popular science writing adopted the "grammar" of premodern narrative conventions to frame the "vocabulary" of scientific knowledge. In Andrew Milner's terms, this is to say that the cultural field defining the selective tradition in which Chinese SF emerged could be mapped out as follows: early twentieth-century SF drew on preexisting prose genres and discourses concerning Western science and technology during the period of its emergence, and its "disappearance" can be described as the sublimation of SF into a new set of genres that again drew upon pre-twentieth-century models. Expanding upon Michel Hockx's adoption of Bourdieu's cultural field, describing Chinese literature in terms of a three-dimensional space along the axes of cultural capital, symbolic capital, and political capital, adding a fourth dimension—time— would help to construct a more accurate map of the emergence and "disappearance" of Chinese SF. During the late nineteenth century the axis of economic capital in publishing saw increasing emphasis with the emergence of mass media in urban centers. In the late 1920s and 1930s, economic capital was de-emphasized as leftists emphasized the political value of literature, and this shift was canonized by literary historiographers after the establishment of the People's Republic of China. Exactly what defined high- and low-value political capital also shifted during these decades, leading to the eventual post-1949 victory of socialist realism. The definition of symbolic capital also shifted, as the vernacular language won out over premodern literary forms and genres. The cultural field of early twentieth-century China understood in terms of change over time was particularly amorphous. Individual elements—genres, styles, and forms—within the cultural field also shifted rapidly. Under these conditions, SF emerged by combining elements of preexisting genre conventions with new ideas about literature from the Western world. It saw a brief period during which its symbolic, cultural, and political capital ascended (and writers hoped it would continue to do so), and it did not disappear so much as it was sublimated into other forms and stylistic conventions.

Dianshizhai huabao

Pictorial representations of news from China and abroad fast became one of the staples of the modern publishing industry of the late Qing dynasty, a hodgepodge of stories that Rania Huntington has argued were "a continuation of the *zhiguai* (tales of the strange) genre" (Huntington, 341). The *Dianshizhai huabao* was originally included as a supplement in the Chinese-language newspaper *Shenbao* (whose inaugural issue was published in 1872), every ten days for fourteen years, comprising over four thousand images. The first issue of *Dianshizhai* appeared on May 8, 1884, and the journal ran through 1898. The pictorial was published by the same team that produced *Shenbao*, under the ownership of Ernest and Frederick Major and their three friends C. Woodward, W. B. Pryor, and John MacKillop. The Major brothers were entrepreneurs involved in a number of enterprises, including lithographic printmaking. Their press was extremely successful from the outset, having published over one hundred thousand copies of the Kangxi Dictionary, which were sold to examination candidates, and with the Shenbao guan produced a reprint of the entire illustrated *Gujin tushu jicheng*[3] (Wagner, 121). The company made a number of reprints of classical works but also encountered great success with the publication of *Shenbao*. The pictorial was one of the first of its kind in China, and numerous imitations sprouted up soon after its popularity became clear (Chen Pingyuan and Xia Xiaohong 2006, 6). Work printed at the Dianshizhai studio was distributed nationwide. Very soon after the initial print run in *Shenbao*, the Majors also began producing bound volumes of the pictorial, each containing twelve issues. The Majors' editorial policy was one of reliance on the marketing instincts of their Chinese editors, often reflecting Chinese points of view and political sentiments in the subject matter and editorial style. Coverage of the Sino-French War, which appeared in the first four volumes, was decidedly pro-Chinese; and likewise in conflicts between China and Great Britain, the editors of the pictorial made no great effort to spare the feelings of the Major brothers or other potential British readers. Continuing the trend in their presentation of the 1884 Kapsin coup in Korea, the editors allowed authors and illustrators to take a decidedly pro-Chinese stance in condemning those involved in the coup (Ye Xiaoqing, 4–9). The Majors did their best to present themselves as Chinese, using Chinese-style editorial content that often focused on the theme of retribution. While the editors did not shy away from nationalistic content, the editorial staff were neither politically radical, nor were they degree holders in the examination system (Ye Xiaoqing, 12–13, 28–29).

The principal artist was Wu Youru (d. 1894), a talented illustrator who lacked a classical education or scholarly background.[4] After his work at *Dianshizhai*, he went on to publish the *Feiyingge huabao*. Very little is known about the rest of the team of Chinese illustrators who worked for the pictorial. The journal was published three times a month, each issue featuring eight illustrations (this number increased to ten after the sixth issue) accompanied by extended prose commentary and a pithy remark in the form of a seal that served as a coda to each illustration.

The journal was distributed by the *Shenbao* in Shanghai and in at least twenty-four other cities across China, including Beijing, Tianjin, Nanjing, and Chongqing. Accurate circulation figures are difficult to pin down, in part because a reliable count of the number of copies of *Shenbao* published in any given year is very difficult to determine, but also because any single issue of *Shenbao* or *Dianshizhai* would have changed hands numerous times, first making its way through a number of readers in the major cities of initial distribution, and then being sent inland by post to more remote and less urbanized areas. Readers could also rent newspapers for approximately one-tenth the cost of their cover price. In short, the actual audience for *Shenbao* and the accompanying pictorial was many times higher than the print run would suggest. Advertisements for the pictorial that appeared in *Shenbao* claimed that *Dianshizhai* was extremely successful, often selling out very quickly and prompting the publisher to rerelease and print bound volumes of the journal (Ye Shaoqing, 9–10). *Dianshizhai*'s success ushered in an era of pictorial journalism. Other publishing ventures were deeply influenced by *Dianshizhai huabao*'s pedagogical mission and artistic format, and the pictorials *Qimeng huabao* (c. 1902), *Shishi huabao* (c. 1905), *Kaitong huabao* (c. 1906), and *Tuhua ribao* (c. 1909) soon followed. By the May Fourth Movement, such journals were firmly established as a major mode of popular publication (Chen Pingyuan and Xia Xiaohong 2006, 6).

Along with its eclectic collection of illustrations, *Dianshizhai* offered tabloid sensationalism, world news, political reportage, current events, ethnography, news of scientific and technological innovations, and local news. One major focus of the journal was the infiltration of Western technologies into Chinese culture and the growing interest in the Western world and associated fields of knowledge. Included in this broad thematic scope were curious events like strange births and animal anomalies, profiles of European leaders, explanations of cultural events both in China and abroad, reports of feats of strength and daring, accounts of the wonders and dangers of urban life, descriptions of folk customs and current events throughout China, the execution or miscarriage of justice, descriptions of other countries and cultures (both real and imagined), and depictions of Western science and technology (also both real and imagined).[5] Among the technological innovations reported on were electronic burglar alarms, X-ray machines, machine guns, various underwater breathing apparatuses, and even an English robot with an image of smoke billowing out of its stovepipe hat.[6]

Reminiscing about the role the journal played in influencing his own artistic sensibilities, Bao Tianxiao, a colleague of Xu Nianci at *Xiaoshuo Lin*, wrote,

> When I was twelve or thirteen, in Shanghai they were producing [a series of] lithographs called *Dianshizhai huabao*, which I really loved reading. . . . Whenever it was published, it would be sent to Suzhou and if it came down to it, I'd spend my lunch money in order to buy a copy. One edition would come out every ten days, and ten editions would be bound together in a book. At the time I had quite a few bound volumes. Although the artists weren't particularly well trained, you could still gain some general knowledge from the illustrations. This was because Shanghai was a leader in changing fads—foreign inventions, foreign things, all came to Shanghai first. For example, steamships and trains—with a copy [of the pictorial] in hand, people from inland who hadn't seen these things could get a sense of what they were. Local traditions, customs, whatever different things there were from all over the world, it all had an impression on me. (Quoted in Chen Pingyuan 2006, 9)

The pages of the pictorial made *boxue* (broad and esoteric learning) into a popular medium, occasionally replacing the "gentleman of broad learning" with the figure of the museum. The similarity between Bao's depiction of a body of work that serves both to edify and to entertain and Xu Nianci's fantastic writing in "New Tales of Mr. Braggadocio" is striking (Huntington, 344). In 1898, an article titled "A Discussion of the Potential for Pictorials to Enlighten" ("Lun huabao keyi qimeng") appeared in the pages of *Shenbao*. This polemic was representative of late Qing discussions of the didactic role of the popular press, and especially of the relationship between visual culture and the printed word. The author argued that accompanying text with images was in keeping with classical modes of learning and that such illustrations could help deepen readers' understanding of the material and attract new audiences (Ye Shaoqing, 12).

The depictions of science and technology in *Dianshizhai huabao* follow a pattern similar to that evinced in scholarly approaches to science, in accounts of the adoption of Western material goods, and soon after in SF. This attitude included a schizophrenic understanding of the Western world, again characterized by stylized representations of the West that convey simultaneously envy and exoticism. At the same time, many of these images of technology are associated with questions of national standing and power. Rudolph Wagner notes that the inaugural issue of the paper took the Sino-French War as its primary focus, and conflicts throughout Asia continued to appear regularly, illustrating the publication's conjunction with nationalistic concerns (Wagner, 122–126).

The journal's titillating catalog of events, anomalies, and innovations treads a thin line between reportage and fiction, often veering over entirely into the realm of fiction, but rarely conceding this to be so. Much of the journal could be seen as having a loosely defined scientific (or pseudo-scientific) orientation, privileging the thrill of the spectacle over the delivery of verifiable facts or education in scientific principles. Even when accounts of the supernatural or spectacular events were debunked, the pictorial continued to emphasize these events as commoditized forms of entertainment. Both rational and supernatural explanations appear on a more or less equal footing, second to the presentation of the spectacle itself. Illustrations depicting animal and plant anomalies, newly discovered species, or species not native to China arguably take up the taxonomic mission of biological science, but they are also regularly brought into dialogue with traditional Chinese catalogs of the natural and supernatural world. Similarly, depictions of cultures, peoples, and customs both foreign and Chinese take on an ethnographic or anthropological tone but also include accounts that are clearly fantastic. *Dianshizhai huabao* and other publications of its ilk existed at a moment prior to the naming of SF (*kexue xiaoshuo*) as a distinct genre but occupied a space in a shifting cultural field that was very near to its future cousin.

More strictly defined, it is difficult to say that any of the reportage in the journal is truly scientific—if SF best describes the content of novels and short stories that depict exploration and imperial conquest in the context of scientific knowledge as discussed above, fictional science might best describe the majority of the *Dianshizhai huabao* that is devoted to scientific discovery. As producers of a sensationalist publication whose primary aim was to appeal to the largest possible audience, the editorial staff focused little attention on journalistic accuracy or fidelity. While many events depicted in the journal corresponded to actual news items (e.g., an illustration of a man swimming the English Channel), almost all the illustrations skirted the line between reality and fiction, and (understandably) the Chinese art staff had to rely on their own imaginations for the majority of the events depicted. Occasionally, retractions of such stories were published, but these were issued less out of fidelity to journalistic excellence and more out of a sense that the events reported were offensive to the moral sensibilities of the Chinese audience (Ye Shaoqing, 22).

These pictorial representations of the world beyond China's borders, especially representations of things scientific and technological, were demonstrative of the publisher's desire to please its readership first and focus on accuracy of reportage second (if at all). The scientific and technological reporting that appears in *Dianshizhai huabao* almost always appears to be at least loosely tied to real-world developments but follows a spectrum that I would argue is as follows: In rare cases, events and objects depicted adhere to actual science. In others, we see what I refer to as "fictional science," or imagined scientific and technological innovations. In many cases, these depictions appear to be relatable to factual developments but have been transformed in the retelling as news made its way from Europe or the United States to East Asia. Finally, some depictions must fall into the category of sf—both for their apparent lack of any relationship to verifiable historical developments and for their repetition of Orientalist discourses. Indeed, even the most accurate scientific reportage in *Dianshizhai huabao* is marked by an anxiety concerning the relationship between foreign epistemology and material culture and the "native" Chinese worldview and social patterns.

Pictorials and the Knowledge Industry

One aspect of *Dianshizhai huabao*'s and other publications' symbiosis with the sf narratives examined in the previous chapters was their attention to museums, exhibitions, and other institutional undertakings related to the knowledge industry. *Dianshizhai huabao* prefigured the attention to the knowledge industry that late Qing reformers-cum-sf-translators-and-authors lavished on knowledge production as an institutionalized, rationalized practice. A depiction of the British Museum contains an extensive textual summary of the location and events, and the illustration features a fish (easily three or four times the size of the cow next to it) housed in a livestock pen (Wu Youru 2001, vol. 3, appendix). This image appeared in a collected reprint of *Dianshizhai huabao*, alongside a textual description of Wang Tao's visit to the British Museum accompanied by James Legge, recorded in his travelogue *Manyou suilu*, a record of his 1867 and 1879 trips to Western Europe, which was also published by the Dianshizhai studio as the *Manyou suilu tuji* (1890).

Wang Tao enumerates such details as the cost of admission, the size of the exhibition grounds and halls, and even how the exhibition grounds were cleaned during the night. In his description of the wonders of the British Museum, he writes,

In the afternoon Mr. Legge arrived, and together we went to visit the Museum. . . . The museum houses the greatest wealth of books, maps of all the five continents, and collected works of past and present. There are no less than 500,000 volumes. Each country is arranged by shelves without any disarray. There are more than a hundred male and female readers every day, coming in the morning and leaving at night, the books can be borrowed for reading though one cannot take them home. . . . Another wing houses rare objects from all over the world. . . . We left there and proceeded up a flight of stairs and were granted access to a great hall lined with more than a hundred pillars. Therein are held all birds, beasts, fish and insects, grasses, trees, grains and fruits, the wonders of the mountains and oddities of the seas, not recorded in *Bowu zhi* [of Zhang

Hua (232–300)], not discerned in *Huayi huamu niaoshou zhenwan kao* [Shen Maoguan, sixteenth C.], nor detailed in the *Gegu [yao] lun* [Cao Zhao, fourth C.]. Nothing has been left out, all reveal their natural essence. (Wang Tao, 102)

Borges, Baudrillard, and McLuhan all offer instructive modes of reading this image and the accompanying text. The museum is a world catalog, a Borgesian simulacrum meant to display imperial power, while Wang Tao's description is a simulacrum of this simulacrum, the *Dianshizhai* image a simulacrum of that, and these simulacra of simulacra of simulacra are infinitely reproduced by the budding mass media industry for the purpose of mass consumption.

Dianshizhai huabao was at the intersection of a number of media: the visual images often featured a pastiche of traditional Chinese and Western illustration styles (Huntington, 359). This visual style was arguably foreshadowed by the hybrid visual style of Chinese genre painting and Western realist illustration used in paintings of flora and fauna produced by Chinese artists and amateur British natural historians and analyzed by Fa-ti Fan (47). The hybrid visual language of *Dianshizhai* was combined with explanatory passages that drew on *biji* and *zhiguai* traditions—premodern prose forms that treaded a vague line between records of real events and sensationalist fantasy—to explicate the images. Wang's narrative in particular drew on premodern Chinese catalogs of "broad learning" to contextualize the comprehensiveness of the British Museum's collection. The marketability of Wang's narrative reflects a broad interest in institutions devoted to cataloging, museumification, and other forms of display—Jones and Rauch's "knowledge industry."[7]

Bennett argues that the development of the museum must be related to the development of other institutions, some of which have no apparent connection with the scientific mission of the museum, but all of which are familiar features of the urban cityscape and all of which became prevalent features of colonial cities like Shanghai at the turn of the last century (Bennett, 6). Alongside museums and gallery displays, exhibitions played a key role in the formation and representation of the modern nation-state, as educational and civilizing institutions engaged in the display of power and knowledge. Qin Shao notes that many nations were anxious to participate in exhibitionary displays of modernity, as symbols of their cosmopolitan participation in the modern imagination of the nation-state (Qin Shao, 687; Bennett, 6–7). Spaces of enjoyment, leisure, and consumption, not commonly associated with the mission of moral education in the way that museums and libraries are, were also sites where modernity and progress were put on display and where the behavioral evolution of the modern citizen could be publicly shaped.[8]

Exhibition grounds, another site for the expression of the modernist drive that received a great deal of attention in late Qing sf (and in the European press), were another regular feature of late Qing print media, the World's Fair in particular. Nineteenth-century exposition culture availed itself of displays of machinery and industrial innovations or procedures under a similar evolutionary rubric to that of the museum, as material symbols of progress (Bennett, 66–67). John Fryer, a major figure in the world of late Qing scientific translations, was instrumental in publishing a booklet on the 1893 World's Columbian Exposition, titled *An Illustrated Account of the World's Columbian Exposition at Chicago, 1893 (Meiguo bowu dahui tushuo)*.[9] The booklet, a reprint from two issues of the *Chinese Scientific and Industrial Magazine (Gezhi huibian*, 1876), was translated into Chinese with the assistance of the Jiangnan Arsenal and a number of unnamed scholar-missionaries. *Gezhi huibian* in itself was the most influential magazine on science published in the late Qing period (Chen Pingyuan and Xia Xiaohong 2006, 18).

An extensive introduction explains why the exposition was held and the significance of such exhibitions in general, before going into the details of the leadership committee and the investment structure. The bulk of the booklet is dedicated to detailed descriptions of the various national and theme-related pavilions and galleries and includes illustrations, annotated in Chinese, of many of these buildings. Extended lists of the items on display at the agricultural, botanical, mineralogical, mechanical, zoological, and other pavilions are given as well.

Trains that moved exhibition-goers around the site, and accommodations such as bathrooms and restaurants, are also described. A significant portion of the booklet is dedicated to the behavioral expectations of exhibitors, including rules for what could be displayed, how power for machines was to be provided, how display items were to be delivered to Chicago, and the proper mode of display. Also included were general rules and regulations for attendees. A frontispiece includes an English-language quote from the *North-China Daily News*: "We trust that [the booklet] will answer [Fryer's] most sanguine expectations, and that the popular and lengthy description he gives in its pages will materially aid in the great work of the enlightenment of China. . . . Every patriotic American resident in China, who feels proud of the World's Columbian Exposition as the greatest achievement of ancient or modern times would do well to present each of his Chinese friends with a copy of the work in question" (Fryer, frontispiece).[10] The booklet was not merely a description of the exhibition but also served as a primer on how to organize and fund such an endeavor, and it makes explicit the relationship between display culture, modernity, and national vitality. Although this publication was overseen by Fryer and makes its scientific and Westernizing missionary aspect explicit, the impact of such publications can be seen in local efforts at exhibitions and in fictional depictions of such exhibitions.

Exhibitions—first recorded in travelogues and pictorials, later imagined in novelization, and finally reproduced in semicolonial China— were used in part to promote economic nationalism. By May 1909, Nanjing, Shanghai, and dozens of other less developed cities had all made arrangements to host local expositions or other cultural displays (Godley, 517). The Nanyang Industrial Exposition (Nanyang quanye hui) of 1910 and other similar exhibitions throughout the Republican period were meant to demonstrate state commitment to industrial modernization. These exhibitions dedicated significant effort to identifying products that were particularly good imitations of foreign goods. One entire week of the 1910 exhibition was dedicated to the subject of aviation (Dikötter 2006, 10–12, 104). The Nanyang exhibition proved to be a failure, but it demonstrates a keen awareness of the relationship between displays of modernity in the form of industrial processes and technological innovations and the status of the nation-state. An important aspect of the modern nation-state is not just to possess or produce knowledge and material goods, but to display them in a way that demonstrates the evolutionary advancement of the society that produced them. Well into the third decade of the twentieth century, museums and other public institutions were seen as critical sites through which China's development as a modern nation could be engineered. China's hosting of the 2011 World Expo in Shanghai was the culmination of a fantasy that was born in late Qing sf[11] and saw a failed attempt in the 1910 Nanjing Expo, and continued to betray an anxiety about China's position on the world stage. The expo was marked in the popular media with the re-release of a number of late Qing works of utopian fiction and sf that feature scenes in which Shanghai is the site of a world exposition, and in which China has returned to a position as a world power, often as the leader of the League of Nations (Wanguo).

These were all forms of display understood to be part of the imperial effort and appear elsewhere in Chinese sf as intense points of interest—Jia Baoyu's museum in the Realm of Civilization in *New Story of the Stone* is one example. In the novel, one of the first signals of the wealth and power of the utopian Realm of Civilization is its vast library and museum. Their comprehensiveness and uniform tidiness make visible the power of the empire, weaving the viewing subject into their classificatory system. Laid out in such a manner as to make the spectator visible to other spectators, to take the spectator through the exhibits in a manner that teaches her about the evolution and order of world cultures, and to inculcate a similar evolution of character in the observer, the museum is both a symbol and bringer of civilization.

In a number of Chinese dystopias—Xiaoran Yusheng's unifinished "Journey to Utopia" ("Wutuobang youji," 1906) and Lao She's *Cat Country*—the disarray of institutions of public education is a marker of civilizational collapse. Wang's anxiety about the comprehensiveness of the displays betrays an anxiety about the insufficiency of native bodies of knowledge, effectively undermining arguments that all Western knowledge is no more than a recapitulation of works known to Chinese antiquity. In this respect, the British Museum becomes a signifier of the insufficiency of China's native episteme.

Dianshizhai huabao and zhiguai as Proto-SF

An impulse related to the rationalized public display associated with the knowledge industry and visible in the *Dianshizhai huabao*, and which I have identified as a key feature of the SF narratives that would soon follow, is the desire to identify and catalog creatures from China's mythical past. Images of Chinese villagers carrying gargantuan feathers over their heads as the mythical *peng* soars above them, and of sailors discovering a hill fish (*ling yu*),[12] suggest that the bestiary of Chinese myth had its own place alongside the scientific and techno-logical wonders of the modern age. In 1895, Kang Youwei expressed a similar desire to substantiate the classical tradition through the use of visual culture.

> Texts (*wenzi*) make clear meaning, but there are meanings which cannot be exhausted in text, which are only made clear in pictures (*tupu*). Pictures make clear the physical aspect of the thing that they depict, but still there are things about pictures which prevent a full understanding, which can only be achieved by [looking at] the artifact itself. The *Shijing* [*Classic of Poetry*] says, "'Guan guan' cries the osprey," and we are familiar with Lu Ji's interpretation and understand Chongyuan's explanation of it. Although scholars con-sume the day describing its shape and colors, however, we still do not know what an osprey is. But if you put an osprey in front of someone, then he or she will know immediately. As for the human body (*ti*), if we read the *Suwen* [Yellow Emperor's Classic of Inter-nal Medicine], study the *Ming Tang* [Bright Hall of Acupuncture Diagrams] or all the new essays, we [still] do not know what it is. Westerners have [put] complete bodies of human beings (*renshen quanti*) [on display in museums]; one look and immediately you know what a body is. (Quoted in Claypool, 595)

Osprey are, of course, real animals, unlike the *peng* and the hill fish, but this passage verbalizes the same desire operating in the depiction of mythical creatures in the pages of *Dianshizhai huabao*. Pictorial representation was understood to have a power exceeding that of textual description. Kang Youwei associates visual teaching materials with Western medicine but does so in order to suggest that Western medical diagrams can aid in the understanding of classical Chinese medical texts. That is to say, there was an expectation that visual culture possessed the capacity to confirm traditional bodies of knowledge, rather than displace them.

Another regularly occurring theme in *Dianshizhai huabao* was new modes of transportation, and these appear in fanciful depictions of many modern marvels of transport, for which the illustrators often had only verbal descriptions and their imaginations to draw upon in their work. These included hot-air balloons, submarines, steamships, and various forms of flying boats, parachutists, and the like (Wang Ermin, 156–157). Colonial modernity was in large part made possible by the speed of global communication, and marveling at the speed of travel was a regular motif of late Qing popular science writing, which also appeared in illustrated form. Depictions included images of newly laid railways in China and elsewhere in East Asia, as well as more farflung marvels. Realistic depictions of steam engines and open-air railcars are not nearly as striking as the fantastical illustrations of multistoried luxury train cars, flying sea-ships, and hot-air balloons bristling with cannons.

The illustrations of various flying apparatuses appearing in *Dianshizhai* paralleled the depiction of new modes of transport that appeared in the *biji* and travelogues of late Qing intellectuals. As Frank Dikötter relates,

One of the earliest references to steam in China appeared in Wei Yuan's well-known geography of the world, circulated in the 1840s: "The most astounding occurrence in today's Western world is steam power, [steam] engines propelling ships and wagons and resembling in force an unstoppable storm. If used to move ships and wagons, [steam] can be of great benefit, moving [objects] as if they were flying without the use of wind, water or human labor." Personal accounts soon followed, Guo Liancheng being among the first in the 1860s to express his amazement when boarding a steam vessel for the journey from Shanghai to Hong Kong, as "the wheel moves the ship as if by flight." Li Jingshan thought in 1872 that the steamer "moves as fast as a bird in the sky," while two residents from Jiaxing eulogised the steamer for being "as fast as a horse." (Dikötter 2006, 75)

In the 1890 diary of Song Xiaolian, a clerk for a gold-mining company, the diarist recounts his impressions of a journey by rail in fantastic terms: "The journey was as fast as lightning, its speed beyond any comparison. But even during the fastest part of the journey the train remained very balanced. Whenever I looked out of the window, it did not feel like being on a flying arrow, although the rural landscapes and dwellings shot past in flight. Within a wink, what was in front of us was suddenly behind! Pure magic!" (Dikötter 2006, 102). Depictions of flight by hot-air balloon and train appearing in *Dianshizhai huabao* also dealt with perils of modern transport, telling stories of horses and elderly men run over by trains, and hot-air balloons catching fire.

Figure 7.1 depicts what was most likely an unmanned, steam-powered aircraft made by Samuel Langley (1834–1906) (Guo Enci, 145). The image is rendered as faithfully as one might expect of an illustration of an airplane done by an artist who had never seen one in person. Again, the commentary marvels at the achievements of Western science and technology. Once again, the image and its textual description tread a thin line between scientific reportage and fiction. The imagery conveys a sense of the spirit of exploration, and of the race to assemble a flying machine, but it is still some distance from actual scientific reportage. While the pictorial and its images lay claim to taking account of facts, editorial policies and the content of the publication clearly did not eschew a slippery slope where factual science devolves into fictional science, and from there makes the final step into SF. One of the key aspects that this pictorial example of SF shares with the narratives that would follow in the early twentieth century is the explicit connections drawn between science, technology, and national stand-

Figure 7.1 "At a certain school in America, an instructor named Mr. Langley recently devised a new method to use aluminum and other light materials to make a flying ship. The ship has an air tank, an air-machine, two hidden propellers, four wings, and a rudder. The wings are two meters wide, and are forty percent [of the body of the plane]. It has been tested out in Washington, and apparently it was very nimble. This craft can be piloted through the air, going up and down. It is able to ride the winds unhindered, and it can reach a height of three hundred meters in the air. Westerners become more proficient in science by the day, and their skill in manufacturing exceeds the imagination indeed. Someone said: 'This transforms the hot-air balloon; great ingenuity has been put to work in its invention. So nimble is this ship in riding the clouds and soaring through the skies without a trace that it is without compare, superior even to Liezi riding the wind.'"

Wu Youru, *Dianshizhai huabao da ketang ban*, ed. Shanghai da ketang wenhua youxian gongsi, 15 vols. (Shanghai: Shanghai huabao chubanshe, 2001), vol. 14 (approx. January 1897–January 1898), p. 110.

ing. The closing line, alluding to the Zhou dynasty *Liezi*,[13] evinces a familiar uneasiness, suggesting a precedence for flying ships in China's literary and philosophical tradition at the same time it acknowledges that such an invention would have surpassed the fictional flights in the *Liezi*.

Other features in the pictorial were much less closely tied to any verifiable reality but demonstrate a similar anxiety about the relationship between the West and the rest. A depiction of a fertilizer factory (figure 7.2) where human remains are used to make compost illustrates this anxiety, but is ambivalent regarding the superiority of science and utilitarian approaches to material problems. To a modern viewer, the image is clearly a fabrication and has already passed over the line between science and fiction, entering into a stylized depiction of the other. The Occidentalist depiction of the West as a place where human corpses are recycled for soda ash, oils, and fertilizers flirts with the notion of the West as an essentialized other, irreducibly different from China. However, the irreducible difference does not turn out to be an illustration of the backward, barbaric practice of cannibalism, illustrating China's moral and cultural superiority. Instead, composting human remains is used to illustrate the powers of scientific knowledge, the practicality of Western funerary practices, and ultimately one of the sources of Western wealth and power. In other words, the cannibalistic recycling of human flesh—a staple of the modern Chinese literary canon that continues to appear in contemporary Chinese SF[14]—is turned on its head, illustrating the intellectual and practical failings of China rather than the intellectual failings of Western civilization. A retraction of this image was eventually published, but the disavowal was based on the notion that the image was offensive to Chinese sensibilities, not that it was a fabrication.

A common thread joining a vast number of the objects, institutions, events, and social phenomena cataloged in the *Dianshizhai huabao* is the thin line between fact and fiction that all these images evince, and the fact that the vast majority of them were understood as helping to explain the difference between China and the West, and were purported to be signs of national standing. These accounts of the world of

Figure 7.2 "Westerners value science and make miracles of decomposition, to the point of not casting any object aside. They bring order to that which cannot be ordered, even making use of human corpses. It is said that they boil them down to make oil and extract alkali, and the grindings of the bones are used to fertilize fields. This notion was advocated by the English chemist Grant. It really is like this, and for this reason, China remains unsophisticated in sciences. We know that the body and soul of the dead are seeking rest, and so not interring the coffin is a crime; and we know the avarice of corrupt men is great, and so the punishment for robbing graves is death. At its most crude, it is necessary, and at its greatest refinement, it is a policy for promoting benevolence. This is recorded in legal codes and it is one aspect of governing the nation. As for Westerners' science, can it be used to rectify a nation? I say: it can. Bodily remains will decompose, so burials can be done away with; when graveyards are eliminated, greater benefit can be reaped from tilling the soil. When a member of a poor family dies, the corpse can be sold, the funeral accoutrements spared, and the remaining profit saved. So long as the seller of soda ash can receive a good price and the diligent farmer can reap bountiful harvests, the country is wealthy and the people affluent, the way of rectification will indeed be achieved. This is Westerners' science." Wu Youru, *Dianshizhai huabao da ketang ban*, ed. Shanghai da ketang wenhua youxian gongsi, 15 vols. (Shanghai: Shanghai huabao chubanshe, 2001), vol. 5 (approx. March 1888–March 1889), p. 170; Rania Huntington, "The Weird in the Newspaper," in *Writing and Materiality in China: Essays in Honor of Patrick Hanan*, ed. Judith T. Zeitlin, Lydia Liu, and Ellen Widmer (Cambridge, MA: Harvard University Press, 2003), 368.

the late nineteenth century fit in alongside sf for three key reasons: First, they attempt to carve out spaces for the coexistence of Chinese and Western epistemologies. Second, their depictions of hard science or objectively verifiable facts are often overshadowed by exoticism and sensationalism as they drift over into the realm of fiction. As works of sf, they are more concerned with exploring the relationship between epistemological modes and with inspiring a sense of inquiry than they are in acting as primers on recent scientific discoveries. Third, one of the most prevalent themes of the paper was its attention to national strength. By far the most common imagery is of a military variety— naval ships, battles, and arms. The truly fictional and pseudoscientific content of *Dianshizhai huabao* also foregrounded issues of national fitness.

The editors of *Dianshizhai huabao* and late Qing popular science publications made attempts to carve out spaces for Chinese bodies of knowledge to stand on an equal footing with Western science, expressing particular consternation at the hegemony of scientific explanation. The efficacy of science was undeniable, but one common approach to this was to deny that science was a universal body of knowledge, which no phenomena stood outside of. *Dianshizhai huabao* was a mirror, reflecting the traumas, anxieties, fads, and debates of late Qing society at large. In these features of late Qing society—emergent consumerism, writing concerning newly available foreign goods, and the institutional structures through which the imperial state was represented and reproduced in the imagination of its subjects—a common ground of shared concerns emerges. This process of negotiation between new and old, foreign and domestic appears in late Qing and Republican sf as an anxious consideration of the value of things foreign. Science is occasionally substituted for technology, but more often depictions of science involve considerations of the implications of evolution and social Darwinism. As in the case of Zheng Guanying's calls for economic warfare (see chapter 3), Chinese sf evinces as much concern with the economic dimensions of empire as it does with its military component; capital is as vital a component of empire as arms or ideology. In works like Wu Jianren's *New Story of the Stone*, a clear line is drawn between objects of real value and the consumption of conspicuous objects of diversion. A book on warships is more valuable than a bottle of brandy. A second consideration is the question of whose hands various technologies are in: whether the captain of a steamship plying the Yangtze River is Chinese or British is as important as the existence of the ship, and rifles are worrisome only when they are wielded by the enemy. While anxieties about the value of technological innovation were very real, in the above readings of early Chinese sf, I have demonstrated that meditations on technophobia and enlightenment took a backseat to questions of the fitness of the body politic.

Science, the New Culture Movement, and a Shifting Cultural Field

Wu Yan has noted that during the early years of the Republic of China, with the establishment of the journal *Science* (*Kexue*, introduced January 1915) and *New Youth* (*Xin qingnian*, August 1915), sf quickly "ceded its position to instrumentalist genres more rich in explanatory quality, the *kexue xiaopin* (science essay) and the *kepu sanwen* (popular science essay)," bringing a sudden end to the first wave of Chinese sf. Paralleling the shift in the literary field at large (their national commitments notwithstanding), sf writers felt an even stronger need to create work that would address immediate social issues and spur on social change (Wu Yan 2011, 234–236). While a number of journals dedicated to the "importation" and dissemination of technical information had existed prior to 1911, the second decade of the twentieth century saw a rapid increase in the number of journals and schools and an emphasis on the journals' accessibility to a nonspecialized audience (Qiu Ruohong, 131–182). The literary revolution, which began in 1917 and was catalyzed by Lu Xun's "Diary of a Madman" and the student protests of the May Fourth Movement, saw the canonization of the vernacular literature of nation-building that early twentieth-century sf writers had struggled to bring into being. The era of "Mr. Science" and "Mr. Democracy" saw a rejection of individuals like Kang Youwei and Liang Qichao as remnants of a feudal past, and the condemnation on the part of intellectuals of genres like chapter fiction even as these remained popular reading material (Chen Pingyuan 1990, 113–120), but it also saw the "disappearance" of SF as fictional accounts of technological know-how, and alien encounters gave way to practical writing on popular science. Like the emergent discourses regarding science appearing in the pages of *Dianshizhai huabao*, and contrary to an emerging discourse condemning the continued use of old literary styles, popular science writing during the 1910s and 1920s was formally influenced by prose genres that predated the rise of fiction as a tool of modernization.

The Science Society of China was organized in 1914 by a group of students at Cornell University and was moved to China in 1918. The founding members included Hu Shi (1891–1962), Yang Quan (1893–1933), Zhao Yuanren (1892–1982), Ren Hongjuan (1886–1961), and about a dozen others (Cheng Min, 9). Part of the Boxer indemnity[15] included fellowships for study of science and engineering in America. One of these fellowship recipients was Zhu Kezhen (1890–1974), who was among seventy students who traveled to the United States in 1910 for the study of science. Zhu studied alongside Hu Shi, and both went on to become among the most influential men in the history of modern China—Zhu as a meteorologist, geographer, and administrator of science and education, and Hu as a writer, philosopher, and diplomat. The Science Society was one of many institutions that fall into the nebulous, liminal space between state and society in China, independent of but often aligned with the goals of the nation-state. It was funded at first through a stock fund, then variously through private, corporate, governmental, and semigovernmental sources. The institution was founded with the promotion of a strong Chinese state in mind, was intimately connected to and supportive of the governing bodies of the Republican period, yet remained independent of these governments. It was an institution dedicated both to "scientific professionalism"—freedom of research, social respect for scientists' intellectual and professional authority, and internationalism—and "scientific nationalism," meaning the desire to foment national autonomy and prosperity through the promotion of science and technology (Z. Wang, 291–299, 308, 313–318).

Following the inaugural issues of *Kexue* and *New Youth*, in October 1915, the Science Society changed its name to the Science Society of China (*Zhongguo kexue she*) and was formally recognized as China's first comprehensive scientific society. Funded by member dues and individual and institutional donations, the society (still headquartered in the United States) was divided into an editorial department, a translation department, and another department dedicated to the establishment of a Science Society library in China. The society expanded its charter to include among its purposes the popularization of science, the promotion of a research tradition among Chinese scientists, the writing and translation of scientific texts, the establishment of Chinese terminologies for scientific terms, lectures to promote popular science, and the construction of libraries, museums, and research institutions to promote the production and dissemination of scientific knowledge. In 1918, the Science Society moved its headquarters to Shanghai, taking advantage of the city's already established publication industry and continuing the city's legacy as a center of scientific progress.[16] The fictional events and institutions of late Qing sf became the policy goals and real institutions of Republican science.

One of the first achievements of the society was to establish the journal *Kexue*, in January 1915. Initially it was printed in Shanghai by the Commercial Press. This semimonthly publication was the first Chinese-language popular science journal, dedicated to making science accessible to nonexperts (Cheng Min, 9). The society's journal included anecdotal short stories and dialogues about science, translations of sf, and dedicated studies of the relationship between science and writing in foreign countries (Cheng Min, 13–14). The journal was envisioned as a vehicle for scientific communication among members of the society and a means of popularizing science and technology among Chinese intellectuals (Z. Wang, 301, 308). The introduction to the inaugural issue stated,

All civilized countries have established scientific societies to promote learning. These societies in turn have sponsored periodicals to publish advances in scholarly research and inventions of new theories. Thus the academic periodicals in these countries are truly records of the rise of their scholarship and, in today's world, the means by which scholars communicate with each other. Because we are all still at a stage of pursuing our studies, we have not been able to make many new discoveries or inventions, but we will try to convey what we have learned. . . . As our scholarship advances in the future, we hope to use this outlet to publish our new ideas and creative works. (Quoted in Z. Wang, 301–302)

The stated goals of the Science Society continued a pattern of attention to the pivotal role of social institutions in the knowledge industry, seen previously in the semifictional reportage in *Dianshizhai huabao* and continuing through works of fiction like *New Story of the Stone* and *Cat Country*. Contemporary with the establishment of the journal, and its modest goals of sharing preliminary scientific findings, was a series of important shifts in the cultural field. *Baihua* became increasingly commonplace, was taken up in the elementary school curriculum in 1920, and literature became increasingly popular (that is, focused on proletarian issues). Chapter fiction was rejected (Chen Pingyuan 1990, 122–123). The move from reform to revolution was signaled most strongly by the new position of *baihua* and by the rejection of literature as entertainment, and a concomitant rejection of literature as economic capital, realigning the very terms that defined the cultural field.

While not explicitly written in the terms of Darwinian struggle, the Science Society's pseudo-manifesto does make clear that scientific societies and popular science publication are an important building block in the foundation of a civilized country. The introduction also takes as a given the notion that China remained an intellectual backwater in the arena of civil institutions dedicated to science and the publications that such institutions would oversee. The writers went on to proclaim, "It is science and only science that will revive the forest of learning in China and provide the salvation of the masses!" (Z. Wang, 302). The founders also stipulated that their primary intent was to develop basic scientific knowledge in the population at large, and that professionalization was a secondary concern. This was encapsulated in the maxim "Popularization is elementary, expertise is supplementary" (*Kepu wei zhu, zhuanye wei bu*). *Kexue*'s mission of scientific popularization was also supplemented by the mission of class consciousness in the pages of Chen Duxiu's magazine *New Youth* (*Xin qingnian*; *La Jeunesse*). The two publications mutually reinforced their respective missions in their inaugural issues, both dedicating front-matter advertising to the other, highlighting their complementary causes in the mission of national renewal.[17] *Kexue* and the Science Society were part of a multipronged approach to raising levels of class consciousness and practical scientific knowledge throughout China.

Science Society members and the society's journal played an active role in the New Culture Movement. Reflecting the mutually reinforcing missions of the two magazines, Hu Shi wrote for both *New Youth* and *Kexue*. As one marker of its modernity and its position in a cultural field that had increasingly little room for classical letters, even in terms of visual layout, *Kexue* was the first journal to adopt horizontal typesetting and Western-style punctuation. Echoing Lu Xun's praise for the iconoclasm (both real and imagined) of European scientists in essays like "Lessons from the History of Science," editors praised Galileo for his desire to seek the truth and for having "fought bloody battles with religion for the freedom of thought." Journal editors went on to call for national openness and social and cultural criticism (Z. Wang, 307). These institutions helped to create a new and vigorous sphere for scientific and cultural debate and were the vanguard of a new set of institutions aimed at fomenting domestic scientific research, interest in practical natural science, and, even more importantly, understanding of social sciences.

Leading intellectuals' shifts of focus were motivated in large part by a reconsideration of the purpose of science in the wake of World War I. Anger over China's treatment in the Treaty of Versailles was not the only point of contention for May Fourth radicals. Disappointment at China's continued second-class status in the post-Versailles world combined with a sense that the fruits of European progress had been little more than protracted and brutal warfare, compounding intellectuals' sense that China's path to modernity had to take a different course. Unprecedented bloodshed and suffering resulting from the new mass-produced weaponry and chemical know-how put to use during the war brought renewed doubts about the benefits of science and modernism, and these misgivings soon found their way into the Chinese debate on science, modernity, and belles lettres.

This period saw a radical critique of the conventional Confucian order, and though vestiges of China's philosophical and intellectual tradition remained relevant, the sense that revolution rather than reform was the answer was stronger than ever before. Benjamin Schwarz has argued that social Darwinism and notions of historical and evolutionary progress continued to enjoy an axiomatic status in the debate on the nation's future. Social Darwinism was not understood as the rule of survival of the fittest among individuals in a society, but as the same rule applied to competition between societies. The answer to the social Darwinist imperative for competition was not rugged individualism but the development of a fitter national polity. Only social cohesion could overcome the threat of becoming an unfit collective species. That is, the answer to social Darwinism was socialism (Schwarz 1983, 99–105). As Chen Pingyuan noted above regarding literary forms during the Republican period, the break with the Confucian past was in some respects not as radical as May Fourth intellectuals saw it to be. Like Yan Fu, for whom T. H. Huxley was made more relevant because of his social focus, leftists of the 1930s were also informed by a Confucian emphasis on social stability that prompted them to focus on social sciences rather than the natural sciences. While Confucian hierarchies were done away with, a focus on immediate social needs, relationships between individuals, and the perfection of the social body through education are "Confucian" values that leftist thinkers continued to espouse, even as their condemnations of the great sage became increasingly vocal.

A familiar set of responses characterized the debates on the significance of science and how this should be communicated to the masses during this era. Science was still seen as the possession of global centers that had to be imported to a Chinese periphery, often at the behest of Chinese intellectuals living or previously stationed abroad. Foreign-educated intellectuals, schooled in the United States and Great Britain as well as Japan, established civil institutions and dedicated themselves to sharing their knowledge with their compatriots. Like Lu Xun, many of these individuals were initially educated in natural sciences (for example, Hu Shi's initial education was in agriculture) and then turned their efforts entirely or in part to the mission of popularizing scientific knowledge and class/national consciousness. From the familiar pattern of foreign education as a means to national renewal came a familiar focus on the value of the written word and a top-down mission for elites to proselytize their program of national strengthening to the masses.

Despite the fact that essays on science began to turn away from hard sciences in order to focus on more everyday social concerns, empire continued to be a theme that loomed large in the background (as seen in the above discussion of *Cat Country*). The rising tide of Japanese aggression in Korea, Manchuria, and Southeast Asia heightened the sense of national peril, reinforcing for many the idea that China remained on the verge of extinction. At the same time that intellectuals were pointing to the intellectual bankruptcy of Western Europe, the perception that China was a laggard on the global stage continued to surface in discussions of the importance of scientific education. These efforts aimed at promoting scientific education were carried out in the context of newly formed but familiar social institutions—left-wing promoters of socialism and scientific popularizers coalesced around the Science Society of China and the publishing industry. Continuity between modern institutions, the demands of industry, and social practices was the guiding intellectual principle of this debate.

In 1923, a debate between Zhang Junmai (Carsun Chang, 1886–1969), a philosopher at Qinghua University, and Hu Shi erupted when Zhang argued in a lecture that given the ravages of the Great War in Europe, the cold rationalism of science was not adequate for producing a worldview that had to be subjective and intuitive. Members of the Science Society understood this as a challenge to both scientism and scientific progress and the mission of Chinese modernization. Hu Shi soon joined the fray, penning an article titled "Science and the Outlook on Life" ("Kexue yu rensheng guan"),[18] in which he argued:

China at the present has not enjoyed the benefit from science, much less [suffered] the "disasters" brought by science. Let us try to open our eyes and look around: the widespread divination altars and temples, the widespread magic prescriptions and ghost photography, and undeveloped transportation, and such undeveloped industry—how do we deserve to refuse science? . . . The Chinese view of life has never even encountered science face-to-face! At this time we are still troubled that science is not being promoted adequately, troubled that science education is not being developed, and troubled that the force of science is not enough to sweep away the evil spirit that spreads all over the country. Who could have expected famous scholars to come out to shout "European science has gone bankrupt," to put the blame on the cultural bankruptcy of Europe on science, to belittle science, to enumerate the crimes of scientists' view of life, and [to demand] that science not have any impact on view of life! How could people with faith in science not be worried about the current situation? How could [they] not come out and defend science in a loud and clear voice? (Quoted in Z. Wang, 308–309)

Initially Hu's tone is familiar, if not entirely predictable, framing the question of scientific research and education in the stark terminology of national annihilation. Likewise, the contention that Europe is spiritually bankrupt is a familiar canard seen throughout the encounter with the Western world. What is notable is the emerging distinction between science, Europe, and Europe's claim to moral superiority. In chapter 2, I demonstrated the degree to which notions such as science, progress, literature, modernity and civilization, and the accompanying terms through which they were introduced to China via Japanese neology, were often conflated with one another in the translingual context of the late Qing. By the second and third decades of the twentieth century, Chinese intellectuals had begun to decouple these terms, coming to an understanding of science, civilization, and Westernization as separate entities. As a body of knowledge independent of the Western world, it was possible to give the science a Chinese face. The simultaneous institutionalization of science in China, the questioning of the value of science and modernism brought about by the excesses of war and the industrial revolution, and the developing understanding and local independence of science, literature, and modernity led to a reconsideration of how science and literature were to play a role in China's project of national strengthening.

At the same time that this reconsideration of the spiritual and moral implications of science and technology was taking place, a new set of philosophical and social theories began to take hold in the Chinese intellectual sphere. May Fourth intellectuals adopted European notions of antirationalism, skepticism, anarchism, and critiques of materialism as new fodder for understanding the relationship between themselves and the Western world. This debate came to a head in 1923 in the form of a polemic titled "science and the outlook on life." The debate, named after Hu Shi's essay mentioned above, was sparked by Zhang Junmai, who argued in his lecture at Qinghua University that science did not fit China's cultural specificities and that a more metaphysical outlook, especially in the realm of ethics, spirituality, philosophy, and psychology, was necessary. Zhang and his colleagues were deeply skeptical of the exclusive focus of science on the material and natural world, and held that moral and metaphysical issues were best understood as an autonomous system outside the purview of scientific investigation. Proponents of science, led by Ding Wenjiang (1887–1936), argued that science provided an objective perspective on life and the natural world, and that only a positivist scientific methodology could lead to a proper worldview. This debate revived questions about the provenance of science and renewed intellectual questions about the applicability of Western science to the Chinese sphere, helping to reinvigorate a sense of cultural relevancy for China's own history and philosophical foundations (Liu Shi, 32–35).

Popular Science, Class Consciousness, and the New Culture Movement: *Taibai*

In the wake of this debate, journals like *Kexue, Kexue zazhi*, and *Chen bao* saw the emergence of a new, hybrid form of writing, the *kexue xiaopin* or "science sketch." The *kexue xiaopin* constituted an admixture of written forms and purposes, combining elements of theoretical treatise, news reportage, and literature, to communicate notions of science, aesthetics, and practicality. By the 1930s, the *xiaopin* became the center of a heated debate in which writers argued the importance of repurposing literary forms previously associated with elite appreciation as tools of social education and transformation. Articles on the interpretation of science, often intended for a broad audience, or even intended to spread scientific knowledge, could have been written by scientists, but were also often penned by nonspecialists. As one might identify precursor elements of SF in *Dianshizhai huabao* and other popular science publications that prominently featured pictorial representations of science and technology, one might also identify the 1920s and '30s low tide of SF as a sign of the genre's sublimation into other forms. In many ways, this sublimation was characterized by SF blending back into premodern genres that had been prominent in the cultural field prior to the literary transformation of the turn of the twentieth century.

Over the course of the first three decades of the twentieth century, writing on science and technology appeared in a number of genres other than pure SF, and a number of these already existing genres were convenient vehicles for sharing awe and apprehension about things Western. Charles Laughlin argues that the *xiaopin*, which emerged in the 1920s and reached the height of its popularity in the 1930s, is a combination of three traditional influences: the Daoist critique of Confucian culture offered by the *Zhuangzi*, the eremetic tradition of poets like Tao Qian, and the Buddhist engagement with desire and transcendence. The *xiaopin* was a genre associated with the cultivation of a meaningful private life. In its modern incarnation, the genre "aligned itself with European belles lettres while distancing itself from premodern *guwen* (ancient style prose) and *bagu wen* ('eight-legged essays')" (Laughlin, 1–7). During the course of its development, *xiao-pin wen* was the subject of a debate over repurposing traditional forms for radical purpose. Those who were critical of its perceived frivolity called for a repurposing of the *xiaopin* as an educational model (12).

The emergence of the *kexue xiaopin* in the late 1920s and early 1930s was also part of an ongoing attempt to nail down the role of science and technology in everyday life and the role of intellectuals in sharing science with the reading public. Writing on popular science could also include magazine articles communicating practical information or detailing simple experiments that could be performed in the home and debates on the merits of science and the best methods for spreading scientific knowledge as a means of national renewal. The *kexue xiaopin* was a marriage of the prose essay (*sanwen*), popular-science explanation, and commentary on scientific methodology, aimed at broadening the understanding of science and its audience, propagating interest in its practice, and continuing the mission of promoting the spirit of inquiry that Lu Xun heralded in his "Lessons from the History of Science." The *kexue xiaopin* was conceived as a form that would be at once more systematic than other *sanwen* but would maintain a focus on aesthetic quality, readability, clarity of thought, ideological content, and humanistic purpose. On the other hand, these works were not intended to be as systematic or as focused and technical as textbooks or science research publications.[19]

In his 1931 book *Birds and Literature* (*Niao yu wenxue*), one of the earliest and most successful proponents of the *kexue xiaopin*, Jia Zuzhang (1901–1988), presented a parallel study of both "the science of birds" and the "literature of birds" (Cheng Min, 16–17). The book included information on different species of birds, typology, and bird behavior, but it also included myths and legends about birds and mention of birds in classical literature. Through the lens of science, the author brought order to the world of classical Chinese literary allusions to birds. Works like this were primers in both science and the arts, intended to be pleasurable and practical. Their real-world relevance was meant to be plainly visible.

One of the most influential journals for the development of the *ke-*

xue xiaopin was the semimonthly *Taibai*. The title of the journal was a play on the traditional Chinese word for the planet Venus (whose visibility low on the horizon signals the coming dawn) and the phrase "very clear." The editors, writers, and left-wing intellectuals observing the emergence of *Taibai* understood its mission to be one of mass education. Mao Dun wrote,

> The journal named *Taibai* is edited by Chen Wangdao. He has explained that *Taibai* is "clearer than clear," meaning it is even more clear than the vernacular [*baihua*]; the characters *Tai* and *bai* have few strokes, in accord with the principle of simplification. Furthermore, Venus [*taibai*], which comes out just before dawn, is also known as the "star of emerging brightness" [*qiming xing*], meaning that daybreak is coming; this also hints that the end of dark rule of the Guomindang is near at hand. Lu Xun lauded this polysemy and said, this can only be known amongst our clique, and can't be revealed to outsiders, in order to avoid it being heard by those old codgers in the censorship bureau.[20]

Both Lu Xun and Mao Dun saw in *kexue xiaopin* a multifaceted form well suited to the purpose of teaching basic scientific and historical principles to the masses and in so doing fomenting the development of class consciousness. The consensus that emerged was that the form should emphasize social sciences and philosophy over natural sciences, and that articles on the natural sciences should have a clear relationship to people's everyday life experiences.[21] Amid leftist calls for focus on social issues, writers like Liu Shi (1903–1968) and Shu Qian (b. ?) further insisted on emphasizing the needs of average members of society: "The subject of a flea, or a woodpecker might come up, and I think that this ought to be [understood] through something real, something with 'social feel.' Upon hearing a woodpecker's pecking, wouldn't one be apt to think of Japan's recent encroachment upon China being referred to as 'woodpecker diplomacy'? If we use this 'social feel,' when it comes to these descriptions of natural phenomena, it ought to be well received by the masses, and indeed there is an objective reality to it" (Shu Qian, 168).

The prominence of *kexue xiaopin*, and the theoretical debate on its social role, were not confined to the realm of work dedicated specifically to science. *Shenbao*'s supplementary opinion page (*ziyoutan*) and magazines such as *Xinren* and *Mangzhong* all featured prominent author's opinions, reader responses, and their own *kexue xiaopin*. Among leftists, a consensus emerged that this form was to be clearly delineated from "hack writing" (*bangxian wenxue*), and the impulse toward restoring tradition, and support for an emphasis on publication of work informed by the principles of dialectical materialism and historical materialism, began to emerge (Cheng Min, 50–52).

Although the journal lasted for only one year (twenty-four issues), it had a profound influence on the intellectual and cultural spheres, helping to create a new generation of *kexue xiaopin* writers and a new generation of publishers dedicated to the form. Publication of *kexue xiaopin* continued after the establishment of the PRC in 1949, had a ten-year hiatus during the Cultural Revolution, and was revived again after 1976, when another wave of interest in science and SF publishing took hold.[22] In this respect, the fortunes of *kexue xiaopin* reflect the fortunes of fiction during the modern period, waxing and waning with the political tides. During these same years, SF did not necessarily fare as well, and this presents a vexing question for scholars of Chinese SF.

The production of *kexue xiaopin* was more sustained than that of SF, beginning in the 1920s and continuing through to the contemporary period. The majority of SF published in China was written in the first decade of the twentieth century, followed by a long drought. Through the teens, twenties, and thirties, very few works of original SF were published in China, and publication remained anemic after 1949. The question of why SF failed to take hold during the utopian moment of the New Culture period has not been adequately addressed. In the late Qing, a marriage of earlier *xiaoshuo* forms like the *biji* and *zhiguai* predated the publication of prose identified as science fiction, though it shared many traits with the genre. During the Republican period, the advent of and the expectations associated with the *kexue xiaopin* were contributing factors in the waning popularity of the genre, as the marriage of prose, popular science, and nation-building was sublimated into a more practical form. Republican period leftists chose to focus their attention on much more quotidian concerns, and the task of scientific education that late Qing intellectuals like Lu Xun had hoped SF would fulfill was instead fulfilled by the *kexue xiaopin*. A smattering of pure SF works was published during the twenties and thirties, among them stories by Gu Junzheng (1902–1980) and Lao She.

CONCLUSION

Reflecting on the potential lessons that Chinese SF has to offer the expanding field of "global science fiction," Veronica Hollinger has noted the parallels between central themes of Lu Xun's work and key themes of a number of recent works of Chinese SF by Liu Cixin and Han Song (Hollinger, forthcoming). In Liu Cixin's short story "The Village School-teacher" ("Xiangcun jiaoshi," 2001), the teacher at a benighted and impoverished rural school lies on his deathbed in the one-room schoolhouse where he teaches, suffering from late-stage esophageal cancer that he cannot afford to treat. He reflects on Lu Xun's iron house metaphor, recalling the passage word for word. Inspired by the closing lines, that one cannot say there is absolutely no hope of destroying the iron house, the teacher pushes his way through one final lesson, asking the students to memorize Newton's Three Laws of Motion. Earth is about to be wiped out in order for the Carbon-Based Federation to establish a quarantine zone that will prevent the Silicon-Based Empire from recovering after a millennia-long intergalactic war. This intergalactic drama unfolds almost completely unbeknownst to the denizens of Liu Cixin's village, a place whose cultural backwardness, naked pursuit of self-interest, isolation from the broader political geography of China as a nation-state, and apparent timeless nature are all too familiar in the broader oeuvre of dystopian work that Jeffrey Kinkley has labeled China's "new historical novels" (Kinkley 2014). The children manage to save Earth by passing a test that proves their status as an advanced carbon-based civilization to the aliens; but of fifteen questions, they answer only three correctly because they have memorized them. The inhabitants of the iron house live on but remain ignorant.

Kinkley notes that in the most prominent Chinese dystopian novels and films of the 1990s, "technological development is not the emphasis" (13). However, he observes that a preponderance of the most prominent and critically acclaimed works of mainstream literature from this period share with late Qing SF a vision of human evolution as tending as easily toward decadence as it does toward progress, noting that both Maoists and those to Chairman Mao's right adopted social Darwinian visions of change driven by conflict as *"groups* struggled for supremacy," but that the ultimate outcome of this state of struggle is not evolutionary progress but "secular and recurring decline, even regression" (180). Elements of magical realism are much more prominent in China's "new historical novel" than themes of techno-scientific development, belying greater affinity to and influence from authors like Gabriel García Márquez and Miguel Asturias than George Orwell or Aldous Huxley. Nevertheless, the theme of social decline as a defining feature of human relationships is a familiar trope beyond the borders of China's SF selective tradition.

In Liu Cixin's "The Devourer" ("Tunshizhe," 2000), an emissary from an alien civilization that sustains itself by consuming planets comes to Earth to inform humanity that its planet will be destroyed. Reminiscent of Tamatarō's theory of colonial subjugation on a universal scale in *Tales of the Moon Colony*, the emissary Big Tooth says, "In the galaxy, one civilization becoming poultry for a stronger civilization is quite common, you will find that being bred for harvest is quite a beautiful existence. There's no need to worry about food or clothing and you can live happily to the end of your days, some civilizations can only wish for this. Your discomfort is entirely the result of your worn out sense of anthropocentrism" (Liu Cixin, *Xiangcun jiaoshi*, 167–168). Echoing the ironic motif of the destruction of inferior civilizations in early Chinese SF, Liu Cixin subverts "civilization" as little more than a euphemism for the power to subjugate others. After the destruction of the planet Earth, Big Tooth says, "What is civilization? Civilization is just devouring, ceaselessly eating and eating, always expanding. Everything else is secondary" (182). The Devourer Empire and the vision of human beings raised as poultry resurfaces in Liu Cixin's story "The Poetry Cloud" ("Shiyun," 1997), which depicts the aftermath of the Devourer Empire's plundering of the planet, where human beings have been forced to live underground. Song Mingwei notes that in Liu Cixin's fiction, "human society is often presented as a minor problem against the extravagant and grandiose backdrop of a universe measured in light years. Human life may be at the mercy of a supremely powerful alien species and human extinction has little impact on the universe" (Song Mingwei, 95). Song argues that in Liu's *Three Body Trilogy* (*San ti*, 2007; *San ti er: Hei'an senlin*, 2008; *Santi san: Sishen yongsheng*, 2010) the depiction of interstellar hierarchies and communion with extraterrestrial life is defined by an amoral eternal struggle, one in which the laws of physics themselves can be bent to serve the needs of superior civilizations (97).

A close cousin of the civilization that sustains itself by subjugating or consuming another is the specter of a society whose sustenance depends upon eating itself. Lu Xun's diagnosis of a cannibalistic society has been an enduring trope in Chinese SF. Hollinger notes that in Han Song's "The Passengers and the Creator" ("Chengke yu changzaozhe," 2005), a group of passengers held captive to a totalitarian society aboard an airplane suspended in eternal flight are similarly unaware of their imprisonment in an iron house. Echoing Lu Xun's "Diary of a Madman," the story takes the form of a journal kept by one passenger aboard the plane as he awakens to his plight, eventually learning that a cannibalistic system of distribution of human flesh is what sustains the passengers in the business-class cabin of the aircraft. Finding himself surrounded by Caucasian soldiers after having destroyed the aircraft, the narrator asks himself, "Just who was it who had banished us to flying through the darkness? Had we actually done this to ourselves?" (Han Song, 172). The ambivalent ending seemingly suggests that a familiar and benevolent totalitarian state may be preferable to the unknown empires outside the iron house. This dismal equivalency calls to mind Lu Xun's story "A Lost Good Hell" ("Shidiao de hao diyu," 1925), in which mankind responds to demons who denounce a dilapidated hell by casting out the devil and making it even worse than it was before.[1]

In "Gloomy China: China's Image in Han Song's Science Fiction" (2013), Jia Liyuan (aka Fei Dao) draws a number of parallels between Han Song's oeuvre and the work of Lu Xun, noting that imagery of closed and cannibalistic societies also appears in Han Song's *Subway* (*Ditie*, 2011), "Rebirth Bricks" ("Zaisheng zhuan," 2011), and other works, adding that "Han Song satirically transforms Lu Xun's metaphor of 'dying in one's sleep' for a new era; it becomes 'prospering in one's sleep'" (107). Song Mingwei frames the collapse of human reciprocity that eventually deteriorates into cannibalism and people transforming into insects lacking self-consciousness in the closed system of *Subway* as a reconfiguration of evolution into "a process of degeneration that is killing humanity" (94).

To commemorate the 2010 World Expo in Shanghai, various volumes collecting stories that had predicted Shanghai playing host to a world exposition, including Wu Jianren's *New Story of the Stone*, Lu Shi'e's *The New China (Xin Zhongguo, 1906)*, and Liang Qichao's *The Future of New China (Xin Zhongguo weilai ji, 1902)*, were released. Ren Dongmei has noted the similarities between the language describing imagined displays of China's cosmopolitan belonging to the global knowledge industry in the early twentieth century as it appeared in fictional utopian writings of the three authors above, and in the real reportage from the event that appeared in China's *People's Daily (Renmin ribao)* in the run-up to the actual event more than a century later, observing that signaling China's belonging to the modern world by playing host to a world expo was practically an indispensable element of late Qing utopian narratives (Ren Dongmei, "Mengxiang Zhongguo," 2, 42–43). The science-fictive imaginings of China putting its national standing on display through a world exposition, of turn-of-the-twentieth-century print reproductions of the knowledge industry in serial visual culture, and of the would-be hosts of the failed 1910 Nanjing Exhibition were brought to life when Shanghai hosted the first World Expo since 1992.

Han Song's assessment of the relationship between China and scientific enlightenment echoes Xu Nianci's fictional search for alternative epistemologies in "New Tales of Mr. Braggadocio" and the general sense of skepticism regarding the adoption of Western epistemology that characterized the late Qing intellectual field. Han writes, "Science, technology, and modernization are not characteristic of Chinese culture. They are like alien entities. If we buy into them, we transform ourselves into monsters, and that is the only way we can get along with

Western notions of progress" (Han Song, 20). This ironic invocation of the imagery of the alien to describe Chinese science and SF as characterized by a sense of difference from its Anglo-American counterparts (Hollinger, 4) is also a reminder of the durability of the perception that the adoption of Western science and technology was incompatible with the preservation of a unique national heritage.

The lessons of late Qing SF speak to developments in contemporary Chinese SF and to the literary field as a whole. Paola Iovene has argued that SF was one of the most prominent genres to experience a resurgence in the early 1980s, and that this enthusiasm "provides an ideal case to explore the rediversification of futuristic genres in an emerging literary market" (Iovene, 31). Michel Hockx's three-dimensional map of the Chinese cultural field stops short of placing any genre or medium within the field, instead leaving an empty cube. This is a wise decision, given the constantly shifting relations between various elements within the field. As observed in chapter 7, not only were elements within the field subject to negotiation, but the axes that defined the contours of the field itself have also been contested over the course of the last century. Looking further backward, Iovene notes that vernacular science journals of the socialist era were characterized by a "remarkable continuum between items presented as fact and those listed as fiction" (33). The cultural field is internally amorphous as the boundaries between given practices and genres shift and evolve, and it is amorphous as the axes that determine their value also shift. I would like to propose understanding the history of Chinese SF in terms of a four-dimensional model that accounts for these transformations. This opens the field up to the various subgenres of the socialist period that have previously been labeled as "children's literature," filling in an apparent lacuna in the history of Chinese SF.

This study cannot claim to be an exhaustive history of Chinese SF between the years 1902 and 1934, much less a comprehensive history of the genre. Given their thematic range, the works studied might just as easily be labeled works of social fiction, utopian, dystopian, or fantastic. However, these works evince participation in and awareness of the development of science fiction as a global genre that was intimately concerned both with the impact of industrial technology on human-kind and with the relationship between science, technology, and empire. The authors examined in this study wrote in many genres, and many of them experimented with literary style in search of a new vernacular language. These early authors and the cultural field that gave rise to their work are an indication of the significance of SF in the history of Chinese science, literature, and culture, and of the relationship between Chinese SF and the global SF tradition.

1 I have chosen this abbreviation for a number of reasons, partly to save paper, but also in part to reflect the ambiguities of the term in both English and Chinese. See later in introduction for an explanation of some of these vagaries. Chinese SF was, and remains, the product of a complex exchange between China, Japan, and the West (the United States in particular). To this day, the bulk of the SF available in China consists of works in translation. Especially in the case of the late Qing, and the practices of translation specific to the era, this issue in itself is deserving of a separate, in-depth study. Unfortunately, this study addresses the issue of translation and its relationship to the history of Chinese SF only obliquely, in my discussion of Lu Xun's translations of Jules Verne in chapter 2.

2 This term is particularly problematic because it has been used in so many different ways, only occasionally in the sense of a discourse in opposition to Orientalism and just as often in reference to positive representations of the West, or representations meant to bolster Chinese nationalism while suppressing behaviors unfavorable to the state (Carrier, 1–29; Xiaomei Chen, 4–11; Buruma and Margalit, 5–12).

3 For a translation see Lu Xun 2009 (trans. Gladys Yang), 19.

4 Xianglin Sao, twice-widowed, believes she will be cut in half in the afterlife in order to allow her late husbands to share her. This and the fact that her son was eaten by a wolf cause her fellow villagers to shun her. While the narrator sees the injustice in her situation, he agonizes over his inability to offer any comforting words (Lu Xun 2009 [trans. Yang], 161–177; *LXQJ*, 2:5–23).

5 While resisting Jameson and Suvin's subsuming of utopia into SF as a whole, Andrew Milner argues that SF, utopia, and fantasy "all three occupy positions within the contemporary global SF field and therefore contribute to the SF selective tradition" (Milner 2012, 115).

6 At its most literal, the discourse of "self-strengthening" and the continuity between national health and the individual was formulated as a

question of physical fitness and training. Liang Qichao and Yan Fu both argued that national well-being was a matter of physical education. The term "physical education" (*tiyu*) was most likely an import of the Japanese *taiiku*, which appeared in documents in 1872 explaining the Meiji educational system, and was associated with translations of Spencer. In both Meiji Japan and late Qing China, a direct line was drawn between national standing and physical strength (Morris, 877–881). Two more of Lu Xun's most famous stories — "Diary of a Madman" and "Medicine" — associate China's political and social failings with mental and physical illness (Lu Xun 2009 [trans. Yang], 21–31, 37–45; *LXQJ*, 1:444–456, 463–472).

7 The common practice of translation by which a text was rendered into oral Chinese by one reader, then copied down in literary Chinese by a second individual, and often rendered into "vernacular" language by a third often led to a series of adaptations through which the format, narrative, and characters were modified for the local audience. Lin Qinnan (1852–1924), for example, translated more than 170 works of American and European fiction using this method (Ye Yonglie, 6; Cheng Min, 10).

8 Gary Westfahl notes, "Critics of all schools can accept [Hugo Gernsback] as the first person to create and announce something resembling a history of SF. Some critics before Gernsback discussed earlier works now seen as SF, but they did not treat SF as a separate category and did not distinguish its texts from other forms of non-mimetic fiction (Westfahl 1992, 40).

9 Born to humble beginnings, Liang Qichao (1873–1929) passed the *xiucai* provincial examination in 1884 and the *juren* examination in 1889. In 1890, after failing the palace examination, he became a follower of reformer Kang Youwei and began to actively promote institutional reforms and modernized education. In 1898, following the bloody crackdown on the Hundred Days' Reform, Liang fled to Japan. It was in Japan that he started the magazines *Xin xiaoshuo* (*New Fiction*) and *Xinmin congbao* (*New Citizen*). Liang engaged in translation of SF; and his own novel, *Xin Zhongguo weilai ji* (*The Future of New China*, 1902) is a utopian vision of China's path to political reform. Tang Xiaobing's *Global Space and the Nationalist Discourse of Modernity: The Historical*

Thinking of Liang Qichao (1996) is an excellent intellectual biography. In Chinese, see Ding Wenjiang and Zhao Fengtian, eds., *Liang Qichao nianpu changbian* (1983).

10 While the English term "science fiction" had appeared in writing as early as 1851, it did not come into general use until the late 1920s and early '30s. Once established, the term was used in retroactive attempts to identify genre categories of older works of fiction, in fan discussions, and in marketing of stories in contemporary publication. The phrase existed alongside such genre terms as "science fantasy," "scientific fantasy," "scientifantasy," "scientific romance," "scientifiction," and others (Prucher, 170–180; Clute and Nicholls, 311–314). Wang Der-wei translates the term as "science fantasy" (Wang Der-wei 1997, 253–255). See also *Oxford English Dictionary Online*, http://www.oed.com/view/Entry /172674. The *OED* defines SF as "Imaginative fiction based on postulated scientific discoveries or spectacular environmental changes, freq. set in the future or on other planets and involving space or time travel."

11 This final category of course refers to length, rather than narrative content.

12 For more on China's position at the center of the Asian tribute system and the various iterations of a Pax Sinica presided over by succeeding Chinese dynasties see Charles Horner (2009). Charles Mann's *1493: Uncovering the New World Columbus Created* explicates the relationship between Spanish imperial power and trade between Spanish colonies and China (Mann, 123–196).

13 For a good history of the fate of clocks and Su Song's (1020–1101) armillary sphere in China from the end of the Northern Song through the Qing see Landes, 15–36. Landes posits in part that while Chinese water clocks were likely superior to eleventh-century European clocks, as Joseph Needham has also argued, the development of the water clock was hindered by its unportability, the fact that it did not function in freezing weather, and the relatively closed nature of exchange in the field of horological calculation.

14 This effort was marked by what is often identified as two failures—the inability to match or exceed the quality of European clockmaking, and the confinement of such knowledge to the imperial court.

15 While I am by no means arguing that China did not have any body of knowledge that we might understand as "science," I should note that unless otherwise indicated, when I use the word "science" in this study I am referring to Western science. The dimensions of the social and political crisis described in this introduction were such that the majority of those writing or studying science were operating under the assumption that science was an ontologically Western body of knowledge.

16 See Furth, "Intellectual Change," 16; Pusey 1983, 2–7; and Schwarz, 42–60.

17 The Jiangnan Arsenal was established in 1865 and the Fuzhou Shipyard in 1866, alongside a number of technical schools. The Fujian Naval Academy was established in 1867 and the Telegraphy School in Tianjin in 1879. Between 1871 and 1905, the Jiangnan Arsenal published 178 translations of works on natural sciences, military science, engineering and manufacturing, medicine, and agriculture (Kwok, 5).

18 For more on the development of science and technology in China between the late nineteenth and early twentieth century and the Yangwu Movement see Qiu Ruohong, 11–43, 71–76.

19 The *Daxue* is one of the four central texts of the Confucian tradition, first assembled and commented upon during the Northern Song dynasty (960–1127).

20 One interesting and rarely discussed effect of Britain's victory in the Opium Wars was the new access that British botanists, previously confined in scope to warehouses in Canton, had to methods of planting and harvesting tea. Working in concert with botanists in India, they were able to identify over a half million acres in India and Ceylon suitable to the production of tea, meaning that by the early 1850s, China's monopoly on tea had been undone in a second way, by the growing of the product on British colonial soil (Brockway, 448–449, 454–455).

21 See Wang Hui, 21–82; Lydia Liu, 83–112.

22 See, for example, Weinbaum et al. (2008) on the plurality of expectations for women as a new class of political participants and consumers generated by the figure of the "modern girl," who cropped up in China, Japan, Germany, France, South Africa, India, and elsewhere.

23 Few of the advantages identified by economic historians and theorists

like Weber and Marx were truly as decisive as previously understood. There were minimal (if any) material or intellectual guarantees of Occidental superiority over the Oriental sphere. Mass production was a critical factor in the military superiority of the European world. The set of advantages that Europe did possess prior to the encounter were limited, both geographically and historically. The key advantage in the project of Britain's colonial empire, industrial capitalism, emerged only in the nineteenth century. In many respects industrialization was limited to Great Britain, and prior to the era of Britain's industrialization, Pomeranz hypothesizes, "there is little to suggest that western Europe's economy had decisive advantages." In many respects, late eighteenth-century European craftsmen were far behind their Chinese (and Indian) counterparts, imitating dyeing and weaving processes and the manufacture of porcelain. Chinese doctors were often more effective in treating illness than their European counterparts, and Asian cities were far ahead of Europe in terms of sanitation (Pomeranz, 16, 45–46).

24 I find the clearest definition of "Orientalism" to be "a distribution of geopolitical awareness into aesthetic, scholarly, economic, sociological, historical, and philological texts; it is an *elaboration* not only of a basic geographical distinction (the world is made up of two unequal halves, Orient and Occident) but also of a whole series of 'interests' which, by such means as scholarly discovery, philological reconstruction, psychological analysis, landscape and sociological description, it not only creates but also maintains; it *is* rather than expresses, a certain *will* or *intention* to understand, in some cases to control, manipulate, even to incorporate, what is a manifestly different (or alternative and novel) world; it is, above all, a discourse that is by no means in direct, corresponding relationship with political power in the raw, but rather is produced and exists in an uneven exchange with various kinds of power, shaped to a degree by power political (as with the colonial or imperial establishment), power intellectual (as with reigning sciences like comparative linguistics or anatomy, or any of the modern policy sciences), power cultural (as with orthodoxies and canons of taste, texts, values), power moral (as with ideas about what 'we' do and what 'they' cannot do or understand as 'we' do). Indeed, my real argument is that Orien-

talism is—and does not simply represent—a considerable dimension of modern political-intellectual culture, and as such has less to do with the Orient than it does with 'our' world" (Said 1979, 12–13).

25 See also Milner 2012, 148.

CHAPTER 1. GENRE TROUBLE

1 The Shanghai Expo of 2010, for example, was marked by the fortunate reprinting of a number of novels published around 1910 that depicted China as the host of a World Expo. *Shibo menghuan sanbuqu* includes stories by Wu Jianren, Liang Qichao, and Lu Shi'e (*Xin Zhongguo*, 1910); and *Xin Zhongguo shengshi yuyan*, which contains the same two stories by Lu Shi'e and Liang Qichao, as well as Cai Yuanpei's short story *Xinnian meng* (1904).

2 Knight's original quotation is the glib observation that "science fiction is what we point to when we say it" (Knight, xiii).

3 For more on the Commercial Press and the development of the vernacular language see Huters 2008; Chen Jianhua; and Judge.

4 Lin Shu, coming at the question from a slightly different angle in the preface to his translation of *Oliver Twist* (*Zeishi xu*, 1908), attributed England's strengths to Dickens's ability to reveal social ills, thereby allowing for their correction: "Without Dickens describing the situation, how would people know about this nest of thieves persisting in their midst? England's ability to be strong, therefore, lies in its ability to reform and follow the good. . . . I regret only that we have no Dickens capable of revealing accumulated social wrongs by writing a novel and thus reporting those wrongs to the authorities, perhaps with results similar" (Quoted in Huters 1988, 253).

5 This argument may be seen as an answer to another of Suvin's central arguments, namely that the "academically most acceptable designation [for SF] has been that of a literature of utopian thought" (Suvin, 13). Utopianism, like imaginary technologies or fantastic settings, is a common feature of SF narratives, but utopianism also may be interpreted as an expression of hegemonic desire. Utopias insist internally on an overarching social order, and externally upon a rigorous exclusion of all members of a community that do not subscribe to that social order. The

satirical nature of Thomas Moore's Utopia should serve as a significant reminder that there are just as many dystopias as there are utopias.

6 As Peter Fitting points out in his analysis of the role of social Darwinism in SF narrative, "'organic analogies' and 'evolutionary schemes' are the result of an ideological choice rather than of a scientific understanding of human social behaviour" (Fitting, 184).

7 For more on the mission and content of these publications see Lee 2002, 142–155.

8 Personal communication, March 31, 2011.

9 See Du Bois, *The Souls of Black Folk* (1965), and Fanon, *The Wretched of the Earth* (1968) and *Black Skin, White Masks* (1967).

CHAPTER 2. LU XUN, SCIENCE, FICTION

1 In *Developmental Fairy Tales*, Andrew Jones offers an excellent summary of some of the allegorical readings of the iron house (36–37). See also Tang Tao, 82–94; Chow, 4–11; Hsia, 30–31. For the preface itself, see *LXQJ*, 1:437–443; for an English translation of the preface, Lu Xun 2006 (trans. Julia Lovell), 15–20.

2 For example, Zeng Pu's (1872–1935) pen name in *Niehai hua* is "The Sick Man of Asia" (Dongya Bingfu).

3 One important difference between Lu Xun's translation and many others was that he did apparently complete the work on his own. Most other works of SF were translated as team efforts, involving two to three people (Ren Dongsheng and Yuan Feng, 74–75).

4 Bao Tianxiao (1876–1973) was born in Jiangsu Province; he also wrote under the names Xiao, Tianxiao, and others. He attained the degree of *xiucai* at nineteen. He worked as an editor and writer for more than ten journals. In 1906, he went to work for the *Shanghai Times* (*Shanghai shibao*), as the editor of the supplement *Yuxing*. In 1931, he became editor of *Xiaoshuo huabao* at *Wenming shuju*, editor of *Xingqi* for *Dadong shuju*, and editor of *Nu xuesheng* at *Wenhua yinshua gongsi* (*Zhongguo jinxiandai renming da cidian*, 111; *Zhongguo jindai wenxue cidian*, 113).

5 Quoted in Takeda 1988, 46; for more on Xu Nianci and the purpose of SF see Ma, 56.

6 Quoted in Wang Shanping, 54; See also Chen Pingyuan and Xia Xiaohong 1997, 1:58–63. For more on the history of translations of SF from Japanese to Chinese see Takeda and Hayashi 2001, 45–72.

7 Kang Youwei (1858–1927) was a noted political theorist and reformer. Wei Leong Tay's "Kang Youwei, the Martin Luther of Confucianism and His Vision of Confucian Modernity and Nation" is an excellent intellectual biography.

8 A great deal of this passage and other translations and analysis of Lu Xun's early essays draws from Jon von Kowallis's unpublished translations of Lu Xun's early work and his personal communications, which I am eternally grateful for.

9 Readers interested in China's great wealth of scientific, mathematical, and technological achievement prior to the twentieth century should consult Joseph Needham's omnibus *Science and Civilization in China*. It is in part because these achievements were so significant that *Yangwu* thinking was sustainable until the late nineteenth century. However, China's defeat in the first Sino-Japanese War effectively overshadowed arguments for indigenous scientific traditions, cementing the perception that science was a purely Western possession.

10 The term first appeared in an index of Japanese books entitled *Riben shumu zhi*, published by Kang Youwei in 1897 (Qiu Ruohong, 63).

11 Like many of his contemporaries, Yan Fu (1854–1921) studied for the imperial examination in early life and then changed course after a family tragedy. A year after the death of his father in 1866, Yan began study at the Fuzhou Arsenal Academy (Fuzhou chuanzheng xuetang), where he was introduced to Western science. Yan is perhaps most well known as the translator of T. H. Huxley's *Evolution and Ethics*, Adam Smith's *The Wealth of Nations*, John Stuart Mill's *On Liberty*, and Herbert Spencer's *Study of Sociology*. See Schwarz 1964.

12 See also Pusey 1998, 2–7; Schwarz, 42–60.

13 Tsutomu's rendering of Verne's novel, *Getsukai ryokō*, was published in 1881. Tsutomu was one of a number of Meiji translators who brought Verne to a Japanese audience, having also translated Verne's *Cinq semaines en ballon* [*Five Weeks in a Balloon*, or, Ahirika naichi sanjūgo nichikan kūchū ryokō] and "Martin Paz." In the last two decades of the nineteenth century, he also published translations of Edward Bulwer-

Lytton's *Strange Stories*, Herbert Spencer's *New Thesis on Women*, Thomas Moore's *Utopia*, as well as *Arabian Nights*, *Robinson Crusoe*, and *The Merchant of Venice*.

14 Liu Hui argues that "at that time, translation and original writing were one and the same" (83).

15 The style is marked by the insertion of narrative commentaries that bookend chapters, reminding readers of what had recently occurred and entreating them to read on; the frequent insertion of verse to explain key events and emotional states; and the appending of a poetic coda to every chapter. These poems were written in the traditional tetra-, penta-, and hepta-syllabic forms and were no longer than a single quatrain. Gu Ming Dong refers to the *zhanghui xiaoshuo* as "the perfected narrative form that earlier forms of narrative—myths, legends, literary anecdotes, folktales, personal biographies, narrative short stories, etc.—have striven to become" (Gu, 62). Liu Hui lists three key ways in which SF translators Sinified the original texts they were working with: (1) adoption of traditional narrative modes, including the *zhanghui* form (as discussed above) and use of conventional phrases that suggest an oral narrator of the story; (2) use of a third-person omniscient narrator (for example, the narrator in Lu Xun's translation is changed from the first-person narration of Pierre Arronax to an omniscient narrator; (3) the Sinification of names and customs, such as eating habits (84–85).

16 For an English translation of the text and a brief biographical sketch of Hu Shi see DeBary and Lufrano, 356–360.

17 *Guwen* is a polysemous term, referring to what are indeed a number of different writing styles spanning nearly two thousand years of literary history, whose main commonality is the notion that they represent a lost linguistic register that has been resurrected for the sake of sagely clarity. The term was first used to describe books purported to have survived the Qin bibliocaust. During the Sui dynasty, it referred to Zhou, Qin, and Han texts. During the Tang, *guwen* was a new prose genre modeled on the style of these old texts. Theoretically, this meant Han and pre-Han-style prose. Han Yu and Liu Zongyuan were the two strongest advocates of this form, hoping the style would replace the parallel prose dominant in official writing. The reform of literary style was to be accompanied by a reinvigoration of classical Confucian principles. In later eras the term

referred to nonparallel, straightforward prose dealing with a single sub-ject that had a moral purpose (Nienhauser, 494–500).

18 This is a paraphrasing of a passage from the opening chapter of the *Zhuangzi*. See *Zhuangzi*, 1:1; and Zhuangzi 1968 (trans. Watson), 30. Watson's introduction to the text provides an excellent overview of Zhuangzi and his philosophy. For another summary of Zhuangzi and his relationship to Daoist philosophy in general see also DeBary and Bloom, 1:77–111.

19 "On Imbalanced Cultural Development" features an extended philo-sophical biography of Nietzsche (*LXQJ*, 1:50–55; Kowallis, forthcom-ing).

20 Viren Murthy notes that from 1865 on, Chinese intellectuals and offi-cials saw the solution to the crisis of nation-building in terms of the de-velopment of modern bureaucracy and technology (Murthy, 51).

21 See also Lu Xun 2009, *Lu Xun zhu yi bian nian quanji*, 27–28. All translations of the preface to Lu Xun's translation of *From the Earth to the Moon* and "Lessons" are my own, although they are made in refer-ence to the *baihua* translation of these articles in *Lu Xun yu ziran Ke-xue* and to Andrew Jones's translations of key passages in *Developmen-tal Fairy Tales*.

22 For more on Lu Xun's profound sense of pessimism and linguistic crisis see Huters 2005, 252–274.

23 Borrowing from Alan Rauch's analysis of the "knowledge industry" (2001), Andrew Jones refers to such texts as "knowledge texts," works including encyclopedias, handbooks, and other comprehensive works that mirrored institutions such as libraries, museums, botanical gar-dens, and zoos in their indexical presentation based on a clear set of organizational principles (Jones 2011, 42–43).

24 My analysis of these three essays owes a great debt to the annotated translations of Jon von Kowallis. I have acknowledged this when any passage is cited specifically, but without his careful scholarship I would have been groping in the dark trying to understand these essays.

25 Haeckel's faith in racial inequality went so far as to lead him to believe that the "lowest races were hardly distinguishable from simians." For this reason and others, Larry Arnhart has argued that Haeckel was "the true founder of the intellectual tradition that gave birth to Hitler

and National Socialism" (Arnhart, 117). What is more striking about Lu Xun's evolutionary epic is what is absent from his history of Haeckel's thought: creationist polygenism. Haeckel was a proponent of the notion that human racial difference could be explained by origins in separate species. The translation of Haeckel's evolutionary chart that Lu Xun includes in his translation goes as far as to differentiate primates and *Homo sapiens*, but it does not go as far as Haeckel's ideas of scientific racism. Darwin did not accept this notion, but the issue is elided entirely in Lu Xun's treatment of evolution and the history of evolutionary thought.

26 Rapid urbanization brought new configurations of social life, necessitating a number of transformations in social protocol, many of which were understood to be subject to conscious intervention. Techniques of behavior management, developed in museums, exhibitions, and department stores, were later incorporated in amusement parks, whose design aimed to reconfigure the fair as a sphere of regulation. Tony Bennett notes that early museums were also "characterized by their proscription of codes of behavior associated with places of popular assembly—fairs, taverns, inns, and so forth. No swearing, no spitting, no brawling, no eating or drinking [etc.]" (Bennett, 27). Relations of space and vision were intentionally designed have a moral influence, compelling the audience to self-regulation. Museum construction was part of a utopian vision of architecture as a "moral science"; Bennett likens the physical layout of museum buildings to that of the panopticon: a conspicuously visible space that shapes its subjects' behavior with the potential for surveillance. One way in which museums helped to regulate the behavior of viewers was by presenting objects in open spaces where one's behavior was subject to the gaze (and reproach) of other museumgoers. Beyond putting objects on display, the structure of the museum renders the crowd visible as well, both to museum staff and to other visitors (Bennett, 48, 68).

27 James Pusey has argued that Lu Xun's own rhetoric of Darwinian struggle and confessions of fears that China would be "eliminated by the cosmic process" were political bombast. Pusey observes that actually extinguishing the entire Chinese nation and all its inhabitants from the face of the earth would have been impossible (Pusey 1998, 16). While it

is perhaps unwise to take Lu Xun's rhetoric literally, the sense of crisis in the face of cultural loss was very real.

CHAPTER 3. WU JIANREN AND LATE QING SF

1 The first eleven chapters appeared in the journal *Nanfang bao* (Southern news) between August and December of 1905. The entire forty-chapter novel with accompanying illustrations, titled *Illustrated New Story of the Stone* (*Huitu xin shitou ji*), was first printed in 1908 (Wu Yan 2011, 242).

2 Nüwa (aka Nü Gua) is occasionally referenced in mythology as the creator of human beings, worshipped during the Han dynasty as a goddess of fertility and appearing in a number of early philosophical and mythic traditions. Her status as a civilizing force and cultural innovator who helps tame the forces of nature (especially through agriculture) and restore order is as prominent as her status as creator (Lewis, 110–133).

3 Wu Bohui's name is a homonym for "nothing he cannot do."

4 Xue Pan's first appearance in *Story of the Stone* centers on his murdering a man and then bribing a judge to have the case dismissed.

5 This situation was a symptom of colonial modernity worldwide, not merely limited to China. As Dikötter notes, "Dominant groups in Asia, Africa and South America believed that modernity had to be brought home in order to propel one's country into the universe of 'civilized' nations and join a universal march towards a better future. 'Foreign' stood for 'modern' as Europe was viewed as the fountainhead of a new world of progress." Terms like "ingenious" or "exquisite" (*qiqiao*) "became inextricably linked to foreign goods" (Dikötter 2006, 27).

6 New objects and the expanded availability of familiar objects as a result of mass production also carried the potential to reinforce, rather than displace, traditional ideas regarding cosmology and society as new epistemologies did. Geomantic and folk beliefs became more visible, and their practice more broadly accessible as once-scarce objects associated with their practice saturated local markets. Dikötter notes, "Mass production of the mirror in the republican era, to take but one example, consolidated rather than displaced cosmological conceptions about spiritual forces, as cheap mirrors were placed outside the door to keep malign spirits from entering the house" (2006, 10). Hierarchies previ-

ously naturalized under the rubrics of cosmological-spiritual order were reified under the rubric of empirical rationality. As Dikötter has argued both in *The Discourse of Race in Modern China* and in *Sex, Culture and Modernity in China*, in many respects science was appropriated as an instrument through which native discourses of racial uniqueness and sexual differentiation, originally phrased in terms of Confucian morality and correlative cosmology, were made "modern," "Western," and "logical" as well. Notions of gendered difference previously framed in terms of *yin/yang* were rephrased in terms of quantitative and qualitative difference, but the set of essential categories that defined these differences remained the same in both discourses (Dikötter 1995, 14–61).

7   To take a contemporary example from the United States, one may purchase a computer whose chips were made in Taiwan and which was assembled in a sweatshop in Shenzhen. The computer company is a transnational corporation with headquarters in Japan, and the global chain where the computer was purchased has invested more capital in Washington to deteriorate environmental and labor laws than it has in health care for local workers. To the extent that a consumer is aware of such considerations of capital, he or she may feel very angry about the situation, but price and necessity are powerful forces in helping consumers forgo concerns of economic nationalism.

8   Lit. "Old Youth."

9   The Realm of Civilization fits the model of what Csicsery-Ronay defines as "future history"—Wu's narrative makes clear that it is a place with its own historical teleology. While it is temporally and spatially at an oblique angle to the real China, the material and intellectual developments there are the fruit of an independent developmental schema (Csicsery-Ronay 2008, 76–110).

10 Andrew Jones has written at length about Wu Jianren's relationship to the iron house metaphor as well, suggesting that the motif comes from the translation of Edward Bellamy's 1888 novel *Looking Backward* (2011, 31–51). Biheguan zhuren's (1871–1919) *The New Era* (*Xin jiyuan*, 1908), the story of a battle between China and Europe over whether to adopt the Gregorian calendar, features an iron house by a slightly different name (*tie fangzi*), invented by a French scientist named Michael (Maike). The device causes those shut inside to simultaneously freeze to

death and suffocate. Conveniently placed where Chinese troops come ashore along the Suez Canal, this iron house again prefigures Lu Xun's iconic metaphor. In the penultimate battle, the nephew of Chinese general Huang Zhisheng (lit. "Flourishing of the Yellow [race]"), Jin Jingwei, and his squadron of soldiers chase a group of enemy soldiers ashore and come upon the iron house. Once inside, they find themselves trapped and begin getting colder and short of breath as a pipe in the ceiling extracts the air from the room. They devise a method of sealing the pipe with their army fatigues and are rescued shortly after by their fellows outside the iron house. Contrary to Lu Xun's allegory, this iron house is clearly the work of foreign powers, and the soldiers trapped inside are well aware of their plight, working actively to remedy their situation at the same time that a unified social body outside the house works to free them. This awareness leads to a solution, and the iron house is escaped. Thus, the iron house becomes a symbol of the Western world's inability to contain China, rather than a symbol of China's domestic psychological illness, putting an optimistic turn on a very familiar metaphor.

11 The "Symptom," defined by Slavoj Zizek in *The Sublime Object of Ideology* as a physical or psychological ailment that becomes a defining characteristic of one's subjectivity, is one of the most prevalent tropes of modern Chinese literature. See Žižek, 1–94. On physical and psychological trauma in modern Chinese literature see David Der-wei Wang 2004; Ban Wang 2004; Braester 2003; and Berry 2008.

12 For the passage in context see Mencius, 148; Mengzi, 905–906.

13 Csicsery-Ronay devotes significant effort (an entire chapter) to a discussion of what he refers to as "fictive neology": the estranging vocabularies of SF that are meant to evoke entire histories, social structures, and technologies of alternate worlds. In Wu Jianren's case and in the case of many other works of late Qing SF, the strongest attention to the language of utopias and the future is devoted to describing what features of language have been lost, rather than how language has transformed or emerged (Csicsery-Ronay 2008, 13–46). Wu's *Xin shitou ji* uses characteristically classical grammar and wording, especially in the second half of the novel, when Jia Baoyu has entered the techno-utopic "Realm of Civilization."

14 Frank McConnell argues that the absence of food is a distinguishing

characteristic of SF, and when food is present, it is often as a pill or some other similarly unpalatable concoction—alimentation rather than gastronomic pleasure. To this, Gary Westfahl adds that food in science fiction most closely resembles hospital food. "That is, if we are living today in a 'sick society,' the solution, then, is to establish a hospital society. And as one consequence, the typical future civilization, like a hospital, offers food as an aspect of medical treatment: it is wholesome, nutritious and awful" (Westfahl 1996, 213–223). See also ibid., 200–212.

15 As David Der-Wei Wang and Song Mingwei have noted, a similar rupture appears in Liang Qichao's *The Future of New China* (*Xin Zhongguo weilai ji*, 1902), a utopian future-history of Chinese political reform. While the novel portrays a "splendidly idealized future" (Song Mingwei, 89), the means by which utopia has been attained are omitted from the unfinished novel (Wang, 304).

16 This is a paraphrase of Inderpal Grewal, who writes, "The British Museum was an imperial project because it embodied a love of order, and an attempt to domesticate the unknown through this ordering" (Grewal, 44–57).

17 Already we are seeing hints that another work of early Chinese myth is about to be proven a matter of historical fact. The mermen are a clear allusion to the text of the *Shanhai jing*: "200 *li* farther northeast stands Dragon-Marquis Mountain. There are no plants or trees here, though much metal and jade. The Bursting River emanates here and flows eastward into the Yellow River. In it dwell many Human-Fish. They resemble catfish with four legs and make a sound like a baby. Eating it will cure idiocy" (Strassberg, 130; *Shanhai jing*, 3:3).

18 Lao Shaonian demonstrates his taxonomic expertise by quoting the following passage: "The *Peng* River emanates from Belt-Mountain, and flows into Hidden-Lake River. In it dwell many *Shu-fish*. The *Shu-fish's* form resembles a chicken, but with red feathers, three tails, six feet and four heads. It makes a sound like a magpie. Eating it will cure melancholy" (Strassberg, 119; *Shanhai jing*, 3:3).

19 Exhibitions were also used in the promotion of economic nationalism. The Nanyang Industrial Exposition (Nanyang quanyehui) of 1910 and other similar exhibitions throughout the Republican period were meant to demonstrate state commitment to industrial modernization. These

exhibitions dedicated significant effort to identifying products that were particularly good imitations of foreign goods. One entire week of the Nanjing exhibition of 1910 was dedicated to the subject of aviation (Dikötter 2006, 10–12, 104).

20 For more on the history of the Jiangnan Arsenal see Elman 2006; David Wright 1998, 661–664; and Yue, 7–13, 23–26.

21 China's imperial collection was most likely established during the Song dynasty, but the contents of the collection and efforts at acquisition waxed and waned throughout the imperial period. The collection also delineated the connection between ruling emperors and their Shang and Zhou predecessors (Watson, 9–10). After 1949, claims to political legitimacy on the part of Taiwan and mainland China were centered on the issue of national museums and their collections (Hamlish, 20–28).

22 While there are clearly vast differences between the taxonomical mission of encyclopedias and compendia, quotation of the *Shijing* was a key element of the construction of Confucian textual authority and in diplomatic exchange and negotiation in early China (Lewis, 148–176).

CHAPTER 4. SF FOR THE NATION

1 A version of this chapter appeared in the March 2013 issue of *Science Fiction Studies*, a special issue dedicated to Chinese SF. The work was originally intended to be a novel but was never finished, having been cut off at the end of chapter 35. All passages appearing here are my own translations.

2 Hsieh translates this phrase as "rotten literati"; the term is a clear reference to the *Xunzi* chapter "Contra Physiognomy" (*Xunzi* 5:8) where Xunzi writes: "Hence, the [*Book of*] *Changes* says: 'a tied sack, nothing to blame, nothing to praise, this describes the corrupt Ru'" (Xunzi 1988 [trans. Knoblock], 208).

3 Dong Zhongshu was a Han dynasty scholar and adviser to the royal throne. Dong, among others, helped to construct a Confucian orthodoxy based on correlative associations between the natural world and statecraft. His essay "Comprehending the State as the Body" correlates the maintenance of physical health with that of the vitality of the state (DeBary and Bloom, 292–297).

4 The "international community" and the ban on the use of chemical

weapons referred to in this passage is most likely the 1899 Hague Peace Conference, which laid the foundation for the establishment of the League of Nations in 1919 in the wake of World War I. Officially, chlorine gas was not used in war until World War I; it was used experimentally and in small quantities by French troops in 1914, and the first major gas attack was launched by Germany at the battle of Ypres on April 22, 1915 (Trumpener, 460–468). However, it appears that this is a matter of semantics, as chlorine gas was used in the Eight Nation Alliance attack on Tianjin in reprisal for the Boxer Rebellion in June of 1900. An entry on the Eight Nation Alliance in the *Qingchao yeshi daguan* reads: "In June, a great attack was carried out on Tianjin. [Generals] Ma Yukun [1838–1908] and Nie Shicheng [1836–1900] fought bitterly for three days. The English troops used chlorine gas bombs in their onslaught. Resistance was futile and Tianjin was soon taken. Chlorine gas is among the most poisonous of chemical agents. Chlorine gas bombs are devastating. The cerebral nerves of a man who comes into contact with it will die instantly. Within a hundred paces [of the blast], there will be no survivors. It has been banned in the era of civilized warfare. To this day, the English have only tried it in Tianjin. Because they saw the Boxer Uprising as an uncivilized movement, they too used uncivilized means in response" (Xiaoheng Xiangshi Zhuren, 4:158–159). For more on the history of attempts to prohibit the use of chemical weapons in war see Levie, 1192–1202.

5 For a comprehensive treatment of the impact of changing perceptions of time and space in the cultural sphere in the West around the turn of the twentieth century see Kern 1983.

6 The *tiangan dizhi* system, also known as the *ganzhi* cycle, "is one of two counting systems used in Chinese culture, the other being decimal. The cycle was formed by combining two sets of counters, one denary and the other duodenary to form 60 unique combinations." These characters, which appear in Shang dynasty (1200–1045 BCE) oracle-bone script, were used to calculate most basic units of time—hours, days, weeks, months, and years (E. Wilkinson, 175).

7 For a thorough treatment of the theme of alien invasion see Csicsery-Ronay 2003 and Kerslake 2007.

CHAPTER 5. MAKING ROOM FOR SCIENCE

1 Xu Nianci was born in Changshu, Jiangsu Province, and also wrote under the names Juewo and Donghai juewo. He mastered Japanese at a young age and also excelled in mathematics and writing. Around 1898 he became involved in the "new studies" movement (*xinxue chaoliu*) and went to work for the China Education Society (Zhongguo jiaoyu hui). He was an active translator and writer, known for mastery of a number of different literary styles and registers. He has also been recognized for his interest in modernism, realism, and Hegelian aesthetics, having published a number of works on the subject, including "My Outlook on Fiction" ("Yu zhi xiaoshuo guan") (*Zhongguo jindai wenxue cidian*, 383; *Zhongguo jinxiandai renming dacidian*, 572).

2 Iwaya Sazanami (1870–1933) helped create the magazine *Shōnen sekkai*, one of the first Japanese-language children's magazines, and is best known for compiling and printing Japanese folktales. He is particularly well known for his 1894 retelling of "Momotarō" ("The Peach Boy"). Although these stories were aimed at a juvenile audience, David Henry notes that stories like "Momotarō" "functioned as an allegory supporting particularly Japanese ideas of empire" (Henry, 218).

3 Takeda notes that Xu Nianci also published translations of work by Jules Verne. See also Ma, 55.

4 Xu Nianci appears to have been inspired by both Iwaya Sazanami and Inoue Tsutomu (the Japanese translator of Verne's *De la terre à la lune*), who were in turn inspired by Johann Wolfgang von Goethe's vision of "a fuller integration of poetic and scientific sensibilities that would provide a way of experiencing nature both symbolically and scientifically, simultaneously" (Goethe 2009, xi [Miller introduction]). See Xu Nianci, "Yu zhi xiaoshuo guan" (My outlook on fiction), in *Xiaoshuo lin*, 9:1–8, 10: 19–15 (page numbering is continuous; individual articles in each issue have their own numbering).

5 See Nienhauser, 494–500.

6 See also Takeda 1988, 445; and Luan, 47.

7 See, for example, a discussion of whether the brain is equivalent to the soul in an explication of the brain's function in the human body appearing in *Xia'er guan zhen* in 1855 (6:23). Discourses on the soul and Christian salvation featured regularly in *Jiaohui xinbao* (Church news

[1868–1875]; later known as *Wan guo gong bao* [1876–1907]) alongside translations of passages from the Bible, but scientific treatises well outnumbered Christian content in the journal. For more on the content of Christian journals like *Jiaohui xinbao*, featuring more scientific and technical content than religious content, see Qiu Ruohong, 26.

8 See Zhuangzi 2001, 1–18; Zhuangzi 1968 (trans. Watson), 30.

9 This famous "debate" in Confucian philosophy centers on the question of whether human nature was inherently good or evil. In *Mencius*, Gaozi argues unconvincingly against his mentor that human nature is neutral (Mengzi, 731–733; 6A.1). Xunzi, on the other hand, argues that man's nature is "evil" (*e*) (*Xunzi jijie*, 434–448; *juan*, 23). For English translations and further summary of the debate see DeBary and Bloom, 114–118, or Eric L. Hutton's translation of the *Xunzi* (2014) and Irene Bloom's 2009 translation of the *Mencius*.

10 Mr. Braggadocio's return to Earth and the reuniting of his corporeal and spiritual selves in the Mediterranean sees him rescued from drowning by the leaders of a vast and newly formed Chinese navy on a mission to restore China to her past glory, though they disappear entirely from the narrative upon reaching Shanghai, gone from the plot as rapidly as they found their way into it. This halfhearted gesture toward imagining a militarily superior Chinese nation-state resonates with the dream narrative analyzed in chapter 4 above and in other novels like Liang Qichao's *Xin Zhongguo weilai ji*, Lu Shi'e's *Xin Zhongguo* (1910), and Xiaoran Yusheng's *Journey to Utopia* (*Wutuobang youji*, 1906) that could only couch their fantasies of a geopolitically ascendant China in terms of dream narrative.

11 For more on the relationship between mesmerism, the Catholic Church, and scientific practice in France in the eighteenth and nineteenth centuries see John Warne Monroe, *Laboratories of Faith: Mesmerism, Spiritism, and Occultism in Modern France* (2008). Barbara Goldsmith's *Other Powers: The Age of Suffrage, Spiritualism, and the Scandalous Victoria Woodhull* (1998) is a fascinating account of the role of these practices in the women's suffrage movement in the wake of the U.S. Civil War.

12 For more on Tan Sitong's theories of ether and the study of chemistry see Qiu Ruohong, 78–79.

13 Tao Chengzhang published his translation on mesmerism in collaboration with Cai Yuanpei, *Cuimianshu jiangyi*, at roughly the same time (Takeda and Hayashi 2008, 87). See also Cai Yuanpei (1906).

14 Antonio Gramsci's "Americanism and Fordism" offers a concise history of the relationship between rationalized production and its political and cultural repercussions in the United States and Western Europe (Gramsci, 275–299).

15 For a detailed account of Everest's naming, early attempts to survey the peak, and the relationship between George Leigh Mallory's first ascent of the mountain and the British imperial project see Davis 2012. On initial surveys and attempts to reach Everest see also Krakauer 1997. On attempts to reach the North Pole in a hot-air balloon see A. Wilkinson 2011.

CHAPTER 6. LAO SHE'S CITY OF CATS

1 Lao She is the pen name of Shi Qingchun. He was born in Beijing to a poor family, and his father was a soldier who was killed when the Eight Nation Alliance forces attacked Beijing in reprisal during the Boxer Rebellion. He would go on to become one of the greatest figures of modern Chinese literature and is best known for his novel *Rickshaw Boy* (*Luoto xiangzi*, 1936), a tragedy about a rickshaw puller, and his play *Teahouse* (*Chaguan*, 1957), both of which make extensive use of Beijing dialect. Below, I detail some of the key midlife experiences that influenced *Cat Country*. It bears noting here that during the Cultural Revolution, Lao She was labeled a counterrevolutionary and beaten by Red Guards, which led to his suicide in 1966. The author and his work were "rehabilitated" in 1978, but *Cat Country* has largely been ignored as part of his legacy.

2 All quotations cite the 2008 Chinese reprint first and the 1970 edition of Lyell's translation second. Both are accurate and more easily accessible versions of the original editions.

3 On the evolving outlook on social Darwinism during the Republican period see Spence, 300–305.

4 *Cat Country*, 1970, 36 (translator's footnote). Guan Jixin argues that the novel is a "cultural allegory" (*wenhua fengyu xiaoshuo*) rather than a "governmental satire" (*zhengzhi fengce xiaoshuo*) because of the de-

gree to which the story is a critique of all aspects of Chinese culture, not just its failing leadership (169). For more on the allegorical content of the novel see Hsia, 165–168, 546. I have made extensive use of William Lyell's translation of *Cat Country*, although in many cases, for the sake of rendering the original Chinese clearer (thus diminishing the literary quality of Lyell's English rendering), my translations differ significantly from Lyell's.

5 See Rojas 2002.

6 Japanese scholars have identified this passage and other repeated references to "writing on the wall" and to fingers as allusions to the biblical book of Daniel (Guan Jixin, 173).

CHAPTER 7. WHITHER SF / WITHER SF

1 See Wu Yan 2011, 11, 233–236, and Han Song 2013, 15–16.

2 While David Der-Wei Wang identifies *Dang kouzhi* (*Quelling the Bandits*, 1853) as an example of "science fantasy," the work is not included in Wu Yan's SF chronology, which identifies Liang Qichao's unfinished utopian work *Xin Zhongguo weilai ji* as the first work of Chinese SF. Wu Yan identifies only four translated SF texts between 1871 and 1900 (D. D. Wang 1997, 252–297; Wu Yan 2011, 240–267).

3 The *Kangxi zidian* (1716) was an imperially commissioned dictionary, containing over forty-seven thousand characters. Until the early twentieth century it was the most comprehensive Chinese dictionary, meant to demonstrate the throne's interest in Confucian culture, and moreover "an expression of government through script unification" (E. Wilkinson, 80). The *Gujin tushu jicheng* (Comprehensive corpus of illustrations and books, from ancient times to the present) was a Qing dynasty, imperially authorized collection originally compiled by Cheng Menglei (1669–1732) in 1726–1728 whose title should make the contents and the work's relationship to China's emergent knowledge industry apparent (E. Wilkinson, 955–960).

4 For more on Wu Youru see Wagner, 127–129.

5 For example, the inaugural issue contains the following illustrations: two depictions of the Sino-French battles at Beining; an illustration of a submarine; a depiction of a hot-air balloon-cum-boat; a demonstration of naval mines in Jiangsu; the collapse of a bridge in Shanghai that oc-

curred when a crowd gathered to watch firefighters deal with a fire; an inquest into the suicide of a brothel patron in Suzhou; and the story of a filial son who cut out his own liver in order to save his father from illness (Wu Youru, vol. 1, plates 1–8).

6 Takeda Masaya's *Tobe!* (and the Chinese translation *Feixiang ba!*) is an extensive study of late Qing visual culture, especially images pertaining to science and pseudoscience. As such, it examines a number of images that appeared in *Dianshizhai huabao*.

7 The publishers at Shenbao also engaged in printing other media arguably belonging to China's premodern "knowledge industry" culture, reproducing works like the *Kangxi zidian* and the *Gujin tushu jicheng* (Huntington, 347).

8 Dikötter also notes: "In a global frame of reference in which emulation and competition led to ever shifting standards, innovations and expectations, museums were established to inspire confidence in the local ability to contribute to the modern: traditional skills and legendary workmanship, organizers believed, could easily be transferred to the production of modern items. . . . In 1927 the Ministry of Industry and Commerce even required that each province and every city should promote national goods by establishing a museum" (Dikötter 2006, 66).

9 Fryer 1892. An online, real-time simulation of the exhibition site, coordinated by Daniel Burham and Lisa M. Snyder, whose expanding database includes virtual tours of the grounds, images from the exhibition, and other published materials is at http://www.ust.ucla.edu/ustweb /Projects/columbian_expo.htm. Viren Murthy notes that Fryer is one of the most (if not the most) important figures in late Qing translation (Murthy, 55; see also Qiu Ruhong, 27).

10 The opening pages also include English and Chinese-language titles of a series of books on science and scientific implements and their respective prices, and direct potential buyers to the Chinese Scientific Book Depot on Hankow Road in Shanghai.

11 Qin Shao notes that "one of the distinct marks of [China's] new era has been the tremendous energy and resources invested in exhibitory institutions and activities, as demonstrated in the national zeal for China to host the 2008 Olympics and the 2010 World Expo" (Qin Shao, 684).

12 See *Shanhai jing*, 12:6; see also Strassberg, 204 (plate LXII.292).

13 The *Liezi* is a Daoist text attributed to Lie Yukou, c. fourth–fifth century BCE. See Barrett, 298–308. See also Liezi 1990 (trans. Graham).

14 Song Mingwei notes two instances of cannibalism / recycling human flesh in his analysis of the work of Han Song (Song Mingwei, 94).

15 In the wake of their defeat in the Boxer Rebellion, the Qing dynasty was ordered to pay, over the course of thirty-nine years, an indemnity of 450 million taels of silver to the Eight Nation Alliance that had quelled the rebellion (Austria-Hungary, Great Britain, Germany, France, Italy, Japan, Russia, and the United States). In 1908, the United States committed a large portion of these payments to funding Chinese students studying in America (Spence, 235, 283).

16 Z. Wang, 302–305. The Science Society's new headquarters was soon followed by the local establishment of other similar institutions. The year 1922 saw the founding of the Biological Institute of the Science Society, complete with resident researchers and laboratories, the first private scientific research institution in China established and run by Chinese scientists. By this time, the society also operated a printing press, a scientific books and implements company, and two science libraries, in Nanjing and Shanghai (Z. Wang, 311–317).

17 See *Xin qingnian*, 1915, 1:2; *Kexue*, 1915, 1:10. See also Cheng Min, 9. The tone of scientific nationalism of Chinese scientists echoes the members of the Royal Asiatic Society, at whose inaugural meeting science was seen as the answer to the question "Shall the great contest, to which the nations seem to be here hastening on, be one of mere physical force or one of intellectual power?" (Claypool, 575).

18 As a number of works covering the question of the debate on science and the outlook on life, and on the question of scientism in Republican China, have already been published in English, I have chosen to leave my analysis of this debate to the summation above. For a full text of the debate as published in *Kexue* see *Kexue yu rensheng guan*, 1927. For more analysis of the debate see Furth 1970; Kwok 1965; and G. Yang, 79–95.

19 Min also lists the five following forms of scientific writing, which he identifies as separate from the *kexue xiaopin*: children's science stories (*kexue tonghua*), science-poetry (*kexue shi*), science cross-talk (*kexue xiangsheng*), and science fables (*kexue yuyan*). In 1929, Hu Shi and

Zhao cowrote music and lyrics for a Science Society anthem, emphasizing the practical use of science and the joy of the pursuit of scientific knowledge (Cheng Min, 18–20). See also Z. Wang, 304. This subset of Chinese science writing is easily worthy of its own specific study, especially in examining the relationship between scientific writing and the leftist movement of the 1930s and '40s. See, for example, *Er Tong Ke Xue Wen Yi Zuo Pin Xuan* (1986) and *Zhongguo kexue wenyi daxi* (1999).

20 Mao Dun, "Wenyi dazhonghua de taolun ji qita," 34:558 (quoted in Cheng Min, 42).

21 See Mao Dun, "Kexue he lishi de xiaopin," 437–438; and Liu Shi, 8–10.

22 See *Zhongguo kexue wenyi daxi* (1999).

CONCLUSION

1 The image of a "lost good hell" is again a topic of extended conversation in Chan Koonchong's dystopian alternate future of China, *The Fat Years: China 2013* (*Shengshi: Zhongguo 2013* [2009]).

GLOSSARY OF CHINESE TERMS

Ailuo bunao zhi 艾羅補腦汁
Aipolaisi 哀波來斯
bagu wen 八股文
baihua 白話
bangxian wenxue 幫閑文學
Bao Tianxiao (1876–1973) 包天笑
Bei Ming 焙茗
Biheguan zhuren (1871–1919) 碧荷
　管主人
biji 筆記
Bowuyuan lu 博物園路
Bowuzhi 博物志
boxue 博學
Cai Yuanpei (1868–1940) 蔡元培
Cao Xueqin (1715–1763) 曹雪芹
Cao Zhao (14th C.) 曹昭
Chen bao 晨報
Chen Wangdao (1891–1977) 陳望道
Cheng Hao (1032–1085) 程顥
Cheng Yi (1033–1107) 程頤
"Chengke yu chuangzaozhe" 乘客與
　創造者
chouru 臭儒
chuanqi 傳奇
chuanqiti xiaoshuo 傳奇體小說
cuimianshu 催眠術
cuimianshu jiangyi 催眠術講義
Da xue 大學
Dadong shuju 大東書局
Dajia fusiji 大家夫斯基
Dalu bao 大陸報

dao 盜
Datong shu 大同書
delüfeng 德律風
Dianshizhai huabao 點石齋畫報
Ding Wenjiang (1887–1936) 丁文江
dongwu ciqixue 動物磁氣學
dongya bingfu 東亞病夫
doupeng xianhua 豆棚閑話
duanpian xiaoshuo 短篇小說
duo shi yu niaoshou caomu zhi
　ming 多識於鳥獸草木之名
Fei Dao 飛氛
Feiyingge huabao 飛影閣畫報
fugu 復古
Fujita Tamataro 藤田玉太郎
Fuzhou chuanzheng xuetang 福州
　船政學堂
gaizao guomin xing 改造國民性
Gaozi (c. 420–350 BCE) 告子
Gegu [yao] lun 格古要論
genbun-itchi 言文一致
Getsukai ryokō 月界旅行
gewu zhizhi 格物致知
gezhi 格致
Gezhi huibian 格致滙編
Guang guo 光國
guanhua 官話
Gujin tushu jicheng 古金圖書集成
Guo Liancheng (19th C.) 郭連城
guomin xiaoshuo 國民小說
guwen 古文

haima 海馬

Haitian Duxiaozi 海天獨孝子

Han Yu (768–824) 韓愈

Hong lou meng 紅樓夢

Hu Shi (1891–1962) 胡適

huaji xiaoshuo 滑稽小說

Huang Zhongzu 黃種族

Huangjiang Diaosou (b. ?) 黃江釣叟

Huayi huamu niaoshou zhenwan kao 華夷花木鳥獸珍玩考

Huitou kan 回頭看

hun 魂

Inoue Tsutomu 井上勤

Iwaya Sazanami (1870–1933) 嚴谷小波

Jia Baoyu 賈寶玉

Jia Xiyi 賈西依

Jia Zuzhang (1901–1988) 賈祖璋

jian 姦

Jiang Jieshi (Chiang Kai-shek, 1887–1975) 蔣介石

Jiaxing 嘉興

Jimmu tennō 神武天皇

jingying 晶瑩

jipi dongwu 棘皮動物

Juewo 覺我

junshi xiaoshuo 軍事笑說

juren 舉人

kagaku 科学

Kaitong huabao 開通畫報

Kang Youwei (1858–1927) 康有為

kepu sanwen 科普散文

kepu wei zhu, zhuanye wei bu 科普為主，專業為補

kexue 科學

kexue shi 科學詩

"Kexue shi jiao pian" 科學史教篇

kexue tonghua 科學童話

kexue xiangsheng 科學相聲

kexue xiaopin 科學小品

kexue xiaoshuo 科學小說

kexue yu rensheng guan 科學與人生觀

Kexue zazhi 科學雜誌

Kuangren riji 狂人日記

kun 鯤

Lao shaonian 老少年

Lao She (1899–1966) 老舍

Le'erlaifu 勒兒來復

Li Jingshan (19th C.) 李靜山

Liji 禮記

Liang Qichao (1873–1929) 梁啟超

Liang Zhangju (1775–1849) 梁章鉅

Liezi 列子

ling yu 陵魚

linghun zhi shen 靈魂之身

lishi xiaoshuo 歷史小說

Liu Shi (1903–1968) 柳湜

Liu Shipei (1884–1919) 劉師培

Liu Zongyuan (773–819) 柳宗元

Liuhe congtan 六合叢談

lixiang xiaoshuo 理想小說

lixue 理學

Long Menghua 龍孟華

Lu Shi'e (1878–1944) 陸士諤

Lu Xun 魯迅 (1876–1935)

lun huabao keyi qimeng 論畫報可以啟蒙

Mangzhong 芒種

Manyou suilu 漫遊隨錄

Manyou suilu tuji 漫遊隨錄圖記

Mao fusiji 貓夫斯基

Maocheng ji 貓城記

maoyan xiaoshuo 冒驗小說

Mazu daxian 馬祖大仙

Mengzi 孟子

mingming huangzu 冥冥黃族

Mingtang 明堂

miye 迷葉

"Moluo shi li shuo" 魔羅詩力說

Muhuade 慕華德

Nahan 吶喊

Nanfang bao 南方報

Nanyang quanye hui 南洋勸業會

naodian 腦電

Niao yu wenxue 鳥與文學

Niehai hua 孽海花

Nu xuesheng 女學生

Nüwa 女媧

peng 鵬

po 魄

"Po'esheng lun" 破惡聲論

Pu Yuhuan 濮玉環

Qimeng huabao 啟蒙畫報

qiming xing 啟明星

qiong chang dongwu 窮腸動物

qiongli zhi xue 窮理之學

qiqiao 奇巧

ququiao zhi shen 軀殼之身

ren ge 人格

Ren Hongjuan (1886–1961) 任鴻雋

"Ren zhi lishi" 人之歷史

Renmin ribao 人民日報

renshen quanti 人身全體

Riben shumu zhi 日本書目志

ruanti dongwu 軟體動物

Santi 三體

Santi II: hei senlin 三體 II 黑森林

Santi III: sishen yongsheng 三體 III: 死神永生

sanwen 散文

Shanghai bowuyuan 上海博物園

Shanghai shibao 上海時報

Shanhai jing 山海經

shehui xiaoshuo 社會小說

Shen Maoguan (16th C.) 慎懋官

Shenbao 申報

Shenbao guan 申報館

shewei xiangxu xuexiao 設為庠序學校

"Shidiao de haodiyu" 失掉的好地獄

Shijie mori ji 世界末日記

Shishi huabao 時事畫報

"Shiyun" 詩云

Shōsetsu 小說

shuyu 鯈魚

Sichang sha'er 司常煞兒

sui shuo yi, qishi nai gaizuo 雖說譯，其實乃改作

Suwen 素問

Taibai 太白

Tan Sitong (1865–1898) 譚嗣同

tanzhen xiaoshuo 探偵小說

Tao Chengzhang (1878–1912) 陶成章

ti 體

tiangan dizhi 天干地支

Tianxiao (See Bao Tianxiao)

tianyan 天演

Tianyan lun 天演論

tie fangzi 鐵房子

Tie shijie 鐵世界

tie wuzi 鐵屋子

Tongcheng 桐城
touguang jing 透光鏡
Tuhua ribao 圖畫日報
"Tunshizhe" 吞食者
tupu 圖譜
Wang Tao (1828–97) 王韜
Wanguo 萬國
Wei Yuan (1794–1857) 魏源
"Wenhua pianzhi lun" 文化偏至論
Wenhua yinshua gongsi 文化印刷公司
wenming 文明
Wenming jingjie 文明境界
Wenming shuju 文明書局
wenyan 文言
wenzi 文字
Wo foshan ren 我佛山人
wu 物
Wu Bohui 吳伯惠
wuli 物理
Wutuobang youji 烏托邦遊記
Xia'er guanzhen 遐邇貫珍
"Xiangcun jiaoshi" 鄉村教師
Xianglin Sao 祥林嫂
xiaopinwen 小品文
Xiaoran Yusheng (b. ?) 蕭然鬱生
xiaoshuo 小說
Xiaoshuo lin 小說林
xieqing xiaoshuo 寫情小說
Xin Xiaoshuo 新小說
Xin Zhongguo 新中國
Xin Zhongguo weilai ji 新中國未來記
Xingqi 興起
Xinmin congbao 新民叢報
Xinren 新人

xin xiaoshuo 新小說
xiucai 秀才
Xiuxiang xiaoshuo 繡像小說
Xue Fucheng (1838–1894) 薛福成
Xue Pan 薛蟠
Xunzi (3rd C. BCE) 荀子
xuwu xiaoshuo 虛無小說
Yan Fu (1854–1921) 嚴復
yan xingzhi 驗性質
Yang Jiyun (1910–1996) 楊霽雲
Yang Quan (1893–1933) 楊銓
yangwu 洋務
yaoguai xiaoshuo 妖怪小說
yeman 野蠻
yitai 以太
yong 用
Yu Lawu 魚拉伍
Yuan Shikai (1859–1916) 袁世凱
Yuanmingyuan lu 圓明園路
Yueqiu zhimindi xiaoshuo 月球殖民地小說
Yueyue xiaoshuo 月月小說
Yulinguo 魚鱗國
Yuxing 餘興
Yuzhou feng 宇宙風
zei 賊
zeishi xu 賊史序
Zeng Pu (1872–1935) 曾樸
zhajiti xiaoshuo 札記體小說
Zhang Hua (232–300) 張華
Zhang Junmai (Carsun Chang, 1886–1969) 張君勱
Zhang Taiyan (1868–1936) 章太炎
zhanghui xiaoshuo 章回小說
Zhao Yuanren (1892–1982) 趙元任
zheli kexue xiaoshuo 哲理科學小說

zheli xiaoshuo 哲理小說

Zheng Guanying (1842–1922)
鄭觀應

zhengzhi xiaoshuo 政治小說

zhiguai 志怪

Zhongguo kexue she 中國科學社

Zhongxue wei ti xixue wei young
中學為體西學為用

"Zhu fu" 祝福

Zhu Kezhen (1890–1974) 竺可楨

Zhu Xi (1130–1200) 朱熹

Zhuangzi (4th C. BCE) 莊子

Ziran lishi bowuyuan 自然歷史博
物園

ziyoutan 自由談

BIBLIOGRAPHY

Alkon, Paul. "Cannibalism in Science Fiction." In *Food of the Gods: Eating and the Eaten in Fantasy and Science Fiction*, edited by Gary Westfahl, George Slusser, and Eric S. Rabkin, 142–159. Athens: University of Georgia Press, 1996.

Altman, Rick. *Film/Genre*. London: British Film Institute, 1999.

———. "A Semantic/Syntactic Approach to Film Genre." *Cinema Journal* 23.3 (Spring 1984): 6–18.

Amelung, Iwo. "Naming Physics: The Strife to Delineate a Field of Modern Science in Late Imperial China." In *Mapping Meanings: The Field of New Learning in Late Qing China*, edited by Michael Lackner and Natasha Vittinghoff, 381–422. Leiden: Brill Academic, 2004.

———. "New Maps for the Modernizing State: Western Cartographic Knowledge and Its Application in 19th and 20th Century China." In *Graphics and Text in the Production of Technical Knowledge in China: The Warp and the Weft*, edited by Francesca Bray, Vera Dorofeeva-Lichtman, and Georges Métailé, 685–726. Leiden: Brill, 2007.

Anderson, Benedict. *Imagined Communities: Reflections on the Origin and Spread of Nationalism*. New York: Verso, 2006.

Anderson, Marston. *The Limits of Realism: Chinese Fiction in the Revolutionary Period*. Berkeley: University of California Press, 1990.

Arnhart, Larry. *Darwinian Conservatism: A Disputed Question*. Charlottesville, VA: USA Imprint Academic, 2005.

Arrighi, Giovanni. *The Long Twentieth Century: Money, Power, and the Origins of Our Times*. London: Verso, 1994.

Bacon, Francis. *Novum Organum*. Translated and edited by Peter Urbach and John Gibson. Chicago: Open Court Press, 1994. First published in 1620.

Barlow, Tani. Introduction to *Formations of Colonial Modernity in East Asia*, 1–21. Edited by Tani E. Barlow. Durham, NC: Duke University Press, 1997.

Barrett, T. H. "Lieh tzu." In *Early Chinese Texts: A Bibliographical Guide*, edited by Michael Loewe, 298–308. Berkeley: Society for the Study of Early China, 1993.

Bellamy, Edward. *Looking Backward, 2001–1887*. New York: Penguin Books, 1986. First published in 1888.

Bennett, Tony. *The Birth of the Museum: History, Theory, Politics*. New York: Routledge, 1995.

Berry, Michael. *A History of Pain: Trauma in Modern Chinese Literature and Film*. New York: Columbia University Press, 2008.

Bihe Guanzhuren 碧荷館主人. *Xin jiyuan* 新紀元. In 中國近代小說大系, edited by Wang Xuquan et al. Jiangxi renmin chubanshe, 1989.

———. *Xin jiyuan*. Guilin: Guangxi shifan daxue chubanshe, 2008.

Bourdieu, Pierre. *The Field of Cultural Production: Essays on Art and Literature*. Edited and introduced by Randal Johnson. New York: Columbia University Press, 1993.

Braester, Yomi. *Witness against History: Literature, Film, and Public Discourse in Twentieth- Century China*. Stanford, CA: Stanford University Press, 2003.

Brashier, K. E. "Han Thanatology and the Division of Souls." *Early China* 21 (1996): 125–158.

Brockway, Lucile H. "Science and Colonial Expansion: The Role of the British Royal Botanic Gardens." *American Ethnologist* 6.3 (1979): 449–465.

Broderick, Damien. *Reading by Starlight: Postmodern Science Fiction*. New York: Routledge, 1995.

Buruma, Ian, and Avishai Margalit. *Occidentalism: The West in the Eyes of Its Enemies*. New York: Penguin, 2004.

Cai Yuanpei 蔡元培, ed. *Cuimianshu jiangyi* 催眠術講義. Shanghai: Shangwu yinshuguan, 1906.

Campany, Robert Ford. *Strange Writing: Anomaly Accounts in Early Medieval China*. Albany: SUNY Press, 1996.

Carrier, James G., ed. *Occidentalism: Images of the West*. Oxford: Clarendon Press, 1995.

Chakrabarty, Dipesh. *Provincializing Europe: Postcolonial Thought and Historical Difference*. Princeton, NJ: Princeton University Press, 2000.

Chan Koonchung 陳冠中. *Shengshi: Zhongguo 2013* 盛世:中國 2013. Taibei: Maitian Chubanshe, 2009.

———. *The Fat Years: China 2013*. Translated by Michael S. Duke. New York: Doubleday, 2011.

Chen Jianhua. "Canon Formation and Linguistic Turn: Literary Debates in Republican China, 1919–1949." In *Beyond the May Fourth Paradigm: In Search of Chinese Modernity*, edited by Kai-Wing Chow, 51–70. Lanham, MD: Lexington, 2008.

Chen Pingyuan 陳平原. "Cong kepu duwu dao kexue xiaoshuo—yi 'feiche' wei zhongxin de kaocha" 從科普讀物到科學小說—以"飛車"為中心的考察. In *Jia Baoyu zuo qianshuiting—Zhongguo zaoqikehuan yanjiu jingxuan* 贾宝玉坐潜水艇—中国早期科幻研究精选, edited by Wu Yan, 136–158. Fujian: Fujian shaonian ertong chubanshe, 2006.

———. *Dianshizhai huabao xuan* 點石齋畫報選. Guiyang: Guizhou chubanshe, 2000.

———. *Zhongguo xiaoshuo xushi moshi de zhuanbian* 中國小說敘事模式的轉變. Taibei: Jiuda wenhua gufen youxian gongsi, 1990.

Chen Pingyuan 陳平原 and Xia Xiaohong 夏曉虹. *Tuxiang wanqing: "Dianshizhai huabao"* 圖像晚清:《點石齋畫報》. Tianjin: Baihua wenyi chubanshe, 2006.

———, eds. *Ershi shiji zhongguo xiaoshuo lilun ziliao* 二十世紀中國小說理論資料. Vol. 1. Beijing: Beijing daxue chubanshe, 1997.

Chen Wangdao 陳望道, ed. *Xiaopin wen he manhua* 小品文和漫畫. Shanghai: Shanghai shudian, 1981.

Chen, Xiaomei. *Occidentalism: A Theory of Counter-discourse in Post-Mao China*. Oxford: Oxford University Press, 1995.

Cheng Min. *Kexue xiaopin zai Zhongguo* 科學小品在中國. Beijing: Kexue chubanshe, 2009.

Chow, Rey. *Primitive Passions: Visuality, Sexuality, Ethnography, and Contemporary Chinese Cinema*. New York: Columbia University Press, 1995.

Clareson, Thomas. "The Emergence of Science Fiction." In *Anatomy of Wonder: A Critical Guide to Science Fiction*, edited by Neil Barron, 3–32. New York: R. R. Bowker, 1981.

Claypool, Lisa. "Zhang Jian and China's First Museum." *Journal of Asian Studies* 64.3 (August 2005): 567–604.

Clute, John, and Peter Nicholls, eds. *The Encyclopedia of Science Fiction*. New York: St. Martin's, 1993.

Cong Cao. *China's Scientific Elite*. New York: Routledge Curzon, 2004.

Csicsery-Ronay, Istvan, Jr. "Science Fiction and Empire." *Science Fiction Studies* 30.2 (July 2003): 231–245.

———. *The Seven Beauties of Science Fiction*. Middletown, CT: Wesleyan University Press, 2008.

Cuvier, Georges, and Charles L. Laurillard. *Recherches sur les ossemens fossiles de quadrupèdes, ou l'on rétablit les caractères de plusieurs espèces d'animaux que les révolutions du globe paroissent avoir détruites*. [With plates.] Paris, 1812.

Daruvala, Susan. *Zhou Zuoren and an Alternative Chinese Response to Modernity*. Cambridge, MA: Harvard University Press, 2000.

Davis, Wade. *Into the Silence: The Great War, Mallory, and the Conquest of Everest*. New York: Alfred A. Knopf, 2012.

DeBary, Wm. Theodore, and Irene Bloom, eds. *Sources of Chinese Tradition*. Vol. 1. New York: Columbia University Press, 1999.

DeBary, Wm. Theodore, and Richard Lufrano, eds. *Sources of Chinese Tradition*. Vol. 2. New York: Columbia University Press, 2000.

Delbourgo, James, and Nicholas Dew, eds. *Science and Empire in the Atlantic World*. New York: Routledge, 2008.

Dikötter, Frank. *The Discourse of Race in Modern China*. London: Hurst, 1992.

———. *Exotic Commodities: Modern Objects and Everyday Life in China*. New York: Columbia University Press, 2006.

———. *Sex, Culture and Modernity in China: Modern Science and the Construction of Sexual Identities in the Early Republican Period*. London: Hurst, 1995.

Ding Wenjiang and Zhao Fengtian, eds. *Liang Qichao nianpu changbian* 梁啟超年譜長編. Shanghai: Shanghai renmin chubanshe, 1983.

Dirlik, Arif. "Orientalism Reconsidered." *History and Theory* 35.4 (Theme Issue 35: Chinese Historiography in Comparative Perspective, December 1996): 96–118.

Duara, Prasenjit. *Sovereignty and Authenticity: Manchukuo and the East Asian Modern*. Lanham, MD: Rowman & Littlefield, 2003.

Du Bois, W. E. B. *The Souls of Black Folk* (1903). In *Three Negro Classics*, by Booker T. Washington, W. E. B. Du Bois, and James Weldon Johnson, 207–389. New York: Avon Books, 1965.

Elman, Benjamin. *A Cultural History of Modern Science in China.* Cambridge, MA: Harvard University Press, 2006.

———. *From Philosophy to Philology: Intellectual and Social Aspects of Change in Late Imperial China.* Cambridge, MA: Harvard University Press, 1984.

———. "From Pre-Modern Chinese Natural Studies 格致學 to Modern Science 科學 in China." In *Mapping Meanings: The Field of New Learning in Late Qing China*, edited by Michael Lackner and Natasha Vittinghoff, 25–73. Leiden: Brill Academic, 2004.

Er tong ke xue wen yi zuo pin xuan 兒童科學文藝作品選. Shanghai: Bianzhe, 1986.

Fanon, Frantz. *Black Skin, White Masks.* Translated by C. L. Markmann. New York: Grove Weidenfeld, 1967. First published in 1952.

———. *The Wretched of the Earth.* Translated by C. Farrington. New York: Grove, 1968. First published in 1961.

Fa-ti Fan. *British Naturalists in Qing China: Science, Empire, and Cultural Encounter.* Cambridge, MA: Harvard University Press, 2004.

Fitting, Peter. "Eating Your Way to the Top: Social Darwinism in SF." In *Food of the Gods: Eating and the Eaten in Fantasy and Science Fiction*, edited by Gary Westfahl, George Slusser, and Eric S. Rabkin, 172–187. Athens: University of Georgia Press, 1996.

Frank, Andre Gunder. *ReOrient: Global Economy in the Asian Age.* Berkeley: University of California Press, 1998.

Freedman, Carl. *Critical Theory and Science Fiction.* Middletown, CT: Wesleyan University Press, 2000.

Fryer, John. *Meiguo bowu dahui tushuo* 美國博物大會圖說. Shanghai: gezhi shushi, guangxu 18 (1892).

Fu Jianzhou 付建舟, ed. *Xiaoshuo jie geming de xingqi yu fazhan* 小說界革命的興起與發展. Beijing: Zhongguo shehui kexue chubanshe, 2008.

Furth, Charlotte. "Intellectual Change: From the Reform Movement to the May Fourth Movement, 1895–1920." In *Intellectual History of Modern China*, edited by Merle Goldman and Leo Ou-fan Lee, 13–96. Cambridge: Cambridge University Press, 2002.

———. *Ting Wen-chiang: Science and China's New Culture.* Cambridge, MA: Harvard University Press, 1970.

Garnett, Rhys, ed. *Science Fiction Roots and Branches: Contemporary Critical Approaches*. London: Macmillan, 1990.

Gilbert, Scott F. "Ernst Haeckel and the Biogenetic Law." In *Developmental Biology*, 10th ed. Companion website, www.devbio.com. Sunderland, MA: Sinauer Associates, 20013.

Godley, Michael R. "China's World's Fair of 1910: Lessons from a Forgotten Event." *Modern Asian Studies* 12.3 (1978): 503–522.

Goethe, Johann Wolfgang von. *The Metamorphosis of Plants*. Introduction and photographs by Gordon L. Miller. Cambridge, MA: MIT Press, 2009. First published in 1790.

Gould, Stephen Jay. *Time's Arrow, Time's Cycle: Myth and Metaphor in the Discovery of Geological Time*. Cambridge, MA: Harvard University Press, 1987.

Gramsci, Antonio. "Americanism and Fordism." In *The Antonio Gramsci Reader: Selected Writings, 1916–1935*, edited by David Forgacs, 275–299. New York: NYU Press, 2000.

Grewal, Inderpal. "Constructing National Subjects: The British Museum and Its Guidebooks." In *With Other Eyes: Looking at Race and Gender in Visual Culture*, edited by Lisa Bloom, 44–57. Minneapolis: University of Minnesota Press, 1999.

Gu Ming Dong. *Chinese Theories of Fiction: A Non-Western Narrative System*. Albany: SUNY Press, 2006.

Guan Jixin 關紀新, ed. *Lao She ping zhuan* 老舍評傳. Chongqing: Chongqing chubanshe, 1998.

Gunn, James, Marleen S. Barr, and Matthew Candelaria, eds. *Reading Science Fiction*. New York: Palgrave Macmillan, 2009.

Gunn, James, and Matthew Candelaria, eds. *Speculations on Speculation: Theories of Science Fiction*. Lanham, MD: Scarecrow, 2005.

Guo Enci 郭恩慈 and Su Jue 蘇珏, eds. *Zhongguo xiandai sheji de dansheng* 中國現代設計的誕生. Hong Kong: Joint Publishing Co., 2007.

Guo Jianzhong 郭建中. *Kepu yu kehuan fanyi* 科普與科幻翻譯. Beijing: Zhongguo duiwai fanyi chubanshe, 2004.

Hamashita Takeshi 浜下武志 and Kawakatsu Heita 川勝平太. *Ajia koekkiken to Nihon kogyoka, 1500-1900* アジア交易圏と日本工業化 1500-1900. Tokyo: Riburopōto, 1991.

Hamlish, Tamara. "Preserving the Palace: Museums and the Making of

Nationalism(s) in Twentieth-Century China." *Museum Anthropology* 19.2 (1995): 20–30.

Hamm, John Christopher. *Paper Swordsmen: Jin Yong and the Modern Chinese Martial Arts Novel*. Honolulu: University of Hawai'i Press, 2005.

Han Song. "Chinese Science Fiction: A Response to Modernization." *Science Fiction Studies* 40.1 (March 2013): 15–21.

———. "The Passengers and the Creator." 2006. Translated by Nathaniel Isaacson, edited by Mingwei Song. *Renditions: A Chinese-English Translation Magazine* 77/78 (Spring/Autumn 2012): 144–172.

Hardt, Michael, and Antonio Negri. *Empire*. Cambridge, MA: Harvard University Press, 2000.

Harrell, Stevan. "The Concept of Soul in Chinese Folk Religion." *Journal of Asian Studies* 38.3 (May 1979): 519–528.

Harris, Trevor. "Measurement and Mystery in Verne." In *Jules Verne: Narratives of Modernity*, edited by Edmund J. Smyth, 109–121. Liverpool: Liverpool University Press, 2000.

Henry, David. "Japanese Children's Literature as Allegory of Empire in Iwaya Sazanami's *Momotarō* (*The Peach Boy*)." *Children's Literature Association Quarterly* 34.3 (Fall 2009): 218–221.

Heroldova, Helena. "Glass Submarines and Electric Balloons: Creating Scientific and Technical Vocabulary in Chinese Science Fiction." In *Mapping Meanings: The Field of New Learning in Late Qing China*, edited by Michael Lackner and Natasha Vitinghoff, 537–553. Leiden: Brill Academic, 2004.

Hockx, Michel, ed. *The Literary Field of Twentieth-Century China*. Honolulu: University of Hawai'i Press, 1999.

Hollinger, Veronica. "Genre vs. Mode." In *The Oxford Handbook of Science Fiction*, edited by Rob Latham, 139–154. Oxford: Oxford University Press, 2014.

———. "'Great Wall Planet': Estrangements of Chinese Science Fiction" "Changcheng xingqiu: Zhongguo kehuan xiaoshuo zhong de mosheng hua" 長城星球: 中國科幻小說中的陌生化. Forthcoming.

Horner, Charles. *Rising China and Its Postmodern Fate: Memories of Empire in a New Global Context*. Athens: University of Georgia Press, 2009.

Hsia, C. T. *A History of Modern Chinese Literature*. 3rd ed. Bloomington: Indiana University Press, 1999.

Hu Shi 胡適. *Hu Shi xuanji: Shuxin* 胡適選記:書信. Taibei: Wenxing chubanshe, 1966.

Huang Jie 黃潔. "Xu Nianci de xiaoshuo meixue sixiang" 徐念慈的小說美學思想. *Yuzhou daxue xuebao* 渝洲大學學報 19.1 (February 2002): 86–90.

Huang Jinzhu 黃錦珠. "*Lun Wu Jianren de Xin shitou ji*" 論吳趼人的《新石頭記.》In *Jia Baoyu zuo qianshuiting—Zhongguo zaoqikehuan yanjiu jingxuan* 賈寶玉坐潛水艇—中國早期科幻研究精選, edited by Wu Yan, 196–215. Fujian: Fujian shaonian ertong chubanshe, 2006.

Huang Kewu 黃克武. "*Minguo chunian Shanghai de lingxue yanjiu: Yi 'Shanghai lingxuehui' weili*" 民國初年上海的靈學研究: 以「上海靈學會」為例. *Zhongyang yanjiuyuan jindai shi yanjiusuo jikan* 中央研究院近代史研究所集刊. Vol. 55 (March 2007), 99–136.

Huang Yong 黃勇, ed. *Huimou wanqing: Dianshizhai huabao jingxuan shiping* 回眸晚清:《點石齋畫報》競選釋評. Beijing: Jinghua chubanshe, 2006.

Huangjiang Diaosou 荒江釣叟. *Yueqiu zhimindi xiaoshuo* 月球殖民地小說. In *Zhongguo jindai xiaoshuo daxi* 中國近代小說大系, edited by Wang Xuquan et al., 1–218. Jiangxi: Renmin chubanshe, 1989.

Huff, Toby E. *The Rise of Early Modern Science: Islam, China and the West*. New York: Cambridge University Press, 2003.

Huntington, Rania. "The Weird in the Newspaper." In *Writing and Materiality in China: Essays in Honor of Patrick Hanan*, edited by Judith T. Zeitlin, Lydia Liu, and Ellen Widmer, 341–396. Cambridge, MA: Harvard University Press, 2003.

Huters, Theodore. *Bringing the World Home: Appropriating the West in Late Qing and Early Republican China*. Honolulu: University of Hawai'i Press, 2005.

———. "Culture, Capital, and the Temptations of the Imagined Market: The Case of the Commercial Press." In *Beyond the May Fourth Paradigm: In Search of Chinese Modernity*, edited by Kai-wing Cow, 27–50. Lanham, MD: Lexington, 2008.

———. "Ideologies of Realism in Modern China: The Hard Imperatives of Imported Theory." In *Politics, Ideology, and Literary Discourse in Modern China: Theoretical Interventions and Cultural Critique*, edited by Liu Kang and Tang Xiaobing, 147–172. Durham, NC: Duke University Press, 1993.

———. "A New Way of Writing: The Possibilities for Literature in Late Qing China, 1895–1908." *Modern China* 14.3 (July 1988): 243–276.

Huxley, Thomas Henry. *The Advance of Science in the Last Half Century*. New York: D. Appleton & Co., 1889.

———. *Autobiography and Selected Essays*. Edited by Ada L. F. Snell. New York: Houghton Mifflin, 1909.

———. Hexuli *tian yan lun* 赫胥黎天演論 (*Evolution and Ethics*). Translated by Yan Fu. Guangxu: fuwen shuju, 1901.

Inoue Tsutomu 井上勤. *Inoue Tsutomu shū* 井上勤集. *Meiji honyaku bungakushuu* 明治翻訳文学集. Vol. 3. Edited by Kawado Michiaki et al. Tokyo: Ozorasha, Shōwa 47 [1972].

Iovene, Paola. *Tales of Futures Past: Anticipation and the Ends of Literature in Contemporary China*. Stanford, CA: Stanford University Press, 2014.

Isaacson, Nathaniel. "Science Fiction for the Nation: *Tales of the Moon Colony* and the Birth of Modern Chinese Fiction." *Science Fiction Studies* 40.1 (March 2013): 33–54.

Jacob, Margaret C. *Scientific Culture and the Making of the Industrial West*. New York: Oxford University Press, 1997.

James, Edward, and Farah Mendlesohn, eds. *Cambridge Companion to Science Fiction*. New York: Cambridge University Press, 2003.

Jameson, Fredric. *Archaeologies of the Future: The Desire Called Utopia and Other Science Fictions*. London: Verso, 2005.

Jenkins, Henry. *Convergence Culture: Where Old and New Media Collide*. New York: NYU Press, 2006.

Jia Liyuan. "Gloomy China: China's Image in Han Song's Science Fiction," trans. Joel Martinsen. *Science Fiction Studies* 40.1 (March 2013): 103–115.

Jia Zuzhang 賈祖璋. *Niao yu wenxue* 鳥與文學. Shanghai guji chubanshe, 2001.

Jiaohui xinbao 教會新報 (Church news). Edited by John Allen. Taibei: Huawen shuju, 1989. First printed 1868–1874.

Jones, Andrew. *Developmental Fairy Tales: Evolutionary Thinking and*

Modern Chinese Culture. Cambridge, MA: Harvard University Press, 2011.

———. *Yellow Music: Media Culture and Colonial Modernity in the Chinese Jazz Age*. Durham, NC: Duke University Press, 2001.

Judge, Joan. *Print and Politics: "Shibao" and the Culture of Reform in Late Qing China*. Stanford, CA: Stanford University Press, 1996.

Kant, Immanuel. *Critique of the Power of Judgment*. Edited by Paul Guyer, translated by Paul Guyer and Eric Matthews. New York: Cambridge University Press, 2007.

Kaske, Elisabeth. *The Politics of Language in Chinese Education, 1895–1919*. Leiden: Brill Academic, 2008.

Katz, Wendy R. *Rider Haggard and the Fiction of Empire*. Cambridge: Cambridge University Press, 1987.

Kern, Stephen. *The Culture of Time and Space, 1880–1950*. New Haven, CT: Yale University Press, 1965.

Kerslake, Patricia. *Science Fiction and Empire*. Liverpool: Liverpool University Press, 2007.

Kexue yu rensheng guan 科學與人生觀. 2 vols. Edited by *Yadong tushuguan* 亞東圖書館. Shanghai: Yadong tushuguan, 1927.

Kinkley, Jeffrey. *Visions of Dystopia in China's New Historical Novels*. New York: Columbia University Press, 2014.

Kioka Nobuo 木岡伸夫 and Suzuki Sadami 鈴木貞美. *Gijutsu to shintai: Nihon "kindaika" no shisō* 技術と身体 日本「近代化」の思想. Kyōto-shi: Mineruva Shobō, 2006.

Knight, Damon Francis. *In Search of Wonder: Essays on Modern Science Fiction*. Chicago: Advent, 1967.

Kowallis, Jon Eugene von. *Warriors of the Spirit: Lu Xun's Early Classical-Style Essays*. Berkeley: University of California, Institute of East Asian Studies, China Research Monographs Series. Forthcoming.

Krakauer, John. *Into Thin Air: A Personal Account of the Mount Everest Disaster*. New York: Villard Books, 1997.

Kuhn, Thomas S. *The Structure of Scientific Revolutions*. Chicago: University of Chicago Press, 1970.

Kurtz, Joachim. "Framing European Technology in Seventeenth-Century China: Rhetorical Strategies in Jesuit Paratexts." In *Mapping Meanings: The Field of New Learning in Late Qing China*, edited by Michael Lackner and Natasha Vitinghoff, 209–232. Leiden: Brill Academic, 2004.

Kwok, D. W. Y. *Scientism in Chinese Thought, 1900–1950*. New Haven, CT: Yale University Press, 1965.

Kwong, Luke S. K. "The Rise of the Linear Perspective on History and Time in Late Qing China, c. 1860–1911." *Past and Present* 173 (2001): 157–190.

Lach, Donald. *Asia in the Making of Europe*. Vol. 2, books 1–3. Chicago: University of Chicago Press, 1977.

Landes, David S. *Revolution in Time: Clocks and the Making of the Modern World*. Cambridge, MA: Belknap Press of Harvard University Press, 1983.

Lao She. *Cat Country: A Satirical Novel of China in the 1930s*. Translated by William A. Lyell Jr. Columbus: Ohio State University Press, 1970.

———. *City of Cats*. Translated by James E. Dew. Ann Arbor: Center for Chinese Studies, University of Michigan, 1964.

———. *Lao She quanji* 老舍全記. Beijing: Renmin wenxue chubanshe, 1999.

———. *Mao cheng ji* 貓城記. Beijing: Renmin wenxue chubanshe, 2008.

———. "Wo zenyang xie Mao cheng ji" 我怎樣寫《貓城記》. In *Lao She yanjiu cailiao* 老舍研究材料, 2 vols., edited by Wu Huaibin 吳懷斌 and Ceng Guangcan 曾廣燦, 544–545. Beijing: Beijing shiyue yishu chubanshe, 1985.

Lao-tzu (Lieh-tzǔ). *The Book of Lieh-tzǔ: A Classic of Tao*. Translated by A. C. Graham. New York: Columbia University Press, 1990.

Latham, Rob, ed. *The Oxford Handbook of Science Fiction*. Oxford: Oxford University Press, 2014.

Laughlin, Charles A. *The Literature of Leisure and Chinese Modernity*. Honolulu: University of Hawai'i Press, 2008.

Lee, Leo Ou-fan. "Literary Trends: The Quest for Modernity." In *An Intellectual History of Modern China*, edited by Merle Goldman and Leo Ou-fan Lee. Cambridge: Cambridge University Press, 2002.

Lem, Stanisław. "Todorov's Fantastic Theory of Literature." In *Microworlds: Writings on Science Fiction and Fantasy*, edited by Franz Rottensteiner, 209–232. Orlando, FL: Harcourt Brace, 1984.

Levie, Howard S. "Humanitarian Restrictions on Chemical and Biological Weapons." *Toledo Law Review* 13 (Summer 1982): 1192–1202.

Lewis, Mark Edward. *Writing and Authority in Early China*. Albany: SUNY Press, 1999.

Li Xin. "Zhongguo lingxue huodong zhong de cuimianshu" 中國零學活動中的催眠術. *Ziran kexue yanjiu* 自然科學研究 28.1 (2009): 12–23.

Liang Qichao 梁啟超. *Liang Qichao quanji* 梁啟超全集. Vol. 10. Beijing: Beijing chubanshe, 1999.

Liezi. *The Book of Lieh-tzu: A Classic of Tao*. Translated by A. C. Graham. New York: Columbia University Press, 1990.

Lightman, Bernard. *Victorian Popularizers of Science: Designing Nature for New Audiences*. Chicago: University of Chicago Press, 2007.

Lin Jianqun 林建群. "*Wan qing kehuan xiaoshuo de shidai lunti yantan*" 晚清科幻小說的時代論題研探. In *Jia Baoyu zuo qianshuiting— Zhongguo zaoqi kehuan yanjiu jingxuan* 賈寶玉坐潛水艇—中國早期科幻研究精選, edited by Wu Yan, 19–36. Fujian: Fujian shaonian ertong chubanshe, 2006.

Liu Cixin 劉慈欣. *San ti* 三體. Chongqing: Chongqing chubanshe, 2007.

———. *San ti er: Hei'an senlin* 三體 II: 黑暗森林. Chongqing: Chongqing chubanshe, 2008.

———. *San ti san: Sishen yongsheng* 三體 III: 死神永生. Chongqing: Chongqing chubanshe, 2010.

———. "The Village Schoolteacher" (2001). Translated by Christopher Elford and Jiang Chenxin, edited by Mingwei Song. *Renditions: A Chinese-English Translation Magazine* 77/78 (Spring/Autumn 2012): 114–143.

———. *Xiangcun jiaoshi: Liu Cixin kehuan zixuanji* 鄉村教師: 劉慈欣科幻自選集. Wuhan: Changjiang wenyi chubanshe, 2012.

Liu Hui. "Qingmo minchu kexue xiaoshuo de zhengzhi xing ji yingxiang" 清末民初 科學小說的政治性及影響. *Huaibei meishiyuan xuebao (zhexue shehui xueyuan)* 淮北煤師院學報 (哲學社會學院) 23.3 (June 2006): 83–85.

Liu Jingmin 劉精民, ed. *Guangxu lao huakan* 光緒老畫刊. Beijing: Zhongguo wenyi chubanshe, 2005.

Liu, Lydia. *Translingual Practice: Literature, National Culture, and*

Translated Modernity — China, 1900-1937. Stanford, CA: Stanford University Press, 1995.

Liu Shi 柳湜. "Lun kexue xiaopin" 論科學小品. *Taibai*《太白》1.1, pp. 8–10 (reprint of original from Shanghai shenghuo shudian, 2 vols). Shanghai: Shanghai shudian, 1981.

Luan Weiping 栾偉平. "Jindai kexue xiaoshuo yu linghun: You 'Xin Faluo xiansheng tan' shuo kaiqu" 近代科學小說與靈魂: 由 '新法螺先生譚' 說開去. *Zhongguo jindai wenxue yanjiu congkan*. Vol. 3 (2006), 46–60.

Luckhurst, Roger. *Science Fiction*. Cambridge: Polity, 2005.

Lu Shi'e 陸士諤. *Xin Zhongguo* 新中國. In *Shibo menghuan sanbuqu* 世博夢幻三部曲, edited by Huang Lin 黃霖. Shanghai: Donfang chuban zhongxin, 2010.

Lu Shi'e, Liang Qichao 梁啟超, and Cai Yuanpei 蔡元培. *Xin Zhongguo shengshi yuyan* 新中國盛世預言. Beijing: Zhongguo Chang'an chubanshe, 2010.

Lu Xun. *Diary of a Madman and Other Stories*. Translated by William A. Lyell. Honolulu: University of Hawai'i Press, 1990.

———. "Kexue shi jiao pian" 科學史教篇. *Lu Xun yu ziran kexue: luncong* 魯迅與自然科學:論叢. Guangzhou: Guangdong keji chubanshe, 1981.

———. "Lessons from the History of Science." Translated by Nathaniel Isaacson. *Renditions* 74 (Autumn 2010): 80–99.

———. *Lu Xun quanji* [*LXQJ*] 魯迅全集. 18 vols. Beijing: Renmin wenxue chubanshe, 2005

———. *Lu Xun zhu yi bian nian quanji* 魯迅著译編年全集. Vol. 1. Edited by Wang Shijia 王世家 and Zhi'an 止庵. Beijing: Renmin chubanshe, 2009.

———. *The Real Story of Ah-Q and Other Tales of China: The Complete Fiction of Lu Xun*. Translated by Julia Lovell. London: Penguin Classics, 2009.

———. "Toward a Refutation of Malevolent Voices." Translated by Jon Kowallis. *boundary 2* 38.2 (Summer 2011): 39–62.

———. "Yuejie luxing bian yan" 月界旅行辯言. *Lu Xun yu ziran kexue: luncong* 魯迅與自然科學:論叢. Guangzhou: Guangdong keji chubanshe, 1981.

Ma, Shaoling. "'A Tale of New Mr. Braggadocio': Narrative Subjectivity and Brain Electricity in Late Qing Science Fiction." *Science Fiction Studies* 40.1 (March 2013): 55–72.

Mao Dun 茅盾. "Kexue he lishi de xiaopin" 科學和歷史的小品. *Mao Dun quanji* 茅盾全集, vol. 20, 437-438. Beijing: Renmin wenxue chubanshe, 1997.

———. "Wenyi dazhonghua de taolun ji qita" 文藝大眾化的討論及其他. *Mao Dun quanji* 茅盾全集, vol. 34, 558. Beijing: Renmin wenxue chubanshe, 1997.

Mathison, Ymitri. "Maps, Pirates and Treasure: The Commodification of Imperialism in Nineteenth-Century Boy's Adventure Fiction." In *The Nineteenth Century Child and Consumer Culture*, edited by Dennis Denisoff, 173–188. Burlington, VT: Ashgate, 2008.

Mauss, Marcel. "Techniques of the Body." In *Techniques, Technology and Civilization*. Edited by Nathan Schlanger. New York: Durkheim, 2006. First published in 1935.

McConnell, Frank. "Alimentary My Dear Watson: Food and Eating in Scientific and Mystery Fiction." In *Food of the Gods: Eating and the Eaten in Fantasy and Science Fiction*, edited by Gary Westfahl, George Slusser, and Eric S. Rabkin, 200–212. Athens: University of Georgia Press, 1996.

Mei Qibo 梅启波. "Lao She Ouzhou wutuobang de huanmie yu Zhongguo wenhua shefen de zhuiqiu—cong *Maocheng ji* dao *Duanhun qiang*" 老舍歐洲烏托邦的幻滅與中國文化身分的追求—從《貓城記》到《斷魂槍》. *Puyang qikan* 普陽期刊, June 2008: 101–104.

Mencius. *Mencius*. Translated by Irene Bloom. New York: Columbia University Press, 2009.

Mengzi 孟子. *Mengzi Zhengyi* 孟子正義 [Correct meanings of the *Mencius*]. Edited by Jiao Xun 焦循. 2 vols. Beijing: Zhonghua Shuju, 1987.

Metzger, Thomas A. *Escape from Predicament: Neo-Confucianism and China's Evolving Political Culture*. New York: Columbia University Press, 1977.

Milner, Andrew. *Locating Science Fiction*. Liverpool: Liverpool University Press, 2012.

———. "Science Fiction and the Literary Field." *Science Fiction Studies* 38.3 (November 2011): 393–411.

Ming, Feng-ying. "Baoyu in Wonderland: Technological Utopia in the

Modern Chinese Science Fiction Novel." In *China in a Polycentric World*, edited by Yingjin Zhang, 152–172. Stanford, CA: Stanford University Press, 1998.

―――. "In Search of a Position: The Paradox of Genre Typology in Late Qing Polygeneric Novel―Romance, Political-Detective, and Science Fiction Novel, 1998–1911." PhD diss., UCLA, 1999.

Monroe, John Warne. *Laboratories of Faith: Mesmerism, Spiritism and Occultism in Modern France*. Ithaca, NY: Cornell University Press, 2008.

Moretti, Franco. *Atlas of the European Novel, 1800–1900*. London: Verso, 1998.

―――. "Conjectures on World Literature." *New Left Review* 1 (January– February 2000): 54–68.

Morris, Andrew. "To Make the Four Hundred Million Move: The Late Qing Dynasty Origins of Modern Chinese Sport and Physical Culture." *Comparative Studies in Society and History* 42.4 (October 2000): 876– 906.

Morse, Donald E., ed. *Anatomy of Science Fiction*. Newcastle, UK: Cambridge Scholars Press, 2006.

Mühlhahn, Klaus, ed. *The Limits of Empire: New Perspectives on Imperialism in Modern China*. New Brunswick, NJ: Transaction, 2008.

Murthy, Viren. "Ontological Optimism, Cosmological Confusion, and Unstable Evolution: Tan Sitong's *Renxue* and Zhang Taiyan's Response." In *The Challenge of Linear Time: Nationhood and the Politics of History in East Asia*. Leiden Series in Comparative Historiography, vol. 7, 49–82. Boston: Brill, 2014.

Nanjing daxue waiguo xuezhe liuxuesheng yanxiu bu Jiangnan jingji shi yanjiushi 南京大學外國學者留學生研修部江南經濟史研究室, eds. *Lun Zhang Jian: Zhang Jian guoji xueshu yantao hui lunwen ji* 論張謇: 張 謇國際學術研討會論文集. Nanjing: Jiangsu renmin chubanshe, 2006.

Needham, Joseph. *The Great Titration: Science and Society in East and West*. London: George Allen & Unwin, 1969.

―――, ed. *Science and Civilization in China*. Vols. 1 and 2. New York: Cambridge University Press, 1954.

Nienhauser, William H., Jr., ed. *Indiana Companion to Traditional Chinese Literature*. Vol. 1. Bloomington: Indiana University Press, 1986.

Nodelman, Perry, ed. "Bibliography of Children's Literature Criticism" (to accompany *Pleasures of Children's Literature*, 3rd ed., by Perry Nodelman and Mavis Reimer). http://ion.uwinnipeg.ca/~nodelman /resources/allbib.htm.

Olson, Richard G. *Science and Scientism in Nineteenth-Century Europe*. Urbana: University of Illinois Press, 2008.

Owen, Stephen. "The End of the Past: Rewriting Chinese Literary History in the Early Republic." In *The Appropriation of Cultural Capital: China's May Fourth Project*, edited by Milena Doleželová-Velingerová and Oldřich Král, 167–192. Cambridge, MA: Harvard University Asia Center, 2001.

Pagani, Catherine. *"Eastern Magnificence and European Ingenuity": Clocks of Late Imperial China*. Ann Arbor: University of Michigan Press, 2001.

Perdue, Peter. *China Marches West: The Qing Conquest of Central Eurasia*. Cambridge, MA: Belknap Press of Harvard University Press, 2005.

Playfair, John. *Illustrations of the Huttonian Theory of the Earth*. New York: Dover, 1956.

Pomerance, Murray, ed. *Cinema and Modernity*. New Brunswick, NJ: Rutgers University Press, 2006.

Pomeranz, Kenneth. *The Great Divergence: Europe, China, and the Making of the Modern World Economy*. Princeton, NJ: Princeton University Press, 2000.

Prucher, Jeffrey, ed. *Brave New Words: The Oxford Dictionary of Science Fiction*. New York: Oxford University Press, 2007.

Pusey, James Reeve. *China and Charles Darwin*. Cambridge, MA: Harvard University Press, 1983.

———. *Lu Xun and Evolution*. Albany: SUNY Press, 1998.

Qin Shao. "Exhibiting the Modern: The Creation of the First Chinese Museum, 1905–1930." *China Quarterly* no. 179 (September 2004): 684–702.

Qiu Ruohong. *Chuanbo yu qimeng: Zhongguo jindai kexue sichao yanjiu* 傳播與啟蒙: 中國近代科學思潮研究. Changsha Shi: Hunan renmin chubanshe, 2004.

Rao Zhonghua 饒中華, ed. *Zhongguo kehuan xiaoshuo daquan* 中國科幻小說大全. Vols. 1–3. Beijing: haiyang chubanshe, 1982.

Raphals, Lisa. "Alterity and Alien Contact in Lao She's Martian Dystopia." *Science Fiction Studies* 40.1 (March 2013): 73–85.

Reardon-Anderson, James. *The Study of Change: Chemistry in China, 1840–1949*. New York: Cambridge University Press, 1991.

Ren Dongmei 任冬梅. "Kehuan wutuobang: Xianshide yu xiangxiangde—*Yueqiu zhimindi xiaoshuo* he xiandai shikongguan de zhuanbian" 科幻烏托邦: 現實的與想像的—月球殖民地小說 和現代時空觀的轉變. *Xiandai Zhongguo wenhua yu wenxue* 現代中國文化與文學, January 2008: 92–110.

———. "Mengxiang Zhongguo—wanqing zhi minguo shehui huanxiang xiaoshuo zhong 'zhongguo xianxiang' de bianhua" 夢像中國—晚清至民國社會幻想小說中 '中國形象' 的變化. PhD diss., Beijing Normal University, 2013.

Ren Dongsheng 人東昇 and Yuan Feng 袁楓. "Qingmo minchu (1891–1917) kehuan xiaoshuo fanyi tanjiu" 清末民初 (1891–1917) 科幻小說翻譯探究. *Shanghai fanyi* 上海翻譯 no. 4 (2010): 72–76.

Repcheck, Jack. *The Man Who Found Time: James Hutton and the Discovery of the Earth's Antiquity*. Cambridge, MA: Perseus, 2003.

Richards, Jeffrey. *Imperialism and Juvenile Literature*. New York: St. Martin's, 1989.

Rieder, John. "Colonialism and Postcolonialism." In *The Oxford Handbook of Science Fiction*, edited by Rob Latham, 486–497. Oxford: Oxford University Press, 2014.

———. *Colonialism and the Emergence of Science Fiction*. Middletown, CT: Wesleyan University Press, 2008.

———. "On Defining SF, or Not: Genre Theory, SF, and History." *Science Fiction Studies* 37.2 (July 2010): 191–209.

Roberts, Adam. *The History of Science Fiction*. New York: Palgrave Macmillan, 2006.

Rofel, Lisa. *Other Modernities: Gendered Yearnings in China after Socialism*. Berkeley: University of California Press, 1999.

Rojas, Carlos. "Cannibalism and the Chinese Body Politic: Hermeneutics and Violence in Cross-Cultural Perception." *Postmodern Culture* 12.3 (May 2002). Project MUSE. http://muse.jhu.edu/.

Rose, Mark, ed. *Science Fiction: A Collection of Critical Essays*. Englewood Cliffs, NJ: Prentice-Hall, 1976.

Said, Edward W. *Culture and Imperialism*. New York: Vintage, 1993.

———. *Orientalism*. New York: Vintage Books, 1979.

———. "Orientalism Reconsidered." In *Literature, Politics and Theory: Papers from the Essex Conference, 1976–84*, edited by Francis Barker, Peter Hulme, Margaret Iversen, and Diana Loxley, 210–229. London: Methuen, 1986.

Schwarz, Benjamin. *In Search of Wealth and Power*. Cambridge, MA: Belknap Press of Harvard University Press, 1964.

———. "Themes in Intellectual History: May Fourth and After." In *The Cambridge History of China*, vol. 12, *Republican China, 1912–1949*, part 1, edited by John K. Fairbank. Cambridge: Cambridge University Press, 1983.

Secord, James A. "Global Darwin." In *Darwin*, edited by William Brown and Andrew C. Fabian, 31–57. Cambridge: Cambridge University Press, 2010.

Shanhai jing 山海經. Edited by Guo Pu 郭璞 et al. Changsha: Yuelu shu she, 1992.

Shibo menghuan sanbuqu 世博夢幻三部曲. Edited by Huang Lin 黃霖. Shanghai: Dongfang chuban zhongxin, 2010.

Shih, Shu-mei. *Visuality and Identity: Sinophone Articulations across the Pacific*. Berkeley: University of California Press, 2007.

Shih, Shu-mei, Brian Bernards, and Chien-hsin Tsai, eds. *Sinophone Studies: A Critical Reader*. New York: Columbia University Press, 2013.

Shu Qian 庶謙. "Muqian kexue xiaopin de gediao he neirong" 目前科學小品的格調和內容. *Xiaopinwen he manhua* 小品文和漫畫, edited by Chen Wangdao, 163–168. Shanghai: Shanghai shudian, 1981.

Slusser, George, and Eric S. Rabkin. *Aliens: The Anthropology of Science Fiction*. Carbondale: Southern Illinois University Press, 1987.

Song Fagang 宋法剛. "Lun Zhongguo kehuan dianying de queshi" 論中國科幻電影的缺失. *Dianying wenxue* 電影文學 19 (2007): 23–24.

Song Mingwei. "Variations on Utopia in Contemporary Chinese Science Fiction." *Science Fiction Studies* 40.1 (March 2013): 86–102.

Song Yongyi 宋永毅. *Lao She yu Zhongguo wenhua guannian* 老舍與中國文化觀念. Shanghai: Xueshu chubanshe, 1988.

Spence, Jonathan D. *The Search for Modern China*. New York: W. W. Norton, 1990.

Spivak, Gayatri Chakravorty. "Can the Subaltern Speak?" In *Marxism and the Interpretation of Culture*, edited by Cary Nelson and Lawrence Grossberg, 271–313. London: Macmillan, 1988.

———. *A Critique of Postcolonial Reason: Toward A History of the Vanishing Present*. Cambridge, MA: Harvard University Press, 1999.

Steinberg, Marc. *Anime's Media Mix: Franchising Toys and Characters in Japan*. Minneapolis: University of Minnesota Press, 2012.

Stott, Rebecca. "Darwin in the Literary World." In *Darwin*, edited by William Brown and Andrew C. Fabian, 58–77. Cambridge: Cambridge University Press, 2010.

Strassberg, Richard, ed. and trans. *A Chinese Bestiary: Strange Creatures from the Guideways through Mountains and Seas*. Berkeley: University of California Press, 2002.

Suvin, Darko. *Metamorphoses of Science Fiction: On the Poetics and History of a Literary Genre*. New Haven, CT: Yale University Press, 1979.

Taibai 太白. 2 vols. Shanghai: Shanghai shudian, 1981. Reprint of original from Shanghai shenghuo shudian, 1934.

Takeda Masaya 武田雅哉. *Tobe! Daishin tekoku: Kindai chūgoku no gensō kagaku* 飛べ～！大清帝国：近代中国の幻想科学. Tokyo: Riburopōto, 1988.

Takeda Masaya and Hayashi Hiskayuki 林久之. Chūgoku kagaku gensō bungakukan 中国科学幻想文学館. 2 vols. Tokyo: Taishūkan Shoten, 2001.

———. *Feixiang ba! Daqing diguo: Jindai zhongguo de huanxiang kexue* 飛翔吧! 大清帝國: 近代中國的幻想科學. Translated by Ren Junhua 任鈞華. Taibei: Yuanliu chubanshe, 2008.

Tang Tao. *History of Modern Chinese Literature*. Beijing: Foreign Languages Press, 1998.

Tang Xiaobing. *Global Space and the Nationalist Discourse of Modernity: The Historical Thinking of Liang Qichao*. Stanford, CA: Stanford University Press, 1996.

Tang Zhesheng 湯哲聲. *Zhongguo xiandai tongsu xiaoshuo sibianlu* 中國現代通俗小說思辨錄. Beijing: Peking University Press, 2008.

Telotte, J. P. *A Distant Technology: Science Fiction Film and the Machine Age*. Hanover, NH: University Press of New England, 1999.

Thompson, E. P. "Time, Work-Discipline, and Industrial Capitalism." *Past and Present* 38.1 (1967): 56–97.

Todorov, Tsvetan. *The Fantastic: A Structural Approach to a Literary Genre*. Translated by Richard Howard. Ithaca, NY: Cornell University Press, 1973.

Trumpener, Ulrich. "The Road to Ypres: The Beginnings of Gas Warfare in World War I." *Journal of Modern History* 47.3 (September 1975): 460–480.

Tso-Wei Hsieh 謝作偉. "The Rhetorical Strategies of Travel Narrative in Late Qing Fiction" (晚清小說中旅途敘事的修辭策略). 聖約翰學報 (Journal of St. John's University) 24 (2007): 193–204.

Tyndall, John. *Advancement of Science: The Inaugural Address of Prof. John Tyndall*. New York: Asa K. Butts & Co., 1874.

Vint, Cheryl, and Mark Bould. "There Is No Such Thing as Science Fiction." In *Reading Science Fiction*, edited by James Gunn, Marleen S. Barr, and Matthew Candelaria, 43–51. New York: Palgrave Macmillan, 2009.

Wagner, Rudolph. *Joining the Global Public: Word, Image, and City in Early Chinese Newspapers, 1870–1910*. Albany: SUNY Press, 2007.

Wakabayashi, Judy. "Foreign Bones, Japanese Flesh: Translations and the Emergence of Modern Children's Literature in Japan." *Japanese Language and Literature* 42.1 (April 2008): 227–255.

Wallerstein, Immanuel. *The Second Era of Great Expansion of the Capitalist World-Economy, 1730–1840s*. Vol. 3 of *The Modern World System III*. New York: Academic Press, 1989.

Walter, E. V., Vytautas Kavolis, Edmund Leites, and Marie Coleman Nelson, eds. *Civilizations East and West: A Memorial Volume for Benjamin Nelson*. Atlantic Highlands, NJ: Humanities Press, 1985.

Wang, Ban. *Illuminations from the Past: Trauma, Memory, and History in Modern China*. Stanford, CA: Stanford University Press, 2004.

Wang, David Der-wei. *Fin-de-Siècle Splendor: Repressed Modernities of Late Qing Fiction, 1848–1911*. Stanford, CA: Stanford University Press, 1997.

———. "Jia Baoyu zuo qianshuiting—wanqing kehuan xiaoshuo xinlun" 賈寶玉坐潛水艇—晚清科幻小說新論. In *Jia Baoyu zuo qianshuiting—*

Zhongguo zaoqikehuan yanjiu jingxuan 中國早期科幻研究精選, edited by Wu Yan, 92–104. Fujian: Fujian shaonian ertong chubanshe, 2006.

———. *The Monster That Is History: History, Violence, and Fictional Writing in Twentieth-Century China*. Berkeley: University of California Press, 2004.

Wang Ermin 王爾敏. *Zhongguo xiandai sheji de dansheng* 中國現代設計的誕生. Hong Kong: Sanlian shudian, 2007.

Wang Hui. "The Fate of 'Mr. Science' in China: The Concept of Science and Its Application in Modern Chinese Thought." *Positions: East Asia Cultures Critique* (Duke University Press) 3.1 (1995): 1–68.

Wang Jianyuan 王建元 and Chen Jieshi 陳潔詩, eds. *Kehuan, hou xiandai, hou renlei* 科幻, 後現代, 後人類. Fujian: Fujian shaonian ertong chubanshe, 2006.

Wang Shanping 王姍萍. "Xixue dongjian yu wanqing kexue xiaoshuo qianlun" 西學東漸與晚清科學小說淺論. *Baoding shifan zhuanke xuexiao xuebao* 保定師範專科學校學報 19.1 (January 2006): 53–56.

Wang Tao. *Man you sui lu* 漫遊隨錄. Changsha: Yuelu shushe, 1985.

Wang Weiying 王衛英. "Kehuan xiaoshuo yu Zhongguo chuantong wenhua" 科幻小說與中國傳統文化. *Xiaoshuo pinglun* 小說評論, February 2008: 147–150.

Wang, Zuoyue. "Saving China through Science: The Science Society of China, Scientific Nationalism, and Civil Society in Republican China." *Osiris* 17 (2002): 291–322.

Watson, Rubie S. "Palaces, Museums, and Squares: Chinese National Spaces." *Museum Anthropology* 19.2 (1995): 7–19.

Wei Leong Tay. "Kang Youwei, the Martin Luther of Confucianism and His Vision of Confucian Modernity and Nation." *Secularization, Religion and the State* (University of Tokyo Center for Philosophy, Booklet 17, 2010): 97–109.

Wei Yang. "Voyage into an Unknown Future: A Genre Analysis of Chinese SF Film in the New Millennium." *Science Fiction Studies* 40.1 (March 2013): 133–147.

Weinbaum, Alys Eve, et al., eds. *The Modern Girl around the World: Consumption, Modernity, and Globalization*. Durham, NC: Duke University Press, 2008.

Westfahl, Gary. "For Tomorrow We Dine: The Sad Gourmet at the Scienticafe." In *Food of the Gods: Eating and the Eaten in Fantasy and Science Fiction*, edited by Gary Westfahl, George Slusser, and Eric S. Rabkin, 213–223. Athens: University of Georgia Press, 1996.

———. "'The Jules Verne, H. G. Wells, and Edgar Allan Poe Type of Story': Hugo Gernsback's History of Science Fiction." *Science Fiction Studies* 19.3 (November 1992): 340–353.

———. *Science Fiction, Children's Literature and Popular Culture: Coming of Age in Fantasyland*. Westport, CT: Greenwood, 2000.

Westfahl, Gary, George Slusser, and Eric S. Rabkin, eds. *Food of the Gods: Eating and the Eaten in Fantasy and Science Fiction*. Athens: University of Georgia Press, 1996.

Wilkinson, Alec. *The Ice Balloon: S. A. Andrée and the Heroic Age of Arctic Exploration*. New York: Alfred A. Knopf, 2011.

Wilkinson, Endymion. *Chinese History: A New Manual*. Cambridge, MA: Harvard University Press, 2013.

Williams, Raymond. "Base and Superstructure in Marxist Cultural Theory." In *Problems in Materialism and Culture: Selected Essays*. London: New Left Books, 1980.

———. *Politics and Letters: Interviews with the "New Left Review."* London: New Left Books, 1979.

Worley, Alec. *Empires of the Imagination: A Critical Survey of Fantasy Cinema from Georges Méliès to "The Lord of the Rings."* Jefferson, NC: McFarland, 2005.

Wright, David. "John Fryer and the Shanghai Polytechnic: Making Space for Science in Nineteenth-Century China." *British Journal for the History of Science* 29.1 (March 1996): 1–16.

———. "The Translation of Modern Western Science in Nineteenth-Century China." *Isis* 89 (1998): 653–673.

Wu Dingbo and Patrick Murphy, eds. *Science Fiction from China*. New York: Praeger, 1989.

Wu Jianren 吳趼人. *Xin shitou ji (XSTJ)* 新石頭記. *Zhongguo jindai xiaoshuo daxi* 中國近代小說大系. Edited by Wang Jiquan 王繼權 et al. Nanchang: Jiangxi renmin chubanshe, 1988.

Wu Kang 吳康, ed. *Xin wenxue de benyuan* 新文學的本原. Changsha: Yuelu chubanshe, 2005.

Wu Qichang. *Liang Qichao zhuan.* Beijing: Tuan jie chubanshe, 2004.

Wu Xianya 吴献雅. "Kexue huanxiang yu kexue qimeng: Wan Qing kexue xiaoshuo yanjiu" 科学幻想与科学启蒙—晚清科学小说. In *Jia Baoyu zuo qianshuiting: Zhongguo zaoqi kehuan yanjiu jingxuan* 贾宝玉坐潜水艇—中国早期科幻研究精选, edited by Wu Yan, 37–91. Fuzhou: Fujian shaonian ertong chubanshe, 2006.

Wu Yan, ed. *Jia Baoyu zuo qianshuiting—Zhongguo zaoqikehuan yanjiu jingxuan* 贾宝玉坐潜水艇—中国早期科幻研究精选. Fujian: Fujian shaonian ertong chubanshe, 2006.

———. *Kehuan wenxue lungang* 科幻文學論鋼. Chongqing: Chongqing chubanshe, 2011.

Wu Yan and Fang Xiaoqing 方曉慶. "Zhongguo zaoqi kexue xiaoshuo de kexueguan" 中國早期科學小的科學觀. *Sixiang bianzhengfa yanjiu* 思想辯證法研究 24.4 (April 2008): 97–100.

Wu Youru 吳友如. *Dianshizhai huabao da ketang ban* 《點石齋畫報》大可堂版. Edited by Shanghai da ketang wenhua youxian gongsi. 15 vols. Shanghai: Shanghai huabao chubanshe, 2001.

Xia'er guan zhen: fu jie ti, suo yin 遐爾貫珍: 附解題, 索引 (Chinese serial). Edited by Matsuura Akira 松浦章 et al. Shanghai: Shanghai ci shu chubanshe, 2005. First printed 1853–1856.

Xiaoheng Xiangshi Zhuren 小橫香室主人. *Qingchao yeshi daguan* 清朝野史大觀. 12 vols. Vol. 4, 158–159. Taibei: Zhonghua shuju, 1959.

Xin qingnian 新青年 (*La Jeunesse*). Edited by Chen Duxiu 陳獨秀. Tokyo: Kyūko shoin, 1970–1971. Reprint of 1915–1921 originals.

Xu Nianci 徐念慈. "New Tales of Mr. Braggadocio." Translated by Nathaniel Isaacson. *Renditions* 75 (Autumn 2011): 15–38.

———. "Xin faluo xiansheng tan" 新法螺先生譚. *Xiaoshuo lin* 小說林, June 1905: 1–39.

———. "Xin faluo xiansheng tan." In *Zhongguo jindai wenxue daxi 1840–1929: Xiaoshuo ji* 中國近代文學大系 1840-1929: 小說集, edited by Wu Zuxiang 吳組緗 et al., 6:323–343. Shanghai: Shanghai shudian.

———. "Yu zhi xiaoshuo guan" 余之小說觀. In *Xiaoshuo Lin* 小說林 (1908). Vol. 9, 1–8; vol. 10, 19–15.

Xun Liu. *Daoist Modern: Innovation, Lay Practice, and the Community of Inner Alchemy in Republican Shanghai.* Cambridge, MA: Harvard University Press, 2009.

Xunzi. *Xunzi: A Translation and Study of the Complete Works*. Translated by John Knoblock. Stanford, CA: Stanford University Press, 1988.

———. *Xunzi jijie* 荀子集解 [Collected commentaries to the Xunzi]. 2 vols. Edited by Liang Yunhua 梁運華. Beijing: Zhonghua shuju, 1988.

———. *Xunzi: The Complete Text*. Translated by Eric. L. Hutton. Princeton, NJ: Princeton University Press, 2014.

Yang, Guorong. "The Debate between Scientists and Metaphysicians in Early Twentieth Century: Its Theme and Significance." *Dao: A Journal of Comparative Philosophy* 2.1 (December 2002): 79–95.

Ye Xiaoqing. *The Dianshizhai Pictorial: Shanghai Urban Life, 1884–1898*. Michigan monographs in Chinese studies, vol. 98. Ann Arbor: Center for Chinese Studies, University of Michigan, 2003.

Ye Yonglie 葉永烈, ed. *Zhongguo kehuan xiaoshuo shiji huimou congshu* 中國科幻小說世紀回眸叢書. Fujian: Shaonian ertong chubanshe, 1999.

Yue, Meng. *Shanghai and the Edges of Empire*. Minneapolis: University of Minnesota Press, 2006.

Zarrow, Peter, ed. *Creating Chinese Modernity: Knowledge and Everyday Life, 1900–1940*. New York: Peter Lang, 2006.

Zhang Guixing 張桂興, ed. *Lao She nianpu* 老舍年譜. Shanghai: Shanghai wenyi chubanshe, 1997.

Zhang Zhi 張治. "Wanqing kexue xiaoshuo chuyi: dui wenxue zuopin ji qi sixiang beijing yu zhishiye de kaocha" 晚清科學小說芻議: 對文學作品及其思想背景與知識野的考察. *Kexue wenhua pinglun* 科學文化評論 6.5 (2009): 69–96.

Zheng Wei 郑為, ed. *Dianshizai huabao shishi hua xuan* 點石齋畫報時事畫選. Beijing: Zhongguo gudian yishu chubanshe, 1958.

Zheng Wenguang 鄭文光. *Zheng Wenguang zuopin xuan* 鄭文光作品選. Guangdong: Renmin chubanshe, 1983.

Zhongguo jindai wenxue cidian 中國近代文學辭典. Edited by Wei Shaochang 魏紹昌 et al. Zhengzhou: Henan jiaoyu chubanshe, 1993.

Zhongguo jinxiandai renming dacixian 中國近現代人名大辭典. Edited by Li Shengping 李盛平 et al. Beijing: Zhongguo guo ji guang bo chubanshe, 1989.

Zhongguo kexue wenyi daxi 中國科學文藝大系. 4 vols. Edited by Zong Jiehua 宗介華 et al. Hunan: Hunan Jiaoyu chubanshe, 1999.

Zhou Liyan 周黎燕. "Fan wutuobang shiye zhong de *Maocheng ji*" 反烏托

邦視野中的《貓城記》. *Chongqing sanxia xueyuan xuebao* 重慶三峽學院學報 26.127 (April 2010): 85–89.

Zhuangzi 莊子. *Zhuangzi jinzhu jinyi* 莊子今注今譯 [The Zhuangzi with contemporary exegesis and translation]. 3 vols. Edited by Chen Guying 陳鼓應. Beijing: Zhonghua Shuju, 2001.

———. *The Complete Works of Chuang Tzu*. Translated by Burton Watson. New York: Columbia University Press, 1968.

Žižek, Slavoj. *The Sublime Object of Ideology*. London: Verso, 2008. First published in 1989.

INDEX

Note: Page numbers with "n" indicate notes. Page numbers in *italics* indicate illustrations.

The Fire in the Stone: Prehistoric Fiction from Charles Darwin to Jean M. Auel
Nicholas Ruddick

The World as It Shall Be
Emile Souvestre

Star Maker
Olaf Stapledon

The Begum's Millions
Jules Verne

Five Weeks in a Balloon
Jules Verne

Invasion of the Sea
Jules Verne

The Kip Brothers
Jules Verne

The Mighty Orinoco
Jules Verne

The Mysterious Island
Jules Verne

Travel Scholarships
Jules Verne

H. G. Wells: Traversing Time
W. Warren Wagar

Star Begotten
H. G. Wells

Deluge
Sydney Fowler Wright

Sisters of Tomorrow: The First Women of Science Fiction
Lisa Yaszek and Patrick B. Sharp, eds.

NATHANIEL ISAACSON is an assistant professor of modern Chinese literature at North Carolina State University. A translator and author, he has written for various journals and contributed essays to *The Oxford Handbook of Modern Chinese Literature* (forthcoming) and *Simultaneous Worlds: Global Science Fiction Cinema* (University of Minnesota Press, 2015). His essays on Chinese SF have appeared in *Science Fiction Studies*.